Counselling

for Depression

SAGE has been part of the global academic community since 1965, supporting high quality research and learning that transforms society and our understanding of individuals, groups and cultures. SAGE is the independent, innovative, natural home for authors, editors and societies who share our commitment and passion for the social sciences.

Find out more at: **www.sagepublications.com**

Counselling
for Depression

A Person-centred and Experiential Approach to Practice

Pete Sanders and Andy Hill

British Association for
Counselling & Psychotherapy

Los Angeles | London | New Delhi
Singapore | Washington DC

Los Angeles | London | New Delhi
Singapore | Washington DC

SAGE Publications Ltd
1 Oliver's Yard
55 City Road
London EC1Y 1SP

SAGE Publications Inc.
2455 Teller Road
Thousand Oaks, California 91320

SAGE Publications India Pvt Ltd
B 1/I 1 Mohan Cooperative Industrial Area
Mathura Road
New Delhi 110 044

SAGE Publications Asia-Pacific Pte Ltd
3 Church Street
#10-04 Samsung Hub
Singapore 049483

Editor: Susannah Trefgarne
Editorial assistant: Laura Walmsley
Production editor: Rachel Burrows
Copyeditor: Helen Skelton
Proofreader: Sarah Cooke
Indexer: Martin Hargreaves
Marketing manager: Tamara Navaratnam
Cover design: Lisa Harper
Typeset by: C&M Digitals (P) Ltd, Chennai, India
Printed and bound by CPI Group (UK) Ltd,
Croydon, CR0 4YY

MIX
Paper from
responsible sources
FSC   FSC® C013604
www.fsc.org

© Pete Sanders and Andy Hill 2014

First published 2014

Library of Congress Control Number: 2013948227

British Library Cataloguing in Publication data

A catalogue record for this book is available from the British Library

ISBN 978-1-4462-7207-7
ISBN 978-1-4462-7209-1 (pbk)

Contents

Figures and tables

Figures

Table

Abbreviations

BACP	British Association of Counselling and Psychotherapy
BAPCA	British Association for the Person-Centred Approach
BCT	behavioural couples therapy
BDI	Beck Depression Inventory
CBT	cognitive behavioural therapy
CfD	Counselling for Depression
CPD	continuing professional development
DALY	disability-adjusted life year
DIT	dynamic interpersonal therapy
DSM	*Diagnostic and Statistical Manual of Mental Disorders*
EBP	evidence-based practice
EFT	emotion-focused therapy
EMDR	eye movement desensitisation and reprocessing
ERG	Expert Reference Group
ES	effect size
FIT	feedback-informed treatment
GAD	generalised anxiety disorder
GDG	Guideline Development Group
GP	General Practitioner
HEPs	humanistic-experiential psychotherapies
IAPT	Improving Access to Psychological Therapies
ICD	*International Classification of Mental and Behavioural Disorders*
IPT	interpersonal psychotherapy
MAOIs	monoamine oxidase inhibitors
MDD	major depressive disorder
NHS	National Health Service
NICE	National Institute for Health and Care Excellence
NIHR	National Institute for Health Research
PCE	person-centred and experiential
PCEPS	Person-Centred and Experiential Psychotherapy Scale
PCT	person-centred therapy
PHQ	Patient Health Questionnaire

PRN	practice-research network
PTSD	post-traumatic stress disorder
PWP	psychological wellbeing practitioner
RCT	randomised control trial
RI	real–ideal
RO	real–ought
SIGN	Scottish Intercollegiate Guidelines Network
SSRIs	selective serotonin reuptake inhibitors
TCAs	tricyclic antidepressants
UPR	unconditional positive regard
WHO	World Health Organization
WSAS	Work and Social Adjustment Scale

About the authors

Pete Sanders worked as a volunteer counsellor for 'Off The Record' in Newcastle-upon-Tyne in the early 1970s whilst a psychology undergraduate. This, and a full time Postgraduate Diploma in Counselling at the University of Aston in Birmingham in 1974–75, set him on his subsequent career as a counsellor, trainer, supervisor and author. During this time he was the course leader on three British Association for Counselling and Psychotherapy (BACP) recognised courses, was centrally involved in establishing and running the BACP Trainer Accreditation Scheme, wrote, co-wrote or edited 15 books, and founded PCCS Training and PCCS Books with his wife Maggie. Apart from his continuing interest in the development of theory and practice in person-centred and experiential therapies, he is dedicated to the demedicalisation of distress. Pete thinks that mental health services are in urgent need of reformation, is an enthusiastic supporter of Hearing Voices Network and he is a Trustee of the Soteria Network, UK.

Having trained as a person-centred counsellor in the late 1980s, Andy Hill has worked as a trainer, counsellor and researcher for over 20 years. He worked originally as a further education lecturer at Oldham College, where he established counsellor training courses and a student counselling service, and subsequently as a senior lecturer at Salford University, where he was programme leader for a BACP accredited counsellor training programme. He has authored systematic reviews in *Counselling Older People* (2004) and *Counselling in Primary Care* (2008) and was lead author for the 2011 evaluation of the Welsh schools counselling strategy. He has played a leading role in the development of competence frameworks in a number of fields: humanistic counselling; Counselling for Depression; counselling young people; online counselling. He is a BACP accredited counsellor and has practised in student counselling, NHS psychotherapy services, NHS primary care and more recently in an Improving Access to Psychological Therapies (IAPT) service. His main area of professional interest is evidence-based practice and how humanistic therapies can engage with this paradigm in order to expand the range of therapies available to service users in the NHS. As part of this work Andy is interested in how stronger links between research, training and practice can produce better therapeutic services and improved outcomes for service users. Andy is currently Head of Research at BACP and so has an ongoing involvement in commissioning projects, undertaking research and disseminating research findings via the association's research journal *Counselling and Psychotherapy Research* and its annual research conference.

Acknowledgements

Pete Sanders: Writing this book has been a team effort in many ways. It would have been impossible without the understanding and support of my wife, Maggie. Close behind is the hard work of my colleagues at PCCS Books, who shouldered the burden of my absence while I was seconded to this project. I would like to thank Peter Pearce and Ros Sewell for their continued assistance, and I am especially grateful for the help, advice and support of Robert Elliott, Kate Hayes and David Murphy. Writing this book has been demanding and exhausting. I have needed many shoulders to lean, if not cry on, so heartfelt thanks to Paul Wilkins, Wendy Traynor, Sandy Green, Heather Allan and the Garronistas: Anthea, Graham, Jerry, Michèle, Tony and Val for their friendship.

Andy Hill: For me this book marks the culmination of around six years' involvement in developing humanistic competences, working with IAPT and attempting to secure a future for person-centred and experiential therapies in the challenging world of evidence-based practice. In this work I'd particularly like to thank my colleagues at BACP for their support and toleration of my absence from the office, Professor Tony Roth for his expert guidance and ability to think creatively across therapeutic modalities, Professor Robert Elliott for his help, particularly in the writing of Chapter 2, all the tutors at the CfD training institutions and my wife, Ilona, for her support and encouragement.

Both Pete and Andy thank Bill Miller and Louise Harper for contributing their experiences of CfD training.

1

Introduction

Counselling in primary care

Counsellors, many of them person-centred, have a long history of working in the UK National Health Service (NHS) primary care, with early reports dating back to the 1970s (Harray, 1975; Anderson and Hasler, 1979). The services they provided tended to arise from local decision-making, based on the popularity of counselling among the public and among GPs (Sibbald et al., 1993), leading to a scenario where by the end of the 20th century approximately 80% of English GP practices had on-site counselling services (Mellor-Clark, 2000). Provision was, however, patchy with access to counselling depending upon where you lived and the attitude of your GP to psychological services (Kendrick et al., 1993). This was a 'grassroots' development resulting from a demand for user-friendly and non-stigmatising psychological services and creative thinking on behalf of GPs about how to respond to this demand within the constraints of NHS resources. At this time, counselling in primary care seemed to be flourishing as a result of its popularity and the widespread availability of a qualified counselling workforce, despite an absence of sustainable central funding from the NHS and clear policy on the general availability of such services. This state of affairs was set to change with the publication of *The Depression Report* (CEPMHPG, 2006). The fact that funding, and therefore treatment, for mental health problems lagged so far behind bio-medical interventions and that the disease burden represented by mental health problems was as significant as, for example, coronary heart disease (Department of Health, 1999), was highlighted in this report and it was noted, 'No NICE[1] guidelines are so far from being implemented as those for depression and anxiety' and that, by way of contrast, 'If the NICE guidelines for breast cancer were not implemented, there would be uproar' (CEPMHPG, 2006: 8). What followed was a successful lobbying of government, followed by large-scale investment in services for people with common mental health problems and the Improving Access to

---

[1] National Institute for Health and Care Excellence.

Psychological Therapies (IAPT) programme was born. This had the benefit of making psychological therapy much more widely available for people with anxiety and depression but, as a centralised, 'top-down' initiative, reversed the 'grassroots' development of primary care counselling based in GP surgeries.

The national roll-out of the IAPT programme was predicated on the implementation of the NICE (2009a) guideline for depression, elevating the significance of this guideline for the psychological therapies: no longer does it simply recommend good practice, it now predicts who will get a job in NHS psychological services. The consequences for primary care counsellors are serious. The guideline recommends cognitive behaviour therapy (CBT)[2] as a frontline therapy, with counselling and other therapies as therapies of last resort should a service user fail to respond to CBT. Following this recommendation, the delivery of the IAPT programme was underpinned by the training of a new CBT workforce as opposed to use of the pre-existing cohort of primary care counsellors, resulting in the loss of counselling jobs and the decommissioning of some counselling services.

The genesis of Counselling for Depression

Notwithstanding the above events, there were those that managed to retain their positions in primary care and a significant number were recruited into IAPT services. It is estimated that approximately 30% (Glover et al., 2010) of the IAPT workforce are counsellors, but often working on lower pay scales than their CBT colleagues and without the kudos of offering evidence-based therapy. This lower status is enshrined in the depression guideline (NICE, 2009a: 16) where healthcare workers, in assessing clients for psychological therapy, are exhorted to 'Discuss with the person the uncertainty of the effectiveness of counselling … in the treatment of depression'.

The threat to person-centred and experiential (PCE) counselling produced by these developments has been significant and it is out of this challenging backdrop that Counselling for Depression (CfD) has been developed, in an attempt to secure continuing employment for counsellors in IAPT services, to gain parity with CBT and, perhaps most importantly, to ensure IAPT service users have a choice of therapies which includes counselling. In developing this model of practice it has been necessary to engage with institutions and philosophical frameworks that are at odds with person-centred and humanistic thinking. Readers of this book will no doubt judge how successful we have been in doing this. One thing that is very clear is that failure to engage would have widespread negative consequences for PCE therapies, counsellors in primary care and those members of the public who may benefit from PCE counselling.

This book is in many ways a culmination of the efforts of many people to develop evidence-based PCE therapy. Several years ago, in the wake of IAPT's implementation,

---

[2] Although there are some unifying principles that distinguish cognitive behaviour therapy, it is important to note that there is a very wide range of theory and practice that comes under the banner of CBT.

a group of people led by Professor Tony Roth met in a room in University College London to develop competences for humanistic counselling/psychotherapy. This in many ways marked the initial step in the development of CfD. Within this group were academics (Professors Mick Cooper, Robert Elliott, Germain Lietaer) and members of professional bodies (from the BACP, Nancy Rowland and Sally Aldridge, and from the British Association for the Person-Centred Approach (BAPCA), Janet Tolan). A second phase of competence development work was led by BACP and involved Helen Coles, Allie Griffiths and others. Involved in the initial roll-out of the CfD training programme were Peter Pearce, Ros Sewell, Maggie Robson, Jane Hunt, Trish Hobman and Lynne Lacock. The support of members of the Four Modalities Group who together developed the therapies additional to CBT within the IAPT programme has been essential to the genesis and delivery of the CfD project – these are Roslyn Hope, Jeremy Clarke, Professor Alessandra Lemma, Roslyn Law and David Hewison. The content of this book in many ways sits on the work of these people and so is the drawing together of the thoughts of many.

This book

We are excited to be presenting this book to introduce this new integrative counselling approach, 'Counselling for Depression'. The book is intended to serve many purposes. First, it introduces the CfD model of therapy, and explains how to implement it in any healthcare setting – although CfD is at the time of writing presented only in terms of the IAPT programme with its associated limits. It is, therefore, intended to be particularly useful to counsellors working in IAPT services and other generic NHS primary care settings. However, there is no reason to limit CfD as an integrative approach to IAPT or the current roll-out of training. Anyone working with people with experiences of depression can use it, adapting it to their and their clients' circumstances.

Second, it is a practitioner textbook supporting students following the CfD training programme. This programme, devised by the BACP and approved by the Department of Health, is briefly described in Chapter 10. Again, we can see no reason to confine training in the theory and practice of CfD to this training programme. It is an integrated approach to working with depression which deserves to be shared. The practice of CfD in IAPT services, however, will require approved training.

Third, the book provides an introduction to the CfD competence framework which underpins the training programme, and is also a key element in the process of developing and implementing the larger CfD project to gather evidence for CfD as an IAPT intervention, described in Chapters 2, 3 and 10. We imagine some readers will not be interested in the place of CfD in the process of gathering data for evidence-based practice research – the theory and practice will stand alone for them, separate from the competences. We, however, are convinced that CfD has an important role to play in establishing a strong evidence base for person-centred and experiential therapies in primary care.

Finally, we expect that the book will introduce other IAPT practitioners, unfamiliar with these humanistic approaches, to person-centred and experiential theory and practice for the first time. Our hope is that they will discover something useful in the traditions from which Counselling for Depression originates and appreciate its thoughtful development.

As we have outlined above, CfD was developed from the work of leading figures in the field of person-centred and experiential therapies, and the task of breathing life into the ideas fell initially to the trainers and early cohorts of students. Since then we have worked on this book as a way of clearly delineating the theory and practice, and making manifest the competences. Lagging somewhat behind the first training cohorts, this book has taken the elements from which CfD was derived, the expertise and experiences of the above constituencies, and integrated them into a cohesive therapeutic model.

We present CfD as a new integrative model, limited to a maximum of 20 sessions, for people suffering from depression. Since CfD is drawn from person-centred therapy (PCT) and emotion-focused therapy (EFT), experienced person-centred therapists are best placed to offer it. The majority of CfD practice – characterised in Chapter 8 as the 'Counselling for Depression Therapeutic Stance' – will be familiar territory for these experienced PCT practitioners. We hope they will be reassured to find a good portion of their established everyday work here, albeit presented in a new integrated therapy for the first time.

Writing this book has been an exciting adventure for us. It is the first time we have worked together since Pete was responsible for Andy's original training in 1986. While exciting on the one hand, it has also been hard work and not without its problems. Many readers will know that ideas such as competence, manualisation, protocols, outcome and adherence measures are troublesome if not anathema for humanistic theory and practice. We had numerous difficulties to surmount as we navigated a course between the sensitive areas of values and principles which underpin counselling philosophy, theory and practice. One thing we can be sure of is that we will not have satisfied everyone. Our determination continues to be fuelled by two desires. First, to see person-centred and experiential counselling available free to patients in the National Health Service via IAPT, and second, for jobs to be available for the thousands of already well-qualified person-centred and experiential practitioners working in primary care. The continuing project will see a randomised controlled trial led by Professor Michael Barkham at the University of Sheffield, comparing CfD with CBT with depressed clients accessing therapy in the Sheffield IAPT service to hopefully further strengthen the evidence base.

2

Evidence-Based Practice and Person-Centred and Experiential Therapies

Andy Hill and Robert Elliott

Evidence-based practice (EBP)

What is EBP?

During the last 20 years the evidence-based paradigm has gained pre-eminence and in the UK context has been enshrined in the process of developing clinical guidelines, as set out by NICE. In the world of UK public healthcare a rigorous assessment of the efficacy – and increasingly the cost-effectiveness – of treatments is necessary before recommendations can be made. This is to ensure that healthcare interventions are effective and represent value for money for the taxpayer. Wasting taxpayers' money by providing ineffective treatments can open governments and their departments to political and ethical criticism, which they are anxious to avoid.

EBP is a scientific paradigm which has been adopted as a defence against such criticism. Originating in the world of medicine, as opposed to psychological therapy, it was described by Sackett et al. (1996: 71–2), as a combination of rigorous science and professional judgement:

> the conscientious, explicit, and judicious use of current best evidence in making decisions about the care of individual patients. The practice of Evidence-based Medicine means integrating individual clinical expertise with the best available external clinical evidence from systematic research. Good doctors use both individual clinical expertise and the best available external evidence, and neither alone is enough. Without clinical expertise, practice risks becoming tyrannised by evidence, for even excellent external evidence may be inapplicable to or inappropriate for an individual patient. Without best current evidence, practice risks becoming rapidly out of date, to the detriment of patients.

The paradigm aims to integrate clinical judgement with the findings of high-quality research to ensure healthcare interventions are guided by the best contemporary knowledge of effectiveness in order to maximise outcomes for service users. The implementation of the paradigm within the UK healthcare context includes a number of elements:

- A definition of what constitutes high-quality efficacy research (i.e. randomised controlled trials)
- A technology for aggregating and synthesising the findings from multiple high-quality research studies (i.e. systematic reviews and meta-analyses)
- A method for translating research findings into practice and identifying where there are gaps in research (i.e. guideline development groups)
- Infrastructure to ensure research is carried out where gaps exist (i.e. grant funding programs)

Randomised controlled trials (RCTs)

As EBP is currently defined in the UK, the RCT has been accorded with significant status as a highly rigorous research design capable of producing reliable evidence on the effectiveness of treatments. In terms of the interventions they provide, practitioners need to know whether a treatment has been shown to produce beneficial effects and which of the wide range of therapies available appears to work best (Bower and King, 2000). Although not without its limitations, the RCT design is well placed to answer these questions, resulting from its ability to establish cause and effect relationships between interventions and outcomes. There are many reasons other than therapy why a client may improve while in therapy. The simple passage of time may be enough to produce recovery (so-called 'spontaneous remission'); extra-therapy factors such as the client's social circumstances may change, leading to greater levels of support and better interpersonal relationships; involvement in new self-help activities such as regular exercise may also be a factor. These variables need to be controlled in order to establish a causal link between therapy and its outcomes. Within a research study, the degree of confidence that a causal link has been established by ruling out other causes is known as the *internal validity* of the study. This contrasts with *construct validity*, the degree to which the therapy delivered is what it is claimed or theorised to be, and *external validity*, the degree to which the relationships within the study can be generalised beyond the research to practical situations: whether the findings of the study hold true in other settings, with other therapists and clients in the real world.

A number of strategies are employed to protect the internal validity of RCTs. Clients need to be selected on the basis of the type of problem that is being targeted and according to specified levels of severity. There may be additional criteria governing the recruitment of clients including the absence of comorbid problems such as drug or alcohol misuse. It is clear to see how these kinds of controls, which are necessary in trials, would be impractical in routine practice. Where a trial seeks to establish whether or not an intervention is effective a *no-treatment control group* will be introduced, primarily to control for the passage of time and spontaneous remission. It is well known that a proportion of psychological problems will improve over time without any professional intervention. Control groups prevent spontaneous remission being confused with the effects of an intervention by ensuring that it affects both the control and the active treatment group. If it is found that the levels of recovery in the intervention group are not significantly different from those in the control group, then, all things being equal, it can be concluded that the intervention did not provide benefits over and above what would have happened anyway without therapy and hence that the treatment was not effective. If participants in the active treatment group did worse than those in the no-treatment control group then it could be concluded that the intervention had negative effects and was harmful. Without a control group it would be difficult to discern these effects with any degree of certainty.

A somewhat different issue is the construct validity of the treatments, whether the therapy is delivered as intended and what the active nature of the therapy is. Thus, adherence and competence checks are used to evaluate whether the therapists within the trial are delivering the therapy they are supposed to. An example of such a check is the Person-Centred and Experiential Psychotherapy Scale (PCEPS), which is described in Chapter 10. A further issue that can threaten the construct validity of trials is the so-called placebo effect of being offered therapy as opposed to being put on a waiting list. Unlike with drug trials where participants receive either a drug or placebo and are unaware of which of these they are receiving, in trials of psychological therapies it is not possible to disguise whether or not participants are receiving therapy. This sets up psychological differences between the groups, where those assigned to the waiting list may feel disappointed and those assigned to treatment may feel hopeful of a resolution of their problems. This instillation of hope may be the actual active ingredient in the treatment rather than the theorised change processes, such as the empathic exploration of depressive experiences. A third important construct validity issue is the fact that there are nonspecific factors common to all therapies that are likely to be responsible for effects. The common factors issue derives from the fact that all therapies share common features such as attention, empathy, supportive listening and a coherent theoretical framework. The extent to which these factors produce benefits as opposed to more technical aspects of therapy is an important question. Some trials have addressed this question by introducing sessions of non-directive, supportive listening to the control group, in an attempt to separate out the effects of the more technical aspects of the therapy. The use of placebo and non-specific control groups in therapy research has been widely criticised, especially when applied to relational therapies such as psychodynamic and humanistic approaches, where it can be difficult, if not impossible, to sort out common factors from those unique to the particular approach.

This leads us on to *comparative trials,* which seek to ascertain whether one type of therapy is superior to another by using two or more different active treatments in order to identify the most effective one. This type of 'horse race' study assumes that psychological therapy is generally beneficial, but aims to establish which type of therapy works best for a particular client population. The advantages of this study design are that the positive expectations that come from receiving treatment (as opposed to being assigned to a waiting list control group) are equal in all groups within the trial and that common factors are controlled as they, by definition, exist in all treatment groups. The main downside of this design is that differences between active treatments are typically fairly small, and so it often takes a large, expensive study with many clients to detect differences.

Another key feature of RCTs is randomisation, used to reduce the likelihood of significant pre-treatment differences between the groups that could produce post-treatment differences in outcomes. As long as the number of participants in a trial is large enough, then the random allocation of participants to the different groups within a trial will make it unlikely that there will be any systematic differences between the groups on any variable (either known or unknown). If this is the case, then between-group differences in post-treatment outcome can be attributed to differences between treatments rather than pre-existing differences between groups.

External validity is a term used to describe the extent to which the findings of a trial can be applied to contexts outside of the study, particularly to routine practice settings. There tends to be an inverse relationship between internal and external validity; high levels of internal validity typically lead to low external validity and vice versa. While both types of validity are desirable for RCTs, the inherent conflict between the two has led to the development of a dichotomy in the design of trials. Those that privilege internal validity, often referred to as *explanatory* trials, emphasise strict control of variables to ensure that the causal relationship between intervention and effects is not compromised. Usually this degree of control is neither feasible nor desirable in routine settings and so such studies are more akin to laboratory-type experiments than evaluations of what happens in routine practice: interventions are clearly specified; the number of therapy sessions is specific; participants are recruited according to rigid criteria. In contrast, *pragmatic* trials seek to strike more of a balance between internal and external validity: therapy is provided more flexibly; recruitment of participants to the trial is more reflective of the clients who would normally present to a service for therapy. The aim here is less to establish a cause-effect relationship between intervention and outcome, and more to evaluate interventions in routine settings to identify benefits to clients using services. In making judgements about the results of trials it is important to take on board the type of trial in question, as different criteria apply in assessing the two different types of trial. For more information on RCT methodology see Torgerson and Torgerson (2008).

Systematic reviews

An individual RCT study, although producing significant results, does not usually represent adequate evidence on which to base major policy decisions that may affect millions of health service users. A body of evidence is required, bringing together multiple studies and weighing their findings. The traditional literature review has in the past provided this function, where a subject expert would select a group of papers and provide a summary of these. The problem with this type of review is that they are open to charges of bias both in the selection of the original papers and the interpretation of their findings. A hallmark of the RCT study design is to reduce bias to a minimum; for the review of such studies to be so susceptible to bias undermines this intention. Systematic review methodology has been developed to address this problem and support EBP.

Unlike traditional reviews, systematic reviews are explicit in their methodology and transparent in how conclusions are derived. They can take the form of narrative reviews, where research evidence is analysed and summarised in verbal form, or they can employ a statistical technique known as meta-analysis. This latter technique aggregates statistical data from multiple studies to produce a calculation of effectiveness and has the benefit of pooling the results of RCTs with small sample sizes that may, in themselves, lack the statistical power to detect small but important effects. When the results of these small studies are pooled, significant and robust findings may emerge. Systematic reviews set out to answer specific questions and follow a detailed protocol for how the review will be conducted. The question should specify who the participants are, the intervention and the outcome(s) of interest. For example:

1. adult users of primary care
2. receiving counselling
3. for depression

A search strategy should specify the search terms used and which of the electronic databases of published literature are to be searched. If a search of the unpublished literature is to be conducted then this also should be specified. Inclusion and exclusion criteria are necessary to clarify how the individual studies were selected for inclusion in the review and what quality criteria were used to ensure that the review findings are based upon the most reliable studies. Given that some degree of bias is inevitable, strategies should be in place to reduce bias and all stages of the review process should be as transparent as possible. While systematic reviews aim to guide healthcare interventions based on robust and reliable evidence, it is important to bear in mind that the quality of a review's findings depends on the quality of the primary research (i.e. the individual RCTs and other studies) on which the review is based. It is therefore quite common, where there is an absence of reliable primary research, for reviews to be inconclusive as regards recommendations for clinical practice, but specific in identifying areas where new research studies are needed. Hence systematic reviews can be very useful in telling what we don't know.

As long ago as 1972, a British epidemiologist, Archie Cochrane, recognised healthcare professionals' need for rigorous and reliable reviews of scientific literature. The Cochrane Collaboration was established in response to this call. It is an international organisation aiming to help health professionals make well-informed decisions by supplying them with up-to-date systematic reviews of RCT evidence. There are a number of groups within the collaboration specialising in particular areas of healthcare, including mental health. A rigorous and standardised method of meta-analysis is used across all the groups to ensure the research evidence is of the highest quality. Reviews are published in the Cochrane Library, which is updated on a regular basis.[1] For more information on systematic review methodology see Petticrew and Roberts (2006).

---

[1] www.thecochranelibrary.com/view/0/index.html (retrieved 04/05/2013).

The National Institute for Health and Care Excellence

The role of NICE is to provide national guidance and advice to improve health and social care. Its scope is very wide, covering bio-medical interventions, mental health, public health and social care. Along with the provision of information services for those working in health and social care, it produces evidence-based guidance and develops quality standards and metrics to measure the performance of services.

Originally set up in 1999 as the National Institute for Clinical Excellence, in 2005, after merging with the Health Development Agency, it began developing public health guidance to help prevent ill health and promote healthier lifestyles, changing its name to the National Institute for Health and Clinical Excellence. In April 2013 NICE took on responsibility for developing guidance and quality standards in social care, and its name changed once more to reflect these new responsibilities. NICE is accountable to the Department of Health, but is operationally independent of government. The National Collaborating Centre for Mental Health has been commissioned by NICE to produce guidelines relating to psychological and other interventions for mental health problems.

NICE guidance and recommendations are made by independent committees. Topics for guidance and appraisals are decided by the Department of Health, based on a number of factors, including the burden of disease, the impact on resources and whether there is inappropriate variation in practice across the country. The process of guideline development uses the best available evidence and includes the views of experts, patients and carers, and industry. Guidance is reviewed regularly to ensure it is up to date and a consultation process is in place to allow individuals, patient groups, charities and industry to comment on recommendations. An independent guideline development group is established for each clinical guideline being developed, including health professionals and patient/carer representatives with relevant expertise and experience. Registered stakeholders are invited to nominate people to join the group. There is a specific protocol for guideline development[2] which uses rigorous systematic review methods, looking at the evidence available and considering comments made on draft versions of the guideline issued for consultation before producing the final version. Not only does NICE provide guidance on health and social care practice, but also it identifies gaps in the evidence base and makes recommendations for future research.

National Institute for Health Research (NIHR)

For new research to take place infrastructure is needed to support it. Funded through the Department of Health and established in 2006, the NIHR[3] aims to set research

---

[2] http://publications.nice.org.uk/the-guidelines-manual-pmg6 (retrieved 12/11/2013).
[3] www.nihr.ac.uk/about/Pages/default.aspx (retrieved 12/11/2013).

priorities and provide funding for social care and public health research in order to improve treatments for the benefit of patients. The Health and Social Care Act 2012 places a statutory duty on the Secretary of State to promote and support research and the NIHR provides a key means through which this duty is discharged. Its role is to develop the research evidence to support decision-making by professionals, policy makers and patients, make this evidence available and to encourage its uptake and use. It is for other organisations, such as NICE, to use the research evidence to provide national guidance on promoting good health and preventing and treating ill health. NIHR's key objective is to improve the quality, relevance and focus of research in the NHS and social care by distributing funds in a transparent way after open competition and peer review. The NIHR funds a range of programmes addressing a broad range of health priorities. Funding is based on the quality and relevance of the research to social services, public health and the NHS.

Criticisms of EBP

Whereas providing therapy to clients provides the foreground for working as a counsellor in health and social care settings, EBP provides the backdrop. A funda-mental assumption in such settings is that practice should be informed by research evidence and so open to revision and adaptation in the light of new findings. The nature of evidence tends to be defined by positivist epistemology, supported by RCT and meta-analytical methods and implemented by organisations established to generate research knowledge and practice guidelines. While laudable in its intentions to improve treatments for patients and avoid harmful and wasteful practices, EBP has presented significant challenges, particularly for counsellors working in NHS settings. A number of criticisms have been levelled at EBP, particularly with regard to its reliance on RCTs.

To begin with, EBP had its origins in evidence-based medicine (Sackett et al., 1996), which means that it uses methods originally developed to test biomedical treatments. These methods are now being applied to the evaluation of psychosocial interventions. Thus, drug-trial methods are being used to test the effectiveness of relational and inter-personal interventions as opposed to those that rely on biochemical mechanisms and direct physical intervention (e.g. surgery). Unlike in drug trials, where those in the control condition receive a placebo, in trials of psychological therapies participants cannot be blinded as to whether or not they are receiving an active treatment. This in itself can produce psychological differences in the control and the intervention group, with those being offered therapy feeling more positive and hopeful for recovery, as discussed previously.

The fact that there are many different 'brands' of therapy (like different brands of drugs) gives the impression that these are all distinctive interventions with their own particular techniques and mechanisms of change. However, they are all talking therapies, relying on interpersonal relating, which means that they share important common or non-specific factors. Examples are: being related to in a warm and collaborative manner; being listened to supportively; being empathised with; being offered hope within a theoretical framework that explains problems and how to get better. These factors are common across therapies and are responsible for a proportion of the positive outcomes experienced by clients. In RCTs it is difficult to disaggregate specific effects (those techniques and methods specific to particular types of therapy) from non-specific effects (those elements common to all therapies) as a therapeutic approach tends to be delivered as a package in a trial. If indeed it is the non-specific factors as opposed to the specific factors which produce the majority of therapeutic change for clients then it follows that all types of therapy will be more or less equally effective, a common finding where different therapies have been tested against each other. In a reference to the story of Alice in Wonderland, this is often referred to as the *Dodo Bird Verdict* (Wampold, 2001). By casting doubt upon exactly what the therapeutic ingredients are that have been tested, the common factors argument tends to undermine RCT evidence supporting the different 'brands' of therapy.

Triallists (that is, people who believe in the centrality of RCTs as a scientific method) have responded to this challenge by creating an *attention/placebo* to be given to the control group, to compensate for common factors. Most often referred to as *supportive therapy* (or sometimes, confusingly, as *non-directive supportive therapy*), this is an invented control treatment in which clients receive various kinds of psychological support, including sympathetic, supportive listening, with varying degrees of empathy, sharing and practical problem-solving; in contrast, those in the intervention group receive a structured and theoretically grounded therapy such as CBT, psychodynamic therapy or person-centred therapy. Supportive therapy conditions often have specific treatment elements such as exploration of traumatic events systematically removed, in a research strategy that has been referred to as 'intent to fail', s o that they can make a contrasting treatment look better. While this represents a useful step towards controlling for common factors, it may still not provide a full placebo effect, if those receiving it are aware that they are not receiving a full, bona fide therapeutic intervention.

A further problem lies in the delivery of the intervention. Whereas in drug trials the health professionals administering the drug are independent of the intervention (generally it does not matter who supplies the drug to the trial participant), in RCTs of psychological therapies the therapist is confounded with the therapy (therapists work in particular ways and have different personal qualities, so it does matter who delivers the therapy). To control for this, for example, where two therapies are being compared, the same therapists may deliver both therapies in the trial. While this helps to eliminate therapist effects it does raise the problem of whether therapists have the ability to deliver different therapeutic approaches with equal amounts of skill and commitment.

Further criticisms levelled at RCTs relate to their lack of external validity and the cost of conducting them. The fact that conditions are often carefully controlled in RCTs (particularly explanatory trials) means the applicability of their findings to routine settings where conditions are generally uncontrolled is questionable.

Therapists in routine practice rarely have the luxury of selecting their clients according to their having single diagnoses and specific levels of problem severity; in routine practice complexity and comorbidity are the norm. Likewise, in routine practice, therapy is delivered flexibly, responding to clients' needs as opposed to according to a manual or therapeutic protocol. This lack of external validity has led to the argument that the findings of RCTs are only applicable to other RCTs and are irrelevant to routine practice. The cost of conducting this type of study is also considerable, making it unfeasible that all models of psychological therapy could be tested in RCTs. The net result of this is we are left with a 'first past the post' scenario with CBT recommended as a frontline therapy, based on its extensive RCT evidence base, and other therapies struggling to find funding for research and occupying very marginal positions in clinical guidelines, or being excluded completely. This state of affairs does not mean that these excluded or marginal therapies do not work (a lack of evidence of effectiveness is not the same as evidence of ineffectiveness). It simply means that they have not yet been tested by RCT methodology; whether, at some point in the future, the funding and resources will become available for this to occur is a moot point. The resulting scenario has resulted in a narrowing of practice within health-care settings and the marginalisation of a range of not yet tested, but likely to be effective, therapeutic approaches, with a consequent reduction in choice of therapies available for service users.

The focus on RCTs has led to two other important kinds of scientific evidence being ignored. First, systematic case studies use rich case records of qualitative and quantitative data to assess client outcome and the causal role of therapy. They can be used by counsellors and psychotherapists to study their own practice and to document the possible effectiveness of new approaches and new client populations. Second, pre-post studies (also known as open clinical trials) are useful for documenting the amount of pre-post client change, which can be useful for evaluating the possible effectiveness of new or emerging treatments and for creating benchmarks against which to assess routine practice. Thus, an exclusive focus on RCT evidence slights both innovative, emerging approaches and also real-world practice.

The RCT design itself suffers from both excessive support, with some viewing it as the only useful type of research on which to base policy decisions, and excessive denigration, with others viewing the method as reductionist and inappropriate for the field of counselling and psychotherapy. A more balanced position would be to recognise the contribution RCTs can make to our knowledge of the field and also their many limitations. RCT evidence can provide a useful counterbalance to clinical judgement, which at times can be flawed, and also an antidote to blind adherence to particular approaches based on faith or ideology. Such evidence also provides some protection for the public in identifying treatments that work and those that may be ineffective or harmful. It should also be recognised that an accumulation of RCT evidence is responsible for psychological therapies now being recommended as frontline treatments for common mental health problems (as opposed to medication alone). Without RCTs this may not have happened.

Research on the effectiveness of PCE therapy with depression

In this section we review two different sets of research on the effectiveness of PCE therapy with depression: the evidence reviewed by the Guideline Development Group (GDG) in constructing the NICE guideline for depression with adults NICE (2009a) and Elliott et al.'s (2013) meta-analysis of 27 studies of humanistic psychotherapy and counselling, the latter having a much broader focus than the former.

Evidence reviewed for the NICE guideline for depression

This section presents a discussion of the evidence for the effectiveness of counselling reviewed by the GDG for the production of the depression guideline. A full summary of the results of the studies is available (NICE, 2009a).[4] Table 2.1 is extracted from the full version of the NICE depression guideline document. (Note that although it had been included in the previous guideline and was used for utility analyses, the Ward et al., 2000 study was excluded from the main analyses in the 2009 update.)

Characteristics of included studies

Several studies reviewed by the depression GDG were rejected as they did not meet the criteria for inclusion. A study using a non-RCT method (Marriott and Kellett, 2009) compared counselling, cognitive analytic therapy and CBT in routine service settings. The study used neither randomisation to treatment group nor a no-treatment control group. Depression pre- and post-treatment was measured using the Beck Depression Inventory (BDI). This study was excluded by the GDG from the analysis on the grounds that its sample size was too small to reach any definitive conclusion on the differential effectiveness of the treatments. Additionally, just 34% of the sample had a diagnosis of depression, making it difficult to draw any conclusions about the interventions' effectiveness as treatments for depression. A further non-RCT study (Stiles et al., 2006) compared CBT, psychodynamic therapy and person-centred therapy in routine NHS settings, using CORE as the outcome measure. As with Marriott and Kellett (2009) randomisation and a control group were not part of the study design. This study was excluded by the GDG because, once again, not all participants in the study met the criteria for depression and other diagnoses were included in the sample, making it difficult to draw conclusions about the effectiveness of the interventions with depression. Ward et al. (2000) was initially excluded on similar grounds; only 62% of the participants

---

[4] www.nice.org.uk/nicemedia/live/12329/45896/45896.pdf (retrieved 12/11/2013).

Table 2.1 Counselling studies reviewed in the Depression Guideline (NICE 2009a)

Study	Participants	Interventions	Depression measures used
Bedi et al. (2000) (RCT)[1] (UK)	clients recruited via GP n=103 diagnosed by GP for depression using RDC[2]	• antidepressants • six sessions of counselling using a flexible approach according to needs of clients	BDI[3] and RDC taken at 8 weeks and 12 month follow-up
Goldman et al. (2006) (RCT) (Canada)	n=38 all with major depression measured by DSM-IV	• client-centred therapy: 9–20 sessions • EFT[4]: 9–20 sessions	SCL-90[5], BDI
Greenberg et al. (1998) (RCT) (Canada)	n=34 all with major depression measured by DSM-III-R	• client-centred therapy: 15–20 sessions • process-experiential therapy (EFT): 15–20 sessions	SCL-90, BDI
Simpson et al. (2003) (RCT) (UK)	clients recruited from 9 GP practices n=145 all with depression score>14 on BDI	• 6–12 sessions of psychodynamic counselling + usual care • usual care (note usual care in some cases involved use of medication)	BDI at 6 and 12 months
Watson et al. (2003) (RCT) (Canada)	n=93 all with major depression measured by DSM-IV	• CBT: 16 sessions • process-experiential therapy (EFT): 16 sessions	SCL-90, BDI
Ward et al. (2000)[6] (RCT) (UK)	clients referred by GPs, n=464, 62% diagnosed with depression (BDI>14)	• usual GP care • CBT • non-directive counselling based on Rogers' approach • Duration of therapy: 6–12 weekly sessions	BDI at baseline, 4 months and 12 month follow-up

[1]randomised control trial
[2]Research diagnostic criteria. See: Spitzer, R.L., Endicott, J. and Robins, E. (1978) 'Research diagnostic criteria: rationale and reliability.' *Archives of General Psychiatry,* 35: 773–82.
[3]Beck Depression Inventory. See: Beck, A.T., Ward, C.H., Mendelson, M. et al. (1961) 'An inventory for measuring depression.' *Archives of General Psychiatry,* 4: 561–71.
[4]Emotion-focused therapy.
[5]Symptom Checklist 90. For more information see: http://psychcorp.pearsonassessments.com/HAIWEB/Cultures/en-us/Productdetail.htm?Pid=PAg514 (retrieved 12/11/2013).
[6]Initially excluded from the review, but a subgroup analysis of the data from the trial was included following this initial decision.

met the diagnosis for depression, and also the study was not completely randomised. However, a subsequent subgroup analysis focusing only on those participants who met the criteria for depression in this trial was submitted and was included in the evidence review. The results of this analysis indicated a significant medium-sized effect on depression scores post treatment but no significant effect at follow-up.

Five studies met the criteria for inclusion and were included in the evidence review (all in Table 2.1 except Ward et al., 2000). These studies form the basis of the evidence for the effectiveness of counselling in the NICE (2009a) guideline. Bedi et al. (2000) compared the effectiveness of counselling versus antidepressants. No significant differences between the two types of treatment were found and at 12-month follow-up clinician-reported depression scores were significantly lower in the antidepressant group when compared with counselling. On this the GDG viewed the study as inconclusive and not supporting a conclusion that counselling and antidepressants were equivalent. They also stated that this study should be treated with some caution as the introduction of a patient preference element to the trial led to considerable differences in baseline severity measures between the two arms.

Two studies (Goldman et al., 2006; Greenberg and Watson, 1998) compared two different types of PCE therapy (client-centred and emotion-focused therapy). In Goldman et al. (2006) the comparison of client-centred counselling and EFT favoured EFT. In Greenberg and Watson (1998) the comparison of client-centred counselling and EFT (referred to as process-experiential counselling)[5] findings indicated that there was no significant difference between treatments in the reduction of self-reported depression scores. The GDG urged caution in the interpretation of these results because of what it considered to be small sample sizes.

Simpson et al. (2003) compared the combination of psychodynamic counselling plus GP care with usual GP care alone and found no important clinical benefit of therapy plus GP care. Watson et al. (2003) compared EFT with CBT. The GDG criticised this study on the basis of its sample size, judging it to be small and concluding that the study produced insufficient evidence to reach any definite conclusion about the relative effectiveness of the two treatments.

Despite a number of studies having major depression as a criterion for the recruitment of participants (see Table 2.1), the GDG concluded that participants in the reviewed studies were predominantly drawn from groups in the mild-to-moderate range of depression (mean baseline BDI scores between 18 and 26) and two trials included people with minor depression (BDI scores starting from 14) (Bedi et al., 2000 and Ward et al., 2000). Because of this the GDG concluded that evidence supported the effectiveness of counselling for mild-to-moderate depression but not for severe depression. The evidence was also seen to be limited by the small size of the samples of participants recruited into the studies, resulting in studies with low *power* to reliably detect differences between groups within trials. The concept of *power* refers to whether the sample size of a trial is large enough to detect differences that might exist between groups. A relatively small sample size can be used where the differences between groups

---

[5] Note: *process-experiential* and *emotion-focused* are two names for the same therapy.

are expected to be large, such as where a therapy is compared with no-treatment. Where two active treatments are compared such as EFT and CBT (Watson et al., 2003) and differences would be expected to be small, a much larger sample size would have been needed to detect differences. The evidence reviewed was thus judged to be limited partly because of small sample sizes. Another issue, relating to sample selection, is whether participants meet the criteria for depression. NICE guidelines are disorder specific and so it follows that the guidelines for depression should be based on studies of participants who were clearly depressed. Hence studies of participants who did not meet the full diagnostic criteria for depression or who had other prominent psychological problems besides depression were excluded from the evidence review.

The fact that some clients may have strong preferences for particular treatments presents a further problem for the randomisation process in RCTs. If allocated to a treatment they do not want, these participants may become demoralised, hence affecting the outcomes of the treatment they receive. Random allocation to groups is thus predicated on the notion that clients have no strong preference for treatment. Where strong preferences exist *patient preference* trials have been designed to enable those without strong preferences to be randomly allocated and those with strong preferences to be given the intervention they wish to receive. Whereas this is more ethical and helps with recruitment, it can have the effect of setting up the differences between groups that random allocation intends to prevent. This is a criticism levelled at the Bedi et al. (2000) study.

The GDG considered studies that compared two different forms of PCE therapy (client-centred and EFT) (Goldman et al., 2006; Greenberg and Watson, 1998) as problematic because they only evaluated the effects of two quite similar interventions. Had these therapies been compared with a no-treatment control group or comparison with a recommended treatment such as CBT, then the effectiveness of these therapies would have been more clearly established.

The definition of *counselling* presented some difficulty in assessing the evidence. A number of terms were used in the studies reviewed for the depression guideline, including client-centred, psychodynamic, process-experiential, emotion-focused (the latter two being different terms for the same therapy). This underlines some of the complexities around how *counselling* is defined. Within the counselling profession the term is viewed as something of an umbrella term embracing a variety of approaches. However, outside of the profession counselling tends to be viewed as a type of intervention distinct from other therapies such as CBT and psychodynamic therapy. This dual perspective tends to perpetuate misunderstandings about the nature of counselling. From an EBP perspective it also presents fundamental difficulties: reviewing research evidence and developing clinical guidelines require a more precise definition of the intervention in question.

Apart from one study (Simpson et al., 2003), the evidence that supports the inclusion of counselling in the NICE depression guideline consists mainly of RCTs of either person-centred therapy or EFT. This would suggest that the term *counselling* as defined in the NICE depression guideline is based on predominantly PCE types of therapy (namely client-centred, based on Carl Rogers' theories, and EFT). The fact that there is evidence for both person-centred and EFT also suggests that elements from both of these approaches are effective in the treatment of depression and should form a basis for a more precise definition of *counselling* as specified in the guideline. The fact that the GDG viewed the evidence for counselling as limited underlines the need for more RCTs with larger samples, more strict selection of participants to meet the criteria for depression, and with more severely depressed populations. Furthermore, the focus should be on comparisons with waiting list control groups or with established treatments such as CBT.

The Elliott et al. (2013) meta-analysis

As noted earlier, a meta-analysis is an analysis of analyses, carried out in a number of stages. Initially, a number of studies examining the same research question are collected and their relevant characteristics coded (for example, number of participants, measures used, whether participants were randomly assigned to treatments). The next step is complex and involves putting the measures in all the individual studies onto the same metric, so that they can be combined and compared. This common metric is called an *effect size* (ES). The most frequently used ES measure is called the *standardised mean difference*, which is, in the case of this meta-analysis, the difference between the average pre-therapy score and the average post-therapy score divided by the *pooled standard deviation*. Standard deviation is a measure of the variability associated with an average.[6] The last step in a meta-analysis is analysing all the analyses (that's the 'meta' part of the process), running various corrections, coming up with summary values, and looking for variables that might explain differences in effect sizes (such as randomisation or level of therapists' experience).

In their meta-analysis of outcome studies of humanistic-experiential therapies, Elliott et al. (2013) took a much more inclusive approach to the evidence review process than was used by the NICE GDG. There were several reasons for this. First, when Elliott and colleagues began meta-analysing person-centred-experiential outcome research (Greenberg et al., 1994), there was very little research available and so they wanted to use all the available data, including evidence for emerging versions of PCE therapy and applications to new client populations. Second, they were concerned that selecting studies based on judgements of quality would introduce bias: if you don't like the results of a study, it is very easy to find faults with the statistics and design. Third, following the original philosophy behind meta-analysis (Glass et al., 1981), a wide range of studies using different methods was included and methodological features of studies were coded in order to make it possible to see what difference these made for the results. For example, there is an assumption that non-randomised studies are biased and thus produce different results from randomised studies.

In any event, Elliott et al. (2013) looked at approximately 200 studies of the outcome of PCE therapies (which they referred to as humanistic-experiential psychotherapies, or

---

[6] For more information on the calculation of standard deviation and effect size see Sanders and Wilkins (2010).

HEPs). Within this data set were five types of client presenting problem: depression, relationship problems, coping with chronic medical problems (e.g. HIV), habitual self-damaging behaviours (substance misuse, eating disorders) and psychosis. Of these, there were more studies of depression than any other client presenting problem. Twenty-seven studies of depression were included in the meta-analysis and form the basis of the discussion here. There were 34 samples of clients within the 27 studies, comprising a total of 1,287 clients. The types of therapy tested were most commonly person-centred therapy (10 samples), supportive therapy (often used as a control condition, as discussed earlier in this chapter) (9 samples), or EFT (8 samples). Other types of experiential therapy, such as gestalt or psychodrama, were also included. For a more detailed analysis of the results see Appendix 2 and Elliott et al. (2013).

The 27 studies fell into two broad categories: those which measured levels of distress pre- and post-therapy without the use of a control or comparison group (n=19) and similar studies which made use of comparison/control groups (n=8). Analyses were based on the calculation of effect size, where 0.2 and is viewed as small, 0.5 as medium and 0.8 as large (Cooper, 2008). The weighted mean pre-post effect size across all 34 samples was large. On the other hand, the effect size across just the 8 comparison/control studies was somewhat weaker, but still a statistically significant weighted effect in the small to medium range. Within this latter group of studies were two outliers (Maynard, 1993; Tyson and Range, 1987), where negative outcomes were found for the interventions compared with no-treatment groups. Both of these studies had small samples and used group interventions which were not bona fide PCE therapies.

Where PCE is compared with other types of therapy (23 studies), most commonly CBT, the outcomes are broadly equivalent: positive and negative comparative results are evenly balanced across the studies. Within the range of PCE therapies there is some preliminary support that process-guiding approaches may have some superiority over approaches that do not use these methods with depressed clients. Four studies made comparisons between more and less process-guiding therapies involving depressed clients (Beutler et al., 1991; Goldman et al., 2006; Greenberg and Watson, 1998; Tyson and Range, 1987). A significant small to medium mean effect size was found across these studies. However there was a degree of heterogeneity in the interventions tested: Greenberg and Watson (1998) and Goldman et al. (2006) compared EFT with client-centred therapy; Beutler et al. (1991) compared focused-expressive group therapy with a supportive group involving bibliotherapy; and Tyson and Range (1987) compared group gestalt therapy with an active expression group.

Two clusters of evidence on depression are worth noting. First, there are the three well-designed comparative treatment RCTs testing EFT for depression (Goldman et al., 2006; Greenberg and Watson, 1998; Watson et al., 2003), comparing EFT with other therapies in the treatment of major depressive disorder, using medium-sized samples and conducted by two different research teams. These studies, also discussed earlier in this chapter, were brought to the attention of the NICE GDG in the review process but were generally dismissed for being relatively small and for comparing related treatments. Goldman et al. (2006) found that EFT had significantly better outcomes (including very low relapse rates) when compared with person-centred therapy. Watson et al. (2003)

found generally equivalent (and on some measures better) results compared with CBT. Second, there were four well-designed RCTs of person-centred therapy for perinatal depression with medium to large sample sizes that either showed superiority to treatment as usual (Holden et al., 1989; Morrell et al., 2009; Wickberg and Hwang, 1996), or no difference in comparison with CBT (Cooper et al., 2003) or short-term psychodynamic therapy (Cooper et al., 2003; Morrell et al., 2009). Both of these clusters of well-controlled studies met Chambless and Hollon's (1998) criteria for *efficacious and specific* treatments: that is, they were well-designed, conducted by at least two different research teams, and were either superior to some other treatment or superior to a recognised efficacious treatment.

Key recent studies include Cooper et al. (2003) and Morrell et al. (2009), both with perinatal depression as mentioned above, and two studies by Mohr and colleagues on depression in a medical population (Mohr et al., 2001; 2005). The other recent substantial study is Stice et al. (2010), in which adolescents with mild to moderate depression were randomised to one of four conditions: supportive group therapy vs. CBT group therapy vs. CBT bibliotherapy vs. controls. Participants seen in supportive therapy showed benefits comparable with those in CBT which were sustained to two year follow-ups and did much better than control group clients.

In summary, the evidence-based paradigm has become part of the fabric of systems of healthcare delivery, both in the UK and elsewhere. The principles of this approach inform clinical guidelines and decisions about the commissioning of treatments. This has presented significant challenges to PCE therapies because of the relative paucity of RCT evidence compared with CBT and the consequential marginalisation of the PCE approach, particularly in healthcare settings. The narrowness of the scope used by NICE for the inclusion of research evidence into clinical guidelines inevitably excludes significant areas of research evidence supporting the effectiveness of PCE therapies, prompting the need for NICE's methods to be reviewed. A more comprehensive review of the research on the effectiveness of PCE therapies with depression, including perinatal depression, suggests PCE therapies have a significant positive effect, with effect sizes varying between small and large depending on the type of studies analysed. In comparisons with other types of therapy PCE approaches have broadly similar outcomes and there is some preliminary support for the superiority of process-guiding approaches, which, in turn, needs to be tested in further studies. Drawing upon this evidence base, and in response to the crisis evidence-based practice has presented to PCE therapies, CfD has been developed in an attempt to delineate an evidence-based form of PCE therapy, which is specifically adapted for working with depression and can help to consolidate the position of PCE therapists in UK healthcare settings.

3

Introducing the Counselling for Depression Competence Framework

The research–practice gap

A key issue in EBP is the gap between research and practice. The intention behind EBP is for clients to receive interventions which have been tested under rigorous, controlled conditions and have been found to be effective, based on the premise that this predicts good outcomes for clients. As discussed in Chapter 2, in the world of RCTs, therapists usually provide therapy according to a manual and have their practice assessed to ensure adherence to the manual. This ensures that all therapists within the trial are delivering the same therapy with as little variation as possible and that the therapy can be replicated both in further research studies and in routine practice. However, in the world of routine practice, adherence to a therapy manual is not common practice and therapy tends to be shaped by any number of factors – personal philosophy, training, supervision, experience of casework with clients – resulting in a disjunction between research and practice. It is one thing for research to identify interventions that are effective, but if these are not delivered by therapists in routine settings then the whole EBP enterprise breaks down. It is important to bear in mind that this does not *in itself* mean that therapists in routine settings are working ineffectively, simply that there is a lack of certainty as to whether they are providing interventions which have been tested and found to be effective and so practice is less evidence-based. The problem is one of *translation*: ensuring that interventions found to be effective in research studies are transported into routine practice; a simple idea in theory, but quite complex in its implementation.

Counselling and the NICE guideline for depression

An initial step in the process of translating research findings into practice is provided by NICE whose role is to review research evidence (particularly from RCTs) and produce guidelines for clinical practice based on this. The NICE (2009a) guideline for depression is of particular importance to the counselling profession, firstly because depression is the single most common mental health problem experienced in the UK (see Chapter 4) and also the guideline recommends counselling for the treatment of depression, albeit with certain caveats. The guideline recommends CBT as a frontline therapy, but states for people who decline antidepressants, CBT, interpersonal psychotherapy (IPT), behavioural activation, or behavioural couples therapy (BCT), health professionals should consider recommending 'counselling for people with persistent subthreshold depressive symptoms or mild to moderate depression; offer 6–10 sessions over 8–12 weeks' (NICE, 2009a: 16). And so the NICE guideline recommends counselling in these circumstances but does not, however, give a particularly clear or detailed definition of what the intervention is.

Defining counselling

The (2009a) NICE guideline's recommendation of 'counselling' for certain types of depressed client immediately throws up complications, as a result of the term's semantic imprecision and variations in its usage. As discussed in Chapter 2, counselling can be used in both generic and specific ways. In the depression guideline the juxtaposition of counselling with other types of therapy (CBT, IPT etc.) suggests a specific definition as opposed to an 'umbrella' term. And so what is required is a meaningful and specific description of counselling as an intervention that can be implemented by practitioners, while still retaining links to the research evidence on which its recommendation is based.

Competence frameworks as a method for bridging the research–practice gap

A methodology with the potential to address the difficulties inherent in the definition of counselling and the complexities of translating research findings into practice was developed by Roth and Pilling (2008). The process involves the establishment of an Expert Reference Group (ERG), comprising experts in research and/or training, with additional representation from professional bodies. Taking responsibility for the review of relevant material and operating on the basis of consensus, the group follows a process of identifying exemplar RCTs supporting the efficacy of therapy and from these locating descriptions of 'best practice'. The therapy manuals from exemplar trials can be viewed as best practice: the things a therapist should be doing to achieve the best outcomes for the client. However, locating these manuals is not always straightforward: some trials provide references to manuals that explain the therapy in detail, others often provide very little detail as to the therapeutic approach. Where detail is scant, authors of the papers are contacted and asked for references to fuller descriptions or to exemplar texts (published or unpublished) which describe the therapeutic approach employed in the trials. From this literature, descriptions of practice can be extracted and written as competences. These are then grouped into areas of practice and built into a coherent model, taking on board how the different areas of practice interrelate and complement each other. The result is a framework of competences providing therapists with clear guidance on how to implement a particular model of therapy which has strong links to research evidence. This completes the process of *translation* referred to earlier.

A central premise of competence frameworks is that therapists need background knowledge relevant to their practice, and it is the ability to draw on and apply this knowledge in therapeutic work that marks out competence. Knowledge provides practitioners with a rationale for applying their skills; not just about *how*, but also *why* they are implementing them. In addition to knowledge and skills, therapists' attitudes are also critical; both in relation to the client, and also to the wider organisational and social context. Appropriate knowledge, skills and attitudes need to be developed by therapists to create the capacity to deliver therapy that is ethical, conforms to professional standards, and is appropriately adapted to the client's needs and cultural contexts. To provide a basis for therapy delivery competences need to be clear, understandable and valid (i.e. they are recognisable as describing the approach). A balance needs to be struck between complexity and simplicity: if defined too simply, or at too general a level, any therapist (or indeed, non-therapist) would be able to implement them, watering down the potency of what the client may receive. Conversely, if competences are too detailed and complex, the framework would lead to a mechanical 'if this-then that' style of practice, which is anathema to most relational therapies and practitioners. Ideally, a competence framework needs to be detailed enough to specify best practice, be set out in a form that is usable and be recognised as valid by its users.

Criticisms of the competence framework methodology

This method of translating the findings of RCTs into routine practice makes the assumption that there is a consensual view of the nature of 'evidence'. Particularly from a humanistic perspective, practitioners have expressed concerns about the RCT study design conventionally used to assess the efficacy of psychological therapies. Particular concerns are that the evidence base places an inappropriate focus on specific techniques of therapy, to the neglect of 'relationship' factors (such as the interpersonal contribution made by the therapist and the client) and the importance of the therapeutic alliance. Additionally, reliance on the RCT as the foundation of evidence-based practice inappropriately narrows the parameters from which evidence can be drawn, partly because such trials may be difficult to initiate (e.g., research funding may not be forthcoming). More fundamentally however, there is a view that trials need to be supplemented by qualitative approaches, or process-oriented research, to provide a more nuanced evidence base. On a more practical note, descriptions of the interventions in papers reporting RCTs are at times very thin and lacking in detail, limiting the quantity and quality of competences that can be drawn from these sources. In such circumstances an ERG may fall back on other published literature and expert opinion, thus providing sets of competences with weaker links to evidence of efficacy, but perhaps with greater utility to practitioners. It is important to acknowledge that while there are flaws in this methodology, the approach still has many advantages over one which relies purely on practitioners describing what they do. It is also important that descriptions of evidence-based interventions are developed rigorously and methodically to ensure they represent descriptions of best practice as accurately as possible.

The humanistic framework

Following this methodology and led by Professor Tony Roth, a number of competence frameworks have been developed across a range of therapeutic modalities, including humanistic therapy and a supervision framework.[1] The humanistic framework (Roth, Hill and Pilling, 2009) drew most extensively on what can best be described as 'counselling' research. A number of sources of evidence were used:

- A Cochrane review of counselling conducted by Bower and Rowland (2006)
- A database of humanistic psychological therapy trials collated by Professor Robert Elliott and colleagues at Strathclyde University. This was a comprehensive and continuously updated database maintaining a record of all humanistic trials, and was not restricted to RCTs
- A search of databases held by the British Psychological Society's Centre for Outcomes Research and Effectiveness[2] (used as part of NICE guideline development), identifying any additional humanistic trials not identified by the above sources of information

A review of these sources resulted in a final list of trials which met, or came close to meeting, NICE standards of evidence. The work was overseen by an ERG that concluded that the evidence base for the efficacy of humanistic psychological therapies was not especially extensive, though there were indications that the volume of research in this area was increasing. The ERG found support for the benefits of humanistic approaches in general, with substantive evidence of efficacy for EFT (Elliott et al., 2004). This, of course, does not indicate that other humanistic approaches are ineffective, rather that, for these approaches, there is an absence of evidence of effectiveness, rather than evidence of ineffectiveness.

---

[1] www.ucl.ac.uk/clinical-psychology/CORE/competence_frameworks.htm (retrieved 12/11/2013).
[2] www.ucl.ac.uk/clinical-psychology/CORE/core_homepage.htm (retrieved 12/11/2013).

A constraint in the development of the humanistic framework was a difficulty in locating therapy manuals from RCTs, with the exception of EFT and a manual used in the counselling study undertaken by King et al. (2000). It was hence necessary to supplement these with a set of core texts considered by the ERG to be representative of person-centred and humanistic practice (see Appendix 3). The competences which emerged were therefore based on an amalgamation of these sources.

The resulting framework (see Figure 3.1) includes a breadth of approaches whose affiliations are humanistic. This includes, for example, the person-centred approach (both 'classical' and more contemporary), together with related approaches such as EFT and integrative-humanistic therapy which combines psychodynamic and humanistic principles. There are significant variations in these different schools of humanistic therapy to the point where it becomes difficult to identify a common 'core' of philosophy and practice with which practitioners can affiliate. In order to accommodate this diversity the framework differentiates competences into:

- **Basic** competences which, broadly speaking, would be shared across all variants of humanistic therapy
- **Specific** competences which describe a number of interventions which would not be shared by all humanistic therapists

This diversity inevitably means that the framework will contain within it elements that therapists of different persuasions may not see as part of their routine practice.

The Counselling for Depression competence framework

The diversity of the humanistic framework rendered it too cumbersome to provide a template for evidence-based counselling as referenced in the NICE (2009a) depression guideline. It is neither feasible nor desirable for an individual therapist to practise across such a wide range of approaches (person-centred, client-centred, EFT, humanistic-integrative), and so further work was needed to narrow down a definition of counselling as an evidence-based intervention.

The next phase came in 2009 when the IAPT programme commissioned the full roll-out of NICE-recommended therapies additional to CBT, having achieved its original objective of building a CBT workforce. These additional therapies were counselling, brief psychodynamic therapy (known as dynamic interpersonal therapy [DIT]), IPT and BCT, all of which were recommended by NICE as second-line treatments for depression, with the exception of IPT, which has a strong evidence base and is viewed as frontline treatment for a number of psychological problems. The process of rolling out these therapies was to follow the model already used in building the CBT workforce: developing a competence framework, designing a training curriculum based on this, and finally training therapists to deliver the therapy. In the case of counselling, BACP was commissioned to carry out this work.

Ability to offer a therapeutic relationship that facilitates experiential exploration within a relational context

Generic therapeutic competences

- Knowledge and understanding of mental health problems
- Knowledge of, and ability to operate within, professional and ethical guidelines
- Knowledge of a model of therapy, and the ability to understand and employ the model in practice
- Ability to engage client
- Ability to foster and maintain a good therapeutic alliance, and to grasp the client's perspective and 'world view'
- Ability to work with the emotional content of sessions
- Ability to manage endings
- Ability to undertake generic assessment (relevant history and identifying suitability for intervention)
- Ability to make use of supervision

Basic humanistic psychological therapy competences

- Knowledge of the basic assumptions and principles of humanistic psychological therapies
- Ability to initiate therapeutic relationships
- Ability to explain and demonstrate the rationale for humanistic approaches to therapy
- Ability to work with the client to establish a therapeutic aim
- Ability to maintain and develop therapeutic relationships
- Ability to experience and communicate empathy
- Ability to experience and to communicate a fundamentally accepting attitude to clients
- Ability to maintain authenticity in the therapeutic relationship
- Ability to conclude the therapeutic relationship

Specific humanistic psychological therapy competences

- Approaches to work with emotions and emotional meaning
- Ability to help clients access and express emotions
- Ability to help clients articulate emotions
- Ability to help clients reflect on and develop emotional meanings
- Ability to help clients make sense of experiences that are confusing and distressing
- Ability to make use of methods that encourage active expression
- Approaches to working relationally
- Ability to maintain a client-centered stance
- Ability to work with the immediate therapeutic relationship

Specific humanistic adaptations

- Process Experiential/Emotion Focused Therapy

Metacompetences

- Generic metacompetences
- Capacity to use clinical judgement when implementing treatment models
- Capacity to adapt interventions in response to client feedback
- Humanistic metacompetences
- Metacompetences specific to humanistic psychological therapies competences

Figure 3.1 The map of the Humanistic Competence Framework

The humanistic psychological framework (Roth, Hill and Pilling, 2009) provided the starting point, with the obvious proviso that it would need to be scoped to identify a model of practice meeting the following criteria:

- The model is supported by evidence of effectiveness
- It is feasible to train UK counsellors in the model of practice within resource limitations
- The model is coherent in both theory and practice

The balancing act was to ensure that the resulting competences were evidence-based, would not create the need for the training of a brand new workforce (as had been the case with CBT) and would not produce an approach that was overly eclectic.

The review of research undertaken by the humanistic ERG had already signalled support for person-centred therapy and EFT. The NICE (2009a) guideline was also scrutinised to identify the types of counselling interventions tested in trials, and hence supported by evidence of effectiveness. While there was some variation in the interventions used, the most widely tested in the RCTs were person-centred (2 RCTs) and EFT (3 RCTs). On the basis of this, albeit fairly limited, RCT evidence, it seemed reasonable to conclude that, of the different areas of practice included in the humanistic framework, person-centred therapy and EFT had the strongest evidence base.

A second consideration was the feasibility of training counsellors in an evidence-based model and so a model of therapy which requires only an adaptation of existing skills and practices was developed. Although counsellors in the UK use a variety of models of practice, a 2010 survey of BACP members (total membership of approximately 40,000) found that 72% of BACP members had trained in either humanistic or person-centred counselling, suggesting that this approach was firmly rooted in routine practice. In contrast EFT is currently much less widely practised in the UK, and so its implementation would require extensive retraining for counsellors, with a consequential large demand on resources. Pragmatically it was important that the model of evidence-based counselling could build on the skills of the existing counselling workforce and be acquired by means of continuing professional development (CPD) training. Taking on board both the evidence base and these pragmatic issues, the task was to find a way to combine person-centred competences with a selection of EFT competences from the humanistic framework to form a coherent model of practice.

A significant area of EFT practice relies upon empathic responding and is fairly consistent with person-centred practice (see Chapter 8). In contrast *chair-work* is a specific method used in EFT (and in gestalt therapy) which is not widely recognised as being part of person-centred practice and so competences relating to this technique were excluded and those EFT competences based on empathic responding included. The *basic competences for humanistic psychological therapies* (see Figure 3.1) in their entirety and certain sections of the *specific humanistic psychological therapies competences* from the humanistic framework were amalgamated to form a new, narrower competence framework describing 'counselling' as referenced in the NICE (2009a) depression guideline. The resulting competence model was therefore an integration of person-centred and EFT interventions which could accurately be described as *person-centred/experiential therapy*, but which was termed *Counselling for Depression* to differentiate this intervention from other forms of counselling and to remain close to the terminology used in the NICE (2009a) depression guideline. The official description of CfD within the IAPT programme is as follows:

> Counselling for depression is a manualised form of psychological therapy as recommended by NICE (NICE, 2009) for the treatment of depression. It is based on a person-centred, experiential model and is particularly appropriate for people with persistent sub-threshold depressive symptoms or mild to moderate depression. Clinical trials have shown this type of counselling to be effective when 6–10 sessions are offered. However, it is recognised that in more complex cases which show benefit in the initial sessions, further improvement may be observed with additional sessions up to the maximum number suggested for other NICE recommended therapies such as CBT, that is, 20 sessions. (BACP, 2010)

CfD aims to address the emotional problems underlying depression along with the intrapersonal processes, such as low self-esteem and excessive self-criticism, which often maintain depressed mood. It aims to help clients contact underlying feelings, make sense of them and reflect on the new meanings which emerge. This, in turn, provides a basis for psychological and behavioural change.

The structure of the CfD framework

The CfD framework is divided into four areas: generic, basic, specific and metacompetences (see Figure 3.2). Within these categories, competences tend to be of three different types: statements of underpinning knowledge, descriptions of the attitude or stance taken by the therapist in relation to the client and descriptions of skill or method. There are distinct differences between the four areas within the framework.

Generic competences are those which would be employed in any psychological therapy. These 'common factors' are associated with the effective delivery of any psychological therapy and often reflect the idea that there is much more to therapy than the application of a set of techniques. A whole package of professional knowledge and activity underpins the provision of a therapy. For example, all therapists should be able to make effective use of supervision in the interests of their clients. Knowledge of ethical principles and the ability to resolve ethical dilemmas are likewise crucial. Regardless of the theoretical model employed it is essential for therapists to build a trusting relationship with clients as a basis for collaborative therapeutic work, the ability to communicate warmth and acceptance being an important part of this. Understanding depression and its associated risk of suicide and self-harm are also key areas of professional knowledge, together with the ability to work competently with culturally diverse client groups.

Basic competences set out a range of activities that are fundamental to CfD. The term is used to indicate that these competences are 'core' to the approach rather than to suggest they are in any way simple to implement. The focus on establishing a relationship which is warm, accepting, honest and empathic is primary in this type of therapeutic work, rather than a focus on technical interventions. For this reason there is some overlap between generic and basic competences where the building of a therapeutic relationship is described. Within the basic competences the activities which contribute to developing, maintaining and concluding the therapeutic relationship are detailed.

Specific competences assume that, in some cases, such as when clients are unable to contact their feelings or, conversely, are overwhelmed by them, both client and counsellor are presented with a context-specific therapeutic task. In the case of the 'out of touch' client the task would be to help the client contact their feelings and experience. With the 'overwhelmed' client, containment of feelings and the ability to reflect on experience would be important tasks. Specific interventions would not necessarily be used in all cases with all clients and so tend to be subject to the counsellor's clinical judgement and the expressed needs of the client. This area of competence has been influenced by experiential approaches, particularly EFT (Elliott et al., 2004). The underlying assumption is that for therapeutic change to take place, clients need to be able to contact their emotional experience, find ways to express this, articulate their experience symbolically, reflect upon experience and in doing so develop new personal meanings.

Metacompetences articulate high-order, abstract competences perhaps best described as clinical judgement and reflective practice. These are constructed to answer the criticism that competence-based approaches to therapeutic work are mechanistic and reduce complex activities to a series of rote operations. Crucial skills are needed in deciding when and under what circumstances an intervention is appropriate and also how to adapt the therapeutic approach to the needs of individual clients. Hence metacompetences describe the skills needed for the judicious implementation of the competence framework while keeping the interests of the client central to the work. Examples of metacompetences are: *capacity to implement the therapeutic approach in a flexible but coherent manner; capacity to adapt interventions in response to client feedback; ability to work with the whole person.*

The map of competences

The map of competences for CfD is shown in Figure 3.2.

Applying the competences

It is important to understand not only the various domains within the CfD competence framework but also how the framework as a whole should be implemented to ensure clients receive a coherent therapy package.

How knowledge, skills and attitudes interrelate

Counsellor competence is underpinned by a need to understand a wide body of knowledge, including a therapeutic model and its underpinning philosophical principles, a

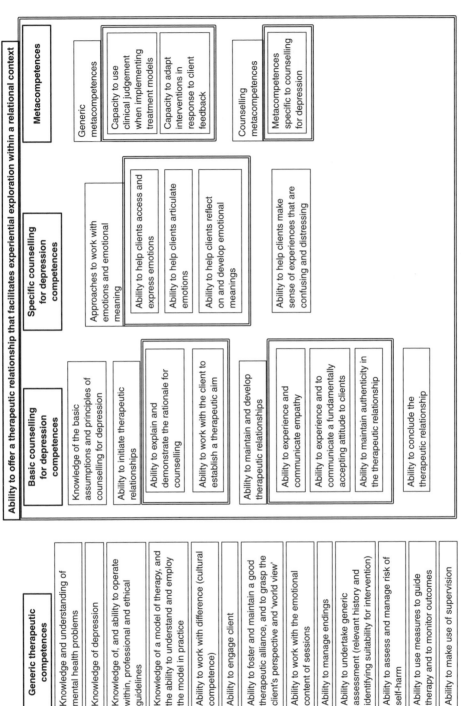

Ability to offer a therapeutic relationship that facilitates experiential exploration within a relational context

Generic therapeutic competences

- Knowledge and understanding of mental health problems
- Knowledge of depression
- Knowledge of, and ability to operate within, professional and ethical guidelines
- Knowledge of a model of therapy, and the ability to understand and employ the model in practice
- Ability to work with difference (cultural competence)
- Ability to engage client
- Ability to foster and maintain a good therapeutic alliance, and to grasp the client's perspective and 'world view'
- Ability to work with the emotional content of sessions
- Ability to manage endings
- Ability to undertake generic assessment (relevant history and identifying suitability for intervention)
- Ability to assess and manage risk of self-harm
- Ability to use measures to guide therapy and to monitor outcomes
- Ability to make use of supervision

Basic counselling for depression competences

- Knowledge of the basic assumptions and principles of counselling for depression
- Ability to initiate therapeutic relationships
- Ability to explain and demonstrate the rationale for counselling
- Ability to work with the client to establish a therapeutic aim
- Ability to maintain and develop therapeutic relationships
- Ability to experience and communicate empathy
- Ability to experience and to communicate a fundamentally accepting attitude to clients
- Ability to maintain authenticity in the therapeutic relationship
- Ability to conclude the therapeutic relationship

Specific counselling for depression competences

- Approaches to work with emotions and emotional meaning
- Ability to help clients access and express emotions
- Ability to help clients articulate emotions
- Ability to help clients reflect on and develop emotional meanings
- Ability to help clients make sense of experiences that are confusing and distressing

Metacompetences

- Generic metacompetences
- Capacity to use clinical judgement when implementing treatment models
- Capacity to adapt interventions in response to client feedback
- Counselling metacompetences
- Metacompetences specific to counselling for depression

Figure 3.2 Map of CfD Competences

framework of ethics, knowledge of mental health problems and how they develop, together with an understanding of culture and how social context impacts on the individual. What is also crucial is an ability to apply this knowledge to practice in the therapeutic context, ensuring that interventions have a clear rationale and practice is thoughtful and deliberate. The judicious combination of knowledge and skill is integral to a definition of competence. In an area of professional activity which is relational and deals with very sensitive and personal issues, the attitudes of the therapist are extremely important and, indeed, central to the therapeutic enterprise, as the client's progress in therapy may depend on these. Outside of therapeutic work with clients, the counsellor's attitudes are equally important in shaping how they relate to the professional, ethical and societal context. Such attitudes will have a central bearing on the provision of professional, ethical and culturally sensitive practice which is centred on the client's needs. What follows is a more detailed description of the different areas of the CfD competence framework. Readers may wish to refer back to the map (Figure 3.2) in order to navigate their way through this section.

Generic CfD competences

Knowledge and understanding of mental health problems: A knowledge of common mental health problems, particularly depression, is vital for counsellors working within the CfD model. An understanding of how problems develop, are maintained and how they present in terms of symptoms is important, particularly when undertaking generic assessments. Knowledge of different types of mood disorder (e.g. depression and anxiety) is essential, both to ensure that clients receive effective therapy and also that clients are signposted to the appropriate type of intervention. In accordance with the NICE (2009a) depression guideline counsellors should be particularly familiar with subthreshold and mild to moderate depressive presentations and how to work with these.

Knowledge of depression: A detailed knowledge of depression is required for the provision of CfD, particularly the cluster of symptoms associated with a diagnosis of the disorder. Counsellors should have an understanding of those factors which may predispose clients to depression, such as emotional neglect in childhood, social isolation and major adverse life-events. Knowledge of the impact of the disorder on the client's functioning and the various psychological and pharmacological treatments available likewise represent key areas.

Knowledge of and ability to operate within professional and ethical guidelines: Competent practice is underpinned by knowledge of national and local codes of practice, professional ethical guidelines and relevant legislation. The ability to apply ethical principles to therapeutic work is also required, particularly with regard to informed consent, confidentiality, avoiding 'dual relationships' and fitness to practise.

Knowledge of a model of therapy, and the ability to understand and employ the model in practice: A comprehensive and in-depth knowledge of a therapeutic model provides a coherent rationale for the interventions used. Clients, in turn, experience a consistent therapeutic approach which supports the building of a collaborative relationship. However, it is also necessary for therapeutic models to be implemented in ways which are flexible and responsive to the client's individual needs. A balance has to be struck between consistency and flexibility.

Ability to work with difference: Ensuring the accessibility of effective therapy is underpinned by the counsellor's 'cultural competence', or ability to work with individuals from a diverse range of backgrounds. Whereas an appreciation of the lifestyle, beliefs and attitudes of various demographic groups is central to the provision of culturally sensitive therapy, the impact of disadvantage and discrimination on such groups is also important. A full appreciation of difference is impossible without counsellors developing an awareness of how their own culture has affected their thinking, attitudes and functioning. Cultural attitudes to help-seeking, the stigma relating to mental illness and beliefs regarding the notion of 'selfhood', will all impact on therapeutic work. The ability to work effectively with an interpreter is also an important area of competence when therapy cannot be conducted in the medium of English. Generally, an understanding of how social and cultural difference can impact on the accessibility, acceptability and effectiveness of an intervention and the ability to mediate for these factors is an important area of competence.

Establishing and maintaining a therapeutic alliance: A significant part of the generic competences is concerned with establishing and maintaining a good therapeutic alliance and a number of competences apply: *ability to engage the client; ability to foster and maintain a good therapeutic alliance, and to grasp the client's perspective and 'world view'; ability to work with emotional content of sessions; ability to manage endings.* A good therapeutic relationship is associated with positive outcomes regardless of the type of therapy offered and for this to be in place the counsellor needs to be able to engage and relate to the client and build a safe atmosphere. An ability to work empathically with a range of emotions expressed by the client helps to build understanding. Likewise when the relationship is under strain and the client may express negative feelings about being in therapy it is important for counsellors to respond openly and constructively in order to explore those factors straining the relationship. Managing the ending of the therapeutic relationship also requires sensitive skills to enable the client to acknowledge significant feelings and be able to disengage in a manner experienced as constructive.

Ability to undertake a generic assessment: This is a core activity for all CfD counsellors, aimed at gaining an understanding of the client's difficulties and how these may have developed over time. The client's social situation with regard to supportive relationships and employment are important factors for consideration, along with personality factors such as their ability to tolerate strong emotions and their level of motivation to change. Assessing the level of risk to self or others is a key ethical concern at this point and to discuss the range of therapeutic options available is appropriate as it supports client choice.

Ability to assess and manage risk of self-harm in clients presenting with depression: As there are elevated levels of risk of suicide and self-harm among depressed populations it is important for counsellors to be able to assess and manage levels of risk in their work with clients. An appreciation of the range of factors associated with risk of suicide and self-harm and an understanding of those markers which may indicate a client is becoming suicidal provide the basis for making an appropriate assessment. Likewise the ability to develop plans to manage levels of risk while continuing to support the client's therapeutic progress is of key importance.

Ability to use measures to guide therapy and to monitor outcomes: The need to measure the outcomes of therapy and evaluate psychological services has become widely acknowledged, particularly since the implementation of the IAPT programme, with its use of session-by-session measures, requiring therapists to be familiar with the questionnaires and rating scales commonly used in routine practice. Counsellors should have a basic understanding of how such measures are constructed and how to interpret results. The benefits of integrating outcome measures into routine practice, in terms of gaining direct feedback from the client and being able to track progress over time should be appreciated by counsellors. This provides a basis for adapting the intervention in the light of such feedback and tailoring the therapy more closely to the client's needs. Counsellors should avoid administering measures in ways that are burdensome to clients and should use them as a basis for active collaboration between client and counsellor. Counsellors should also support clients in making use of the process as a form of self-monitoring, helping clients reflect on their levels of distress and track progress.

Ability to make use of supervision: Supervision is an important factor in the delivery of effective therapy, providing support, guidance and professional development for the counsellor. Effective supervision requires collaboration and an active engagement on the part of the counsellor. Hence counsellors must be able to reflect on themselves and their work, offer an open and honest account of their work and also be able to make constructive use of feedback, which at times may be critical. The ability to adapt practice in the light of supervisory guidance is likewise an essential ability.

Basic CfD competences

This domain of competences describes the range of activities that are fundamental to CfD practice. It begins with the underpinning knowledge necessary for the delivery of interventions and goes on to describe the skills and abilities necessary to engage in, maintain and conclude therapeutic relationships.

Knowledge of the basic assumptions and principles of CfD: Underpinning knowledge has been grouped into three areas, based on the assumption that to work effectively within this model a counsellor needs a thorough understanding of:

- the philosophy and principles that inform the approach
- how the modality explains human development and psychological distress, the rationale for therapy and how this relates to therapeutic change
- the conceptualisation of depression by means of the principles and philosophy of the theories from which the model is drawn

Together these help the counsellor to develop formulations of the client's problem and to focus on the issues and processes that may be maintaining depressed mood.

Ability to initiate therapeutic relationships: Focusing on application, as opposed to knowledge, this area of competence describes activities essential in the early stages of therapeutic work. To explain to the client the rationale for treatment is an ethical priority, as it supports the principle of informed consent, as well as being necessary for the initiation of a collaborative relationship. Additionally to help the client develop a focus or aim for the therapy is associated with good outcomes and so is a priority. It is important that the therapeutic aim[3] is meaningful to the client and is subject to renegotiation as therapy proceeds. Particularly important in the early stages of therapy is that establishing a therapeutic aim does not detract from the building of a therapeutic relationship.

Ability to maintain and develop therapeutic relationships: Three areas of activity are fundamental to the achievement of this area of competence. Often referred to as the 'core conditions' and derived from Rogers (1957), empathy, unconditional acceptance and authenticity are central to CfD (see Chapters 5 and 6).

Ability to conclude the therapeutic relationship: The concluding phase of the therapeutic relationship is a time to review progress in therapy and look to the future. Clients may be reminded of previous endings in their lives and experience quite strong feelings. It is important for counsellors to support the client in expressing these feelings. As Counselling for Depression is a relatively brief therapy (recommended in courses of up to 20 sessions) it is possible that some clients may not feel ready to come to an ending within this timescale. In such cases it is important for counsellors to facilitate the expression of such feelings, explore with the client how to manage any difficulties which may persist and ensure as far as possible that the ending is an opportunity for increased autonomy and self-awareness rather than one which the client experiences as negative.

Specific CfD competences

This domain of competence presumes the establishment of a therapeutic relationship based on authenticity, unconditional acceptance and empathic understanding as described in the basic competences. It supplements this with a set of more specific skills which may be relevant with particular clients in particular circumstances. When and under what circumstances these competences should be applied is dependent to a large extent on the counsellor's clinical judgement and the client's preferences in terms of how they wish to work. The overarching theme of approaches to work with emotions and with emotional meanings, suggests a more intentional focus on working with emotional processes than that outlined in the basic competences. It also emphasises the client developing new meaning and understanding resulting from the process of putting feelings at the centre. The relevance of the specific CfD competences is contextual and related to each individual client, requiring more nuanced intervention. It is noteworthy, however, that the intended outcome for the specific competences is the same as for the

---

[3] CfD encourages clients to consider their aims in therapy and this is covered in Chapter 8.

basic competences; that is to help clients process their emotional experience and expand their self-awareness. The methods used to achieve these objectives, however, may be slightly different.

The ability to help clients access and express emotions: This area of competence is based on the notion that clients may have developed habitual ways of managing their feelings. To identify and explore such habitual processes can help the client to contact underlying feelings and become aware of their characteristic ways of managing their emotions. This set of competences also acknowledges that an optimal level of emotional arousal, or contact with feelings, is important for counselling to progress; too little contact or excessive contact (being consistently overwhelmed by feelings) is likely to make therapeutic progress difficult.

Ability to help clients articulate emotions: CfD theory has it that feelings have a personal significance and potentially can prompt us to act in ways which support our growth and development. However at times clients may not be aware of the significance of their emotions, especially where feelings are distressing or conflicting. To help the client find appropriate language to describe how they feel is a subtle therapeutic skill which often uses imagery and metaphor to help clients apprehend the essence of their emotional experience.

Ability to help clients reflect on and develop emotional meanings: This set of competences indicates the next step in this process where having put a feeling into words the client reflects on its significance in the context of their wider perceptions and beliefs relating to self, others and the world. The theory point here is that emerging emotional meaning may lead the client to revise their view of who they are and how they want to be in the world. The client may wish to make adjustments to the way they relate to others, abandon old habits and embark upon new projects. The role of the counsellor here is to support this process of reflection and the development of new perspectives.

Ability to help clients make sense of experiences that are confusing and distressing: At times clients may express puzzled reactions to situations or events. They may have under- or over-reacted, or behaved in ways they experience as being out of character. In some cases, situations may have been stressful or distressing, leaving the client with a need to 're-visit' the situation in order to reflect on how they feel and how the event has affected them. In these cases it can be useful for counsellors to help the client describe the situation in more detail, creating a richer narrative of events and focusing on underlying feelings which at the time did not come to the surface. Such puzzling experiences which clients keep returning to often signal significant therapeutic issues which the client may identify as ones they want to address.

Metacompetences

Effective counselling competences cannot be delivered in a mechanistic manner. The interrelationship of the different areas of competence is complex and subtle, necessitating the high-order, abstract skills and abilities associated with clinical judgement. This domain of the framework sets out various high-order skills which often relate to the need to strike a judicious balance between different areas of competence in order to maintain a consistent and coherent approach. It also involves the ability to respond creatively and idiosyncratically to the client in order to address the complexity of issues which arise in the unique landscape of each client's needs. This domain is divided into two sections, **generic metacompetences,** which apply to all therapists regardless of modality, and **counselling metacompetences,** which are specific to CfD.

Generic metacompetences are those high-order skills which therapists practising any modality should possess. For example, the ability to adhere to a model of therapy while at the same time working flexibly to meet the individual client's needs is a complex skill. A comprehensive knowledge of the model is required along with the ability to apply this coherently even when circumstances are challenging. At the same time, the therapist needs to be sensitive to how the client is responding to the therapy and whether there are any indications, explicit or implicit, that the client is finding interventions unhelpful or unacceptable. As with most metacompetences, what is signalled here are two areas of competence which may potentially pull the therapist in opposing directions, to the detriment of the therapeutic enterprise. To strike a thoughtful balance and resist being pulled to one extreme or another is the mark of a competent therapist.

Counselling metacompetences are those high-order skills which relate specifically to the implementation of CfD. Similar to the generic metacompetences these skills often refer to the ability to balance different aspects of the competence model. Examples of this are maintaining a holistic perspective while applying a variety of specific skills; balancing a focus on therapeutic task with the need to maintain a therapeutic relationship; balancing a non-directive stance with the need to intervene should issues of client risk or safety arise. On a slightly different tack, the high-order skill of metacommunication doesn't involve the balancing of opposites, but rather the ability to talk reflectively with the client about the nature of client–counsellor communication in the therapeutic dyad and its impact on the participants. The focus of this talk should always be to maintain the therapeutic relationship and support the client's progress.

Using the competence framework

Although competence frameworks inevitably describe therapeutic work in terms of specific skills and abilities there is scant evidence supporting the view that some skills are more important than others in relation to outcomes. Hence counsellors should be competent in all areas of the framework. To maximise effectiveness it is probably more important to view the framework holistically, rather than as a collection of unrelated activities, and implement the entire therapy in a single, seamless, fluid, consistent and coherent manner. The concepts of clinical judgement and therapeutic flexibility are inherent to the application of the framework.

Effective therapy depends upon the availability of good-quality training and rigorous supervision. These are crucial to the delivery of the CfD framework. The framework can be used to support the supervisory process by providing a set of competences known to be associated with positive outcomes. Both supervisors and counsellors can map practice against the framework in order to identify areas for development and further training. With this in mind, the framework is supported by a curriculum, which describes how counsellors can be trained to implement the competences and an adherence scale (PCEPS) which can be used in training, supervision and research to assess to what extent counsellors are delivering the model. These are discussed in Chapter 10.

Conclusion

The translation of 'counselling' as specified in the NICE (2009a) depression guideline into a clear and accessible form of therapy for service users has been a complex and painstaking task. Every attempt has been made to follow evidence-based principles, using the findings of RCTs as the starting point, but supplementing these with expert opinion and the wider research and training literature where necessary. Pragmatic decisions were also necessitated as part of the process to ensure that the therapy can be made available to the public without the demand for large amounts of funding and resources. The result is a clear and coherent description of practice which can be feasibly implemented and monitored to ensure the therapy is practised as intended.

4

Depression

'I hate myself, nobody likes me, I'm worthless. It would be better if I wasn't here. Nobody listens to me; I might as well be dead. I'm a total failure. I take pills all the time, I cut my arms. I don't care what happens to me. I hate everyone and everyone hates me. You can't help me, nobody can, it's pointless. I hope I die.'

Introduction

'Depression' has to be one of the most commonly used words to describe a set of human experiences or an area of human distress in the early 21st century. Having originated as a medical term, it brings with it a certain authority into popular use. When a term is used like this, we are invited to think that it describes a set of well-defined experiences and it is reliably identifying a single, professionally agreed psychological phenomenon. Unfortunately counselling and psychotherapy have shown us that understanding human experience is more complicated than that, if we want to take it seriously. Human experience is not so amenable to theory as to deliver a single set of predictive descriptions (scientific or otherwise) that the majority of practitioners can agree on. We have an abundance of descriptions and explanations which, in turn, gives rise to a plethora of treatments.

Although the term 'depression' has been in common usage only since the 1950s, human beings have almost certainly always had experiences that are currently labelled as such. Since the relationship between language and experience is both important for therapists to engage with and complex, it is useful to take a moment to explore the genesis of the term and how experiences of this type have been and are currently symbolised.

The history of understanding 'depression'

Without chasing terminology back to the earliest writings, it's helpful to go back at least to ancient Greece when Hippocrates elaborated on the description of 'melancholia' as follows: 'If a fright or despondency lasts for a long time, it is a melancholic affection' (Hippocrates, *Aphorisms, Section VI, 26*, http://classics.mit.edu/Hippocrates/aphorisms. mb.txt, retrieved 01/10/2012).

Parenthetically, it is worth noting that Hippocrates specifies two features of the experience which are still thought of as important today, i.e., that it involves an internal state or mood (despondency) which is not transitory, but endures ('lasts for a long time'). The term 'melancholy' has been used for centuries to describe an experience of feeling sad, low, dejected, down in the dumps, miserable, demoralised or to use Hippocrates' term, despondent. Refining the understanding of distressing experiences almost always leads to new vocabulary, sometimes more suited to the zeitgeist. The term 'depression' had been in use since the late 1800s as a way of helping discriminate the detail of the experience of melancholia. The influential psychiatrist Emile Kraepelin coined the phrase *depressive states* as an umbrella term covering many types of melancholia, and Kraepelin's authoritative work proposed a system whereby all problems with moods were grouped together as *manic-depressive insanity* (as distinct from *dementia praecox* – now considered to be the equivalent of schizophrenia).

Kraepelin further distinguished between endogenous (originating from inside the person) and exogenous (caused by external events) depression, though this distinction was not accepted by all – some psychiatrists could find no real distinction in the symptomatology. However, the idea that certain symptom sets can be caused on the one hand by external events, and on the other by an internal (largely unknown) process translates into the commonly held view that depression can be a normal reaction to life events (e.g., bereavement), or an abnormal disease process starting inside the person, possibly with some biological origin – with few apparent external referents, it comes 'out of the blue'. At different points in the 20th century, these ideas have been more or less prominent as ways of understanding depression, depending upon treatment trends, such as the discovery of a new class of medications and their overenthusiastic prescription. Such trends in psychiatry were influential – it was not uncommon for benzodiazepines to be dispensed when a close family member died – demonstrating a disjunction between treatment (chemical) and cause (life event). Thankfully, however well-intentioned, this particular treatment trend did not last long.

The training and predispositions of practitioners also influenced, and continues to influence, definitions and treatment. Amongst practitioners who favoured disease-centred ways of thinking, it was more likely that a sustained period of low mood would have been treated as endogenous depression and treated with medications. Amongst practitioners interested in finding meaning in experiences, a sustained period of low mood would have been treated with talking therapies.

Whatever theoretical position an individual practitioner held, the vocabulary of depression slowly took precedence over melancholia to describe *mood disorders* in psychiatric circles. It was clear that mood disorders covered a wide range of experiences and early diagnostic systems noted the disabling effect of symptoms including:

- feelings of overwhelming sadness
- loss of interest and pleasure in things
- inappropriate guilt
- difficulty sleeping and/or waking early or not being able to fall asleep
- feeling very tired, no energy to get out of bed
- difficulty concentrating
- changes in appetite
- paying less attention to personal hygiene
- recurrent thoughts of death or suicide

These symptoms are sometimes divided into those showing negative affect or emotion (low mood, feeling tired, thoughts of death or suicide) and those showing a lack, or absence of positive affect or emotion (loss of interest and pleasure).

The term depression was installed in more popular everyday use in the 1950s largely as a result of the introduction of a wide range of drugs in the pharmaceutical revolution that also brought antihypertensives and antibiotics. We might have been prescribed antimelancholics, rather than antidepressants, had the pharmaceutical industry taken a slightly different linguistic turn.

Depression in the 21st century

It is important to remind ourselves that practically every aspect of depression is continuously changing – our understanding and definitions of what it is, the methods of diagnosis, the way we collect data, the rates of occurrence and so on. The data presented in this book represents a still from a motion picture. It is certain to change, and might have changed between the time of writing and time of publication. Some will take this to be evidence of the invalidity and unreliability of the entire conceptual basis, others will take it as evidence of our scientific progress to more refined and useful constructs. Regardless of their viewpoint, Counselling for Depression practitioners are required to periodically update their understanding by reviewing the available data.

This note is particularly apposite since the American Psychiatric Association published the fifth edition of the *Diagnostic and Statistical Manual of Mental Disorders (DSM-5)* in May 2013. Later in this chapter we review the changes that affect the diagnosis of depression.

In the past 20 years, depression has become a term frequently used in everyday conversations describing a variety of mood-related experiences which bear little real relation to the terms used to describe experiences of clinical significance. Although there has also been a dramatic increase in the rates of prescription of antidepressants,[1] there has not been a corresponding increase in the rate at which depression is diagnosed (Moore et al., 2009). Using the UK general practice research database, Moore et al. reported a doubling of the prescribing of antidepressants between 1993 and 2005, with no increase overall in diagnoses. New cases rose slightly in young women, fell slightly in all other groups and on average showed no change. There is some evidence that depression is more prevalent among members of the black and minority ethnic (BME) community, and this seems to vary according to geographical location. Research uncovering differences in the prevalence[2] of depression between, for example, rural and urban environments most frequently concludes multivariate causes when other factors are controlled for (e.g. Probst et al., 2005) and Helfin and Iceland (2009) are not alone in reporting strong links between social factors such as employment, education and income and the prevalence of depression. Interesting though these data are, it is not the purpose of this book to unearth the details of dynamics of this particular puzzle.

In the 21st century, depression is presented to us all on a daily basis in the broadcast, printed and online media. Whether it is presented accurately and fairly or not is not the issue; our encounters with depression are manifold in western culture and we are compelled to engage or ignore it daily. The ensuing zeitgeist is suffused with the concept of depression in its various media-determined guises, and so the role of entertainment media, films, television series, theatre and novels all help to construct the concept of depression in the 21st century, regardless of the realities of diagnosis or treatment.

The literature on mental health regularly uses the terms disease, disorder and syndrome.

A **disease** is an impairment, cessation or interruption in the normal functions of the organism, with a known cause. It is identifiable by uniquely distinguishing signs and symptoms.

A **disorder** is an abnormal mental condition which produces dysfunctional mental processes – a *disturbance* in function.

A **syndrome** is a collection of symptoms that consistently occur together to collectively indicate a condition, disorder or disease.

The incidence and prevalence (see Box, p. 44) of depression is not globally homogenous. Andrade et al. (2003) reported a wide range of differences in the lifetime prevalence of

---

[1] Psychiatrist and pharmacologist David Healy takes a radical view of this trend in *The Antidepressant Era* (Harvard University Press, 1997).

[2] We explore the important differences between incidence and prevalence of depression on p. 44.

major depressive disorder between countries – the range being from 17% in the USA to 3% in Japan. Clearly cultural, diagnostic and clinical differences all play a part, indeed the authors even call attention to the absence of common diagnostic protocols. Such differences and problems implicit in the investigation and understanding of all types of depression, including moderate and subthreshold depression[3] lead us to the clinical utility of phenomenological approaches to assessment and treatment based on, and working with, client narratives and individual experiences.

The medicalisation of distress

The 20th century heralded an era in which controlling our world no longer seemed a dream, indeed it could even be believed that it was our destiny to subjugate the natural world. Some diseases appeared to have been banished from the human population, we had travelled to the moon and we could tame the climate in practically every part of the planet, but this hope lasted no more than a few decades. New diseases, epidemics and the unpredictability of climate has led to our trust in the scientific method being accompanied by the awareness that in order to work with the non-linear dynamical systems of the world and living things, it is helpful to observe without intervention, understand and live in concert with them, rather than simply control and manipulate them.

Of particular interest to the place of psychology in western culture is the undoubted fact that medical science has worked to the benefit of humankind. This embracing of medical science has extended, via the medical specialism of psychiatry, to the way we understand human mental life – we talk easily about mental health and mental illness. In the past 50 years we have witnessed an increasing tendency to understand distressing and disturbing experiences as medical conditions or diseases.

This medicalisation of distress has both positive and negative consequences. Medicine as a metanarrative supersedes the divisions inherent in race, class, age and gender. It provides a unitary framework for understanding difference, namely a diagnostic system built from the assumed neutral elements of signs and symptoms. It is also a reassuring framework which takes the responsibility for the symptoms away from the environment and the psychology of the individual and locates it in the biology of the individual. It is a relief to many to have their distress identified and named within a familiar framework – one of health and illness. Furthermore, properly functioning medicalised systems of treating distress mean that access to treatment follows diagnosis, and diagnosis can also lead to sympathetic reactions from family, friends and work colleagues.

Notwithstanding this difficult-to-understand picture of depression in the 21st century, what remains true is that people suffer distressing periods of crushing, enduring low mood, along with other debilitating symptoms – whether over- or under-diagnosed – and a significant number of these people seek help.

---

[3] These and other diagnostic categories are described on pp. 50–5.

The course of depression

Whilst it is necessary to continue to assert the unique lived experience of each person suffering from depression, some commonalities in the course of the disorder are instructive:

1. The average age of the first episode of major depression is the mid-20s. The onset is varied, sometimes rapid, sometimes preceded by a range of symptoms such as anxiety or panic attacks, often associated with a major stressful life event (Fava and Kendler, 2000).
2. Depression is not necessarily a short-term disorder. Half of patients still had a diagnosis of depression one year later (Simon et al., 2002) and at least 10% had persistent symptoms (Kessler et al., 2003). Following a first episode of major depression, more than half will go on to have at least one more episode (Kupfer, 1991) and, after further relapses, the risk of continuing relapse rises, in some cases up to 90% (Kupfer, 1991). This data is important in highlighting the value of good interventions with low relapse rates in first episodes.
3. Clients' history of elevated mood should be assessed, but no more than 10% develop into related manic episodes (Kovacs, 1996).

There are various estimates for the number of people who suffer experiences which would be diagnosed as depression but do not present themselves to primary care or mental health services. There are further estimates that whilst a number of this undiagnosed group recover without treatment, approximately 20% remain undiagnosed and in distress after three years (Kessler et al., 2002). So in spite of the media coverage of mental health issues and depression in the 21st century in particular, we find a large number of people not identifying themselves to helping professions, possibly because of the undoubted stigma attached to suffering mental distress.

Another notable feature of depression is its persistence, as evidenced by the frequency of relapse. At least half of those who recover from a first episode of depression will have one or more further episodes during their lives, and approximately 80% of those who have two episodes will have another recurrence (*DSM IV-TR*, 2000[4]; Kupfer et al., 1996). Across all levels of severity, once depression is established, recurrent episodes will usually begin within five years of the initial episode, and between five and nine depressive episodes is average during the life of a typical sufferer. The following factors increase the likelihood of relapse and we would expect them to be picked up at assessment. The CfD practitioner can then be mindful of the prognosis and possible increased risk of relapse for each client (Timonen and Liukkonen, 2008):

- The client has previously suffered from three or more episodes of major depression
- There has been a high prior frequency of recurrence
- The client has suffered an episode in the previous 12 months
- The client suffered residual symptoms during continuation of treatment

---

[4] American Psychiatric Association (2000) *Diagnostic and Statistical Manual of Mental Disorders. Text Revision – Fourth* (Washington, D.C.: American Psychiatric Association).

- Previous episodes have included severe symptoms, e.g. suicidality, psychotic features
- Previous episodes have been lengthy
- The client has suffered relapse after drug discontinuation in previous episodes

This level of relapse adds to the burden imposed by depression on individuals, families and services. There is little evidence that medication intervenes in this cycle of recurrence in subthreshold or mild to moderate depression, notwithstanding the poor risk to benefit ratio for such diagnoses. Psychological treatments, on the other hand, show evidence of reducing the relapse rate.

The prevalence and incidence of depression

Incidence and prevalence are two different measures used to describe the distribution of disease in a particular population.

Prevalence is the number of people in a population who have the disease of interest in a particular time period. The prevalence *rate* is a measure of the *proportion* of a population affected by a specific illness in a specified time period. Since the larger the number of people in the population, the more people might have the illness, so a prevalence *rate* is the more helpful statistic, i.e. the *proportion* of the population affected.

The **incidence** of disease is the number of *new* cases occurring in a population *over a defined time interval*. Porta and Last (2008: 124) define incidence as 'the number of instances of illness commencing, or of persons falling ill, during a given period in a specified population'. As with prevalence, it is more helpfully expressed as a *rate* (incidence rate) or proportion to account for different population sizes (different towns, countries, genders, ethnic groups, etc.).

For an accurate understanding of these measures when presented in the literature, the sociodemographic and environmental parameters of the population in question need to be carefully noted.

At the turn of the century, the World Health Organization (WHO) estimated that major depression is the leading single cause of disability (WHO, 2001), and, regarding 2012 World Mental Health Day, declared that:

… This year the theme for the day is 'Depression: A Global Crisis'.

Depression affects more than 350 million people of all ages, in all communities, and is a significant contributor to the global burden of disease. Although there are known effective treatments for depression, access to treatment is a problem in most countries and in some countries fewer than 10% of those who need it receive such treatment.

(WHO, 2012)

Although the incidence and nature of depression in the landscape of mental health in the UK and worldwide can be debated, there is overwhelming evidence that the diagnosis of depression is widespread. It is best to steer clear of data supplied by sources either intrinsically skewed or with a vested interest,[5] but even so, the Office for National Statistics Psychiatric Morbidity Survey, 2007 (published in 2009) noted:

- more than half of people with a Common Mental Disorder presented with mixed anxiety and depressive disorder

And the 2000 survey (published in 2001) revealed:

- Between 8–12% of the population experience depression in any year (Office for National Statistics Psychiatric Morbidity Report, 2001)

Within these figures pointing to the widespread incidence of depression, the distribution amongst different groups adds to our understanding of the experience. The following findings illuminate the search for consensus regarding the aetiology of depression, whilst proving nothing conclusive:

1. Diagnosis of depression in women has consistently been found to be between 1.5 and 2.5 times higher than in men – an episode of depression serious enough to require treatment occurs in about one in four women and one in ten men at some point in their lives. These differences are reasonably stable between the ages of 18 to 64 (Waraich et al., 2004).
2. Ethnicity does not seem to affect diagnosis of depression in the UK (Singleton et al., 2001), but unlike other mental health issues, there are insufficient data on the effects of migration on the diagnosis of depression.
3. The diagnosis of a depressive episode is associated with being unemployed, belonging to social classes 4 and below, having no formal educational qualifications and living in social housing/accommodation, having moved three or more times in the last two years and living in an urban environment (Singleton et al., 2001).
4. In a study of 55 GP practices in Hampshire, Ostler et al. (2001) concluded: 'The unemployed, temporarily away from work or permanently unable to work, and those looking after home and family, were significantly more likely to be depressed than those in employment … The retired and student groups were at lower risk than employees.' http://bjp.rcpsych.org/content/178/1/12.long (retrieved 14/11/2013).

Further information on the incidence of common mental health problems in general, and depression in particular, can be found on the 'Mental Health Statistics' page of the Mental Health Foundation website.[6] Whilst the search for physiological substrates for depression continues, it is clear that, as the NICE depression guideline 90 (updated

---

[5] E.g. estimating the incidence of depression by number of prescriptions of antidepressants issued, or data gathered by pharmaceutical companies.
[6] See www.mentalhealth.org.uk/help-information/mental-health-statistics/ (retrieved 22/01/2013).

edition, National Collaborating Centre for Mental Health, 2010: 23) declares, 'The evidence therefore overwhelmingly supports the view that the prevalence of depression, however it is defined, varies according to gender, and social and economic factors'.

The burden of depression

The burden of depression falls upon the individuals suffering distress, their family and friends, employers and society at large. This burden as it relates to individuals and those close to them will be known to practitioners, regardless of their chosen therapeutic approach. In this short section we will look at the burden in terms of employment and economic cost to society. These measures are important to governments when deciding on the allocation of resources in terms of research, prevention and service provision.

A number of ways of estimating and quantifying the economic and social burden on society have been used over the years. A popular metric for physical disease is 'Years of Life Lost', but this is clearly too severe a measure – although it is more sensitive than a crude mortality figure – for any kind of mental distress, the vast majority of which does not result in death. Instead, the WHO use the more comprehensive disability-adjusted life year (DALY) as a measure of overall disease burden which is expressed as the number of years lost due to ill-health, disability or early death. It is a measure of the effects of chronic illness (mental, physical or any combination) in terms of time – time lost due to premature death and/or disability – one DALY being equal to one year of equivalent healthy life lost.

The DALY is an important measure for representing the burden of psychiatric distress more accurately. In 1990 the WHO reported that five of the ten leading causes of disability were psychiatric conditions – accounting for some 28% of all years lived with disability. However, they only account for 1.4% of all deaths and 1.1% of years of life lost. Thus, psychiatric disorders, while hitherto not regarded as a major problem, are shown to have a huge impact on societies.

WHO projections suggest that depression will be the largest cause of disease burden in developed countries by the year 2020. Currently (unipolar) depressive disorders account for 4.4% of the global disease burden or the equivalent of 65 million DALYs.

Estimates for the UK, not using the DALY metric, provide data that are difficult to compare, but as an example, McCrone et al. (2008) estimated the total cost of services for depression in England in 2007 to be £1.7 billion, while lost employment increased this total to £7.5 billion. By 2026, these figures were projected to be £3 billion and £12.2 billion, respectively. Unsurprisingly, the indirect costs of depression – lost employment and productivity – were, in 2000, found to be 23 times larger than the health service costs (Thomas and Morris, 2003). Furthermore, there are ongoing debates regarding the degree to which depression can be considered to be a disability and therefore qualify for incapacity benefit, thus representing a further considerable economic burden. These debates are bound to shift as do the sands of qualification for, and amount of, state benefits.

Regardless of the metrics used, the countries studied or the method of data collection, depression is a substantial burden to us all, individually and collectively, in all domains of life from the emotional to the financial – one which demands a response.

Depression and suicide

The Office for National Statistics suicide figures are as follows:[7]

- In 2011 there were 6,045 suicides in people aged 15 and over in the UK, an increase of 437 compared with 2010
- The UK suicide rate increased significantly between 2010 and 2011, from 11.1 to 11.8 deaths per 100,000 population
- There were 4,552 male suicides in 2011 (a rate of 18.2 suicides per 100,000 population) and 1,493 female suicides (5.6 per 100,000 population)
- The highest suicide rate was seen in males aged 30 to 44 (23.5 deaths per 100,000 population in 2011)
- The suicide rate in males aged 45 to 59 increased significantly between 2007 and 2011 (22.2 deaths per 100,000 population in 2011)
- Female suicide rates were highest in 45 to 59-year-olds in 2011 (7.3 deaths per 100,000 population)

Offering some different demographic detail, the Mental Health Foundation website[8] provides the following information about suicide:

- Suicide remains the most common cause of death in men under the age of 35 (Appleby, 2004)
- More than 5,700 people in the UK died by suicide in 2010 (*Samaritans Information Resource Pack*, 2012)
- The suicide rate among people over 65 has fallen by 24% in recent years, but is still high compared to the population overall (*Samaritans Information Resource Pack*, 2004)

The *Samaritans Suicide Statistics Report*, 2013, reports that:

- British men are three to five times more likely than British women to die by suicide
- The suicide rate for males in the UK is its highest since 2002
- The female rate has also significantly increased since 2007
- Overall, between 2010 and 2011 there was a significant increase in the UK suicide rate

Some suicide statistics are quite stable (e.g. the gender differences) and some do show movement over periods of a few years (e.g. the overall suicide rate). The number of

---

[7] *Suicides in the United Kingdom, 2011.* Office for National Statistics, released January 2013, www.ons.gov.uk/ons/rel/subnational-health4/suicides-in-the-united-kingdom/2011/index.html (retrieved 15/07/2013).

[8] www.mentalhealth.org.uk/help-information/mental-health-statistics/suicide/ (retrieved 12/02/2013).

people committing suicide rose by approximately 6% in 2008 and some commentators have attributed this to the economic crisis. Whilst it is difficult to find cast-iron causal links regarding suicide, the rate does appear to be affected by changes in the social and material world and subsequent changes in the lived experiences, quality of life, hopes and aspirations of the population. Suicide, suicidality (the likelihood to commit suicide) and suicidal ideation are all associated with depression, with the increase in suicidal ideation understood to be the linking factor. Since depression is also frequently a reaction to adverse life events, we might also expect the incidence of depression and suicide to vary in tandem, but that would be dependent upon consistency in the diagnosis of depression. Such consistency cannot be relied upon.

Whilst the dynamics of the relationship between depression and suicide is not straightforward, CfD practitioners should be alert to the increased risk of suicidality in people who have been diagnosed with subthreshold and mild to moderate depression. This increased risk in a particular client might have been identified during assessment – the role of the CfD practitioner in the assessment would then be dependent upon the service protocols regarding triage. In an NHS setting it is necessary to focus on suicidal ideation in the practice of CfD, since even in a well-established relationship, routine empathic responses would not be expected to be sufficient to help the client explore and unfold any distressing suicidal thoughts. More active intervention in the form of risk assessment and support is routine practice. Nevertheless, empathic following is still the substrate for all of this work.

Aetiology of depression

The majority view in the early 21st century is that there is no single cause for the diagnostic category of depression. Acknowledging the huge range of individual presentations and navigating the plethora of theories – genetic, physiological, developmental, psychological, social and environmental – leads the vast majority of commentators and clinicians to a multi-factorial causal pathway. Some factors associated with a diagnosis of depression are described above in the subsection on 'incidence of depression', but these are associations, not cause-and-effect relationships. The fact that no clear causal factors – genetic, physiological, psychological or social – have been identified is not for want of trying.

Once established, a number of factors are linked to the continuation of the experience of depression. Outcome is adversely affected by:

- onset at a young age
- the severity of symptoms in the first episode
- ongoing social stresses
- other psychiatric or physical/medical disorders

Beyond these findings there is little understanding regarding what dictates the length or persistence of a depressive episode and the factors which cause such wide variation of experience between individual sufferers. It is clear, though, that depression, notably in persistent episodes, has a tendency to be a precursor to, or be associated with, further disorders that become incorporated into and compound, the original depression. These include loss of self-esteem and independence, feelings of helplessness and hopelessness (which increase the risk of suicide) and the loss of engagement in outside activities that accompanies social withdrawal. Whilst it is very difficult to evidence a causal relationship between these factors and the maintenance of a depressive episode, self-help opportunities can provide some benefit in the face of scant systematic research evidence of their efficacy.

The medical model of mental illness is propelled by the notion of a single diagnostic category pointing to a single cause or discrete set of causal events, but in the case of depression (as with all mental health difficulties), this is frustrated by the frank lack of evidence for a neat causal theory. Nor does one seem to be just over the horizon. For a recent summary relevant to Counselling for Depression practitioners, see *The NICE Guideline for the Treatment and Management of Depression in Adults: Updated Edition* (National Collaborating Centre for Mental Health, 2010).

What remains are theories from all quarters, not least in the psychosocial domain of psychotherapies. This book concerns person-centred and experiential psychology and although in common with all other psychological theories these ideas remain unverified, we do know that the treatment options offered in Counselling for Depression are evidence-based (see Chapter 2), and it is on that basis that we proceed. In Chapter 6 we discuss the aetiology of depression in terms of person-centred therapy and emotion-focused therapy, and readers will be invited to interrogate these theories with respect to the evidence available from all sources, including their clinical experience and the experience of their clients.

The diagnosis of depression

NICE uses the *Diagnostic and Statistical Manual of Mental Disorders Fourth Edition (DSM-IV)*[9] in its guidance to diagnose depression. NICE explains:

> It should be noted that classificatory systems are agreed conventions that seek to define different severities of depression in order to guide diagnosis and treatment, and their value is determined by how useful they are in practice. After careful review of the diagnostic criteria and the evidence, the Guideline Development Group decided to adopt DSM-IV criteria for this update rather than ICD-10, which was used in the previous guideline (NICE clinical guideline 23). This is because DSM-IV is used in nearly all the evidence reviewed and it provides definitions for atypical symptoms and seasonal depression. Its definition of severity also makes it less likely that a diagnosis of depression will be based

---

[9] The American Psychiatric Association published the *Diagnostic and Statistical Manual of Mental Disorders Fifth Edition (DSM-5)* in May 2013, but this has yet to influence NICE guidelines.

solely on symptom counting. In practical terms, clinicians are not expected to switch to DSM-IV but should be aware that the threshold for mild depression is higher than ICD-10 (five symptoms instead of four) and that degree of functional impairment should be routinely assessed before making a diagnosis. Using DSM-IV enables the guideline to target better the use of specific interventions, such as antidepressants, for more severe degrees of depression.

(NICE, 2009b)

The *DSM-IV* is one of two diagnostic frameworks in use in the UK (the other in popular use is the *International Classification of Mental and Behavioural Disorders* (*ICD-10*) published by the WHO). The systems are very similar – both distinguish between degrees of severity according to a number of factors, including the type and severity of symptoms, the duration of the symptoms and the context of the symptoms. The *ICD-10* tends to be used by clinicians, whereas the *DSM-IV* tends to be used in research largely because it is used in the US and has been adopted as an international research standard in an attempt to make diagnoses equivalent across the world.

We are not concerned with training practitioners to use these diagnostic systems, nor advocating one over the other. We acknowledge that whilst the definition of depression is ultimately a somewhat arbitrary decision, the diagnostic systems are attempts, however flawed, at regularising the decision-making process. We must remind ourselves that all clients are different with unique presentations of symptoms and each diagnoser brings their idiosyncratic understanding of the protocols. With this in mind, we are going to look briefly at the *DSM-IV* since it will be helpful for CfD therapists to know enough about the diagnostic and referral process in order to be able to understand the position of their work in primary care and take an active part in case discussions in multidisciplinary teams.

Diagnosing depression using DSM-IV

Diagnostic protocols are used in both clinical work and research, and there is some overlap in the aims of these areas of use. As mentioned above, when evaluating the effects of a particular treatment upon a particular client group, i.e. people with depression, the methodology is predicated on the idea that the client group is homogenous – that is that they all do indeed suffer from an equivalent form of depression. In many respects, the United States leads the way in psychotherapy research, if only by sheer volume of work being done, and so the *DSM-IV* is the international standard diagnostic protocol. Having said that, many studies hedge their bets by making sure that clients fulfil the criteria in both *DSM-IV* and *ICD-10* where possible.

In clinical work in the NHS, diagnosis is required to ensure that the appropriate treatment is offered to the patient. Since depression is a set of experiences which is critically determined by the degree or severity of the experiences, diagnosis must also identify the severity of the condition. This is the basis on which Counselling for Depression engages with the diagnostic protocols – CfD is obviously a therapy for depression, is effective for that specific group of clients with a certain severity of depression, so requires that they be accurately identified. Furthermore CfD must be continuously evaluated in order to maintain its status as a recommended treatment, and for these reasons, not to mention common sense, the diagnostic protocol needs to be consistent or reliable. How do the diagnostic protocols achieve this?

Signs and symptoms

Diagnostic protocols for physical diseases commonly refer to 'signs' and 'symptoms'.

A **symptom** is subjective experience of the patient such as aches and pains, fatigue, feelings of fear or panic, sensed by the patient – others are only aware of a symptom if the patient tells them about it.

A **sign** is objective evidence of a disease, such as bleeding, skin rash or weak pulse – it can be observed by the doctor, nurse, family members and the patient.

Diagnostic protocols for psychological disturbance rely almost exclusively on symptoms.

The processes are similar for both *DSM-IV* and *ICD-10*, but we will use the *DSM-IV* to illustrate the process since this has the added advantage that NICE has adopted the *DSM-IV* as noted above. As a background to considering the diagnosis of depression, NICE further explains:

Depression is a broad and heterogeneous diagnosis. Central to it is depressed mood and/ or loss of pleasure in most activities. Severity of the disorder is determined by both the number and severity of symptoms, as well as the degree of functional impairment. A formal diagnosis using the ICD-10 classification system requires at least four out of ten depressive symptoms, whereas the DSM-IV system requires at least five out of nine for a diagnosis of major depression (referred to in this guideline as 'depression'). Symptoms should be present for at least 2 weeks and each symptom should be present at sufficient severity for most of every day. Both diagnostic systems require at least one (DSM-IV) or two (ICD-10) key symptoms (low mood, loss of interest and pleasure or loss of energy) to be present.

Increasingly, it is recognised that depressive symptoms below the DSM-IV and ICD-10 threshold criteria can be distressing and disabling if persistent. Therefore this updated guideline covers 'subthreshold depressive symptoms', which fall below the criteria for major depression, and are defined as at least one key symptom of depression but with insufficient other symptoms and/or functional impairment to meet the criteria for full diagnosis. Symptoms are considered persistent if they continue despite active monitoring and/or low-intensity intervention, or have been present for a considerable time, typically several months.

(NICE, 2009b)

The *DSM-IV* divides depression into a number of subtypes, including major depressive disorder (MDD), post-partum depression, psychotic depression, chronic depression, dysthymia, and so on. Although CfD practitioners should be aware of the range of types of depression, in CfD practice, we need only concern ourselves with a limited range, determined by the NICE Guideline (below). Of particular interest are subthreshold depression and dysthymia. The threshold in question is that which signals the diagnosis of MDD (major depressive disorder). So subthreshold is some symptoms of depression but not sufficient to indicate MDD and people diagnosed with subthreshold depression have an increased likelihood of developing MDD (Broadhead et al., 1990; Cuijpers et al., 2004). Dysthymia[10] used to be more commonly known as 'neurotic depression', and is also likely to be called mild-to-moderate depression. It has less severe symptoms than MDD, but the symptoms endure for long periods, i.e. people experience the symptoms for most of the day for most days and for a diagnosis of dysthymia in *DSM-IV*, symptoms need to be present for two years – it is a chronic condition.

The accurate diagnosis of types depression using frameworks such as *DSM-IV* requires taking a detailed case history. For example, periods of mania or major depressive episodes have to be eliminated before a diagnosis of dysthymia can be reached. Importantly, it is possible, indeed completely normal and arguably healthy, to experience several of the listed symptoms for a very short period of time following an upsetting life event, but much more distressing and troubling to experience several symptoms over a number of weeks/months.

The *DSM-IV* lists nine symptoms and a protocol for diagnosing depression based on the number, combination and duration of the listed symptoms. The form and detail of the symptoms can be seen here, for example:

- Markedly diminished interest or pleasure in all, or almost all, activities most of the day, nearly every day (as indicated by either subjective account or observation made by others)
- Feelings of worthlessness or excessive or inappropriate guilt (which may be delusional) nearly every day (not merely self-reproach or guilt about being sick)
- Recurrent thoughts of death (not just fear of dying), recurrent suicidal ideation without a specific plan, or a suicide attempt or a specific plan for committing suicide

The diagnostic process should be attentive and sensitive, not just a counting and box-ticking exercise. The clinician should use their knowledge of the patient and make allowances for any special circumstances that pertain. So, the *DSM-IV* further advises clinicians as follows:

- Do not include symptoms that are clearly due to a general medical condition, or mood-incongruent delusions or hallucinations
- The symptoms should cause clinically significant distress or impairment in social, occupational, or other important areas of functioning

---

[10] *DSM-5* has removed dysthymia as a diagnosis, but until the NICE guideline takes up *DSM-5* in preference to *DSM-IV*, we will continue to use the term. See p. 55.

- The symptoms are not due to the direct physiological effects of a substance (e.g., a drug abuse, a medication) or a general medical condition (e.g., hypothyroidism)
- The symptoms are not better accounted for by bereavement, i.e., after the loss of a loved one, the symptoms persist for longer than 2 months or are characterized by marked functional impairment, morbid preoccupation with worthlessness, suicidal ideation, psychotic symptoms, or psychomotor retardation

Diagnosis of the 'degree' or 'severity' of depression, i.e. if it is mild, moderate or severe, is the key to matching the appropriate recommended treatment. NICE abbreviates the *DSM-IV* comprehensive diagnostic instrument in *Clinical Guidance 90: Appendix C: Assessing Depression and its Severity* (2009b). CfD practitioners should familiarise themselves with this appendix so that they understand the framework within which (a) referrals are made to them for CfD and (b) they might make referrals to other professionals if a more serious manifestation of depression or other disorder is indicated by the symptoms. Whilst good practice emphasises an understanding of the diagnostic framework, it should be emphasised that CfD practitioners are not expected to make *diagnoses* as part of CfD, but in as much as *assessments* are a routine part of primary care counselling, CfD is no different.

Clinical Guideline 90: Appendix C (NICE, 2009b) lists the symptoms and instructions as follows:

Key symptoms:

- persistent sadness or low mood; and/or
- marked loss of interests or pleasure.

At least one of these, most days, most of the time for at least 2 weeks.

If any of above present, ask about associated symptoms:

- disturbed sleep (decreased or increased compared to usual)
- decreased or increased appetite and/or weight
- fatigue or loss of energy
- agitation or slowing of movements
- poor concentration or indecisiveness
- feelings of worthlessness or excessive or inappropriate guilt
- suicidal thoughts or acts.

As noted above, the *DSM-IV* expects clinicians to use the symptom list sensitively and the NICE guideline similarly instructs 'Then ask about duration and associated disability, past and family history of mood disorders, and availability of social support' before explaining how clinicians should match treatments to symptoms:

1. Factors that favour general advice and active monitoring:

- four or fewer of the above symptoms with little associated disability
- symptoms intermittent, or less than 2 weeks' duration
- recent onset with identified stressor
- no past or family history of depression
- social support available
- lack of suicidal thoughts.

2. Factors that favour more active treatment in primary care:

- five or more symptoms with associated disability
- persistent or long-standing symptoms
- personal or family history of depression
- low social support
- occasional suicidal thoughts.

3. Factors that favour referral to mental health professionals:

- inadequate or incomplete response to two or more interventions
- recurrent episode within 1 year of last one
- history suggestive of bipolar disorder
- the person with depression or relatives request referral
- more persistent suicidal thoughts
- self-neglect.

4. Factors that favour urgent referral to specialist mental health services

- actively suicidal ideas or plans
- psychotic symptoms
- severe agitation accompanying severe symptoms
- severe self-neglect.

NICE further helps clinicians navigate the diagnostic process by providing what it calls 'pathways'. The Depression Pathway is a series of flowcharts which help the clinician determine the recommended treatment for a given patient (see http://pathways.nice. org.uk/pathways/depression/).

Finally, and importantly, NICE continues to develop understanding of depression from diagnostic criteria through to management and treatment. A recent publication, *The NICE Guideline for the Treatment and Management of Depression in Adults: Updated Edition* (National Collaborating Centre for Mental Health, 2010: 17), illustrates this when it announces:

In this guideline update the scope was widened to cover the substantial proportion of people who present with less severe forms of depression. Therefore, this updated guideline covers 'subthreshold depressive symptoms', which fall below the criteria for major depression (and which do not have a coding in ICD–10), and subthreshold depressive symptoms persisting for at least 2 years (dysthymia; F34.1).

Readers are encouraged to seek and read this publication and any further updates.

The DSM-5, published May 2013

The fifth edition of the *DSM* has attracted much debate about the validity and reliability of diagnosis, which can be followed in professional journals, worldwide. Whether prompted by the publication of *DSM-5* or not (although it does seem too much of a coincidence) professional bodies in the UK have released statements declaring their position regarding diagnosis and CfD practitioners can easily stay abreast of developments.

Of relevance to CfD practitioners are the changes to the categorisation and diagnosis of depressive disorders, although unless and until NICE adopts *DSM-5* for the depression guideline,[11] we suggest practitioners maintain only a watching brief.[12] Whilst *DSM-5* has added several new depressive disorders, of most interest to readers will be the removal of dysthymia as a separate disorder and included under the heading of persistent depressive disorder, i.e. chronic major depression. This was done because no scientifically meaningful *differences in degree* between the two could be found. What did seem important was the *episodic* versus the *chronic* nature of the symptoms.

Finally, there has been much media attention drawn to the removal of the 'bereavement exclusion' for major depressive episodes. In *DSM-IV*, the experience of many severe symptoms of depression following the death of a loved one would not result in the diagnosis of MDD, whereas in *DSM-5* MDD would be diagnosed after 2 weeks of experiencing sufficient symptoms, even following a bereavement.[13] However, this is accompanied by an extensive footnote to guide practitioners' differential diagnosis of normal grief.

---

[11] *NICE Guideline for the Treatment and Management of Depression in Adults: Updated Edition* (National Collaborating Centre for Mental Health, 2010).

[12] Neither online nor print versions of DSM-5 are necessary for everyday CfD practice. Readers can access information and a very helpful 'Highlights of changes from DSM-IV-TR to DSM-5' from the APA website: www.psychiatry.org/practice/dsm/dsm5 (retrieved 15/07/2013).

[13] See p. 5, 'Highlights of changes from DSM-IV-TR to DSM-5' www.psychiatry.org/practice/dsm/dsm5 (retrieved 15/07/2013).

The experience of depression

In addition to understanding the objective descriptions of depression which make up the diagnostic systems, it is essential to explore the phenomenology of depression – the experiences of clients that bring them to their GPs or other referring body which in turn might lead to a referral to a CfD therapist. We want to engage with clients' narratives of depression, and of course we acknowledge that this is the task of therapy as we understand it – the task of listening to *what it is like to be depressed*.

There are two difficulties with which we must struggle. First, it is important that we proceed to follow the narratives in the session as free as possible from the baggage of theory. Second it is also important that we free ourselves from other assumptions about depression, and having just presented readers with a list of symptoms and a formula for their consideration, readers will appreciate how difficult it is to approach a bottom-up phenomenology. We will revisit this when we look at the practice of CfD.

Actively acknowledging the complex nature of both depression as a constructed disorder and as a set of lived human experiences is not exclusive to person-centred therapy, emotion-focused therapy or Counselling for Depression. The *NICE Guideline for the Treatment and Management of Depression in Adults: Updated Edition* (National Collaborating Centre for Mental Health, 2010) gives an illuminating and detailed overview of the symptomatology, aetiology and economic costs of depression.

Here are some experiences of depression, written in clients' own words. First 'Re' tells their story, briefly summarising the experience of depression, therapy and restoration. Then we look at five more ways of talking about depression.

'Re'

Each day was an ordeal. I could not smell or taste or feel, any enthusiasm. Having a bath or talking to others exhausted me. I was a shell of my former self, surviving an existence that fluctuated between emptiness and emotional torture. I felt no peace. I watched the world through an invisible window and felt alone and unreachable. I did not want to exist but fought on out of the responsibility of limiting the pain of others. Sometimes I felt disconnected, sometimes sad. I looked at those around me who appeared 'normal' and felt mystified at their apparent ease in living a full life.

I was like a robot, I followed the ritual of dragging myself to therapy – getting there took all of my energy. I was beyond caring what others thought. My therapist was warm, patient and consistent and I felt able to be a mess there. This helped me – I realised how my depression had been triggered by recent events that were linked to childhood abuse. Eventually I moved slowly out of depression and then I had a sort of awakening. I felt the richness of existence and I inhaled the aroma of flowers like drugs. Such a connection re-established now felt like a privilege. The memory of the depression will always stay with me and now I take nothing for granted.

'Pa'

My life's a grey fog, like flat-lining. I don't care about anything – can't be bothered to get up, don't want to go out or to talk to people, given up my job – it's no use anyway, it's all boring, can't get interested in anything. I haven't got any energy. There's no point to living. I don't think I've ever been happy.

'Ay'

I just suddenly couldn't cope, it was all too much, it was impossible and I just couldn't stop crying. I felt hopeless, incapable, and panicked. I wanted to kill myself – I went to the railway track but couldn't even pluck up the courage to jump. Now I can't go near a train line as I'm scared that I will. I don't know what to do, I can't decide anything. Normally I am making decisions all day at work, but I can't even decide what to wear. I am falling deeper and deeper and I am so scared of not being able to get out. Sometimes I don't want to go out. I get annoyed with myself of being so useless and that makes me feel worse.

'Ra'

I hate myself, nobody likes me, I'm worthless. It would be better if I wasn't here. Nobody listens to me; I might as well be dead. I'm a total failure. I take pills all the time, I cut my arms. I don't care what happens to me. I hate everyone and everyone hates me. You can't help me, nobody can, it's pointless. I hope I die.

'Va'

My whole world fell apart when my mum died six months ago. I carried on and finished my course like a robot, but I don't know how I did it or how I passed the course. Now I can't find the energy to do anything. I've been off sick since the exams. There is no reason to get up in the morning and I think it was my fault my mum had her heart attack because we had been arguing about me going out rather than studying. I have tried to motivate myself out of it by, in my mind, going to a brighter place, but when I get up and move, the cloud follows me. There is no brighter place.

'Te'

I felt completely lost and without purpose. I actually felt physical pain, as though someone had punched me in the chest or stomach. It doubled me up. Without my wife I could see no future. I couldn't sleep at night and couldn't keep awake during the day. I didn't want to eat anything because I wasn't hungry – it just never occurred to me. Then I got this creeping feeling inside me of damage. It spread out like an ink stain, another actual physical feeling that I felt grip me as missing my wife turned into a sort of rotting, decaying, spreading stain inside me because it was my fault she had left. Every time I thought of her I couldn't see any future now because I was worthless.

Whilst it is not the job of the CfD therapist to make diagnoses, it should be clear that these people are experiencing distress which fulfils the diagnostic criteria. These experiences share some common factors – readers will no doubt be aware of the themes which repeat in these and other accounts – yet are all different.

It is noteworthy that these accounts (all from real people's experiences, appropriately anonymised) have several similarities in the terms used to describe depression. Lack of energy, lack of purpose, helplessness, lack of colour, thoughts of committing suicide, unpleasant physical symptoms, mechanical actions, inescapability and loss of agency all repeatedly figure in these descriptions. These commonalities in the accounts are the starting points for any diagnostic system, and in particular the idiopathic anecdotal frameworks which humanistic therapists work with in order to honour the unique experience of their clients. In other words, it is impossible to ignore these commonalities of experience, yet important to not let them divert us from attention to the lived experience of the client in front of us.

As we naturally search for patterns in data, it is also interesting to note the urge to want to know who is telling the story. Is it a man or a woman? How old are they? Are they in employment and if so what job do they do? And so on. What difference to your perceptions of these experiences does it make to learn that:

Re is Rebecca, a professional woman in her late 30s.

Pa is Paul, a 44-year-old who has had several episodes of depression, but these periods are interspersed with periods of being motivated and happy, periods which he can acknowledge when reminded of them, but can't remember the actual feeling of happiness when in one of these depressed periods.

Ay is Aysha. She is 50 and works as nurse. Here she describes her experience of a single episode of depression.

Ra is Rab. He is 19 and failed to get in to university. Even though his teachers predicted good grades, his work at college had been poor for the six months prior to his exams.

Va is Vantrice, a 22-year-old woman who has just completed her nurse training whilst living at home with her mother and father. Her older brother has moved away and now lives several hundred miles away.

Te is Terry, a 48-year-old self-employed man whose wife of 25 years left him three months ago. He has lost weight and his performance at work raised alarms amongst his colleagues, even though he is self-employed. His business partner and colleagues, although initially sympathetic, have reached the end of their collective tether.

CfD is a way of working that acknowledges and indeed honours the uniqueness of the individual experiences, whilst understanding them within a coherent theoretical framework and offering a consistent respectful, collaborative practice. Moreover, CfD *requires* therapists actively attend to and value the individual expressions of distress, and this is the starting point of its therapeutic method.

Person-centred and experiential psychotherapies and diagnosis

There is an inevitable tension between working in a system of psychological therapy delivery based on diagnostic categories and working with clients' individual, subjective experience. One way CfD practitioners can manage this tension is by considering a number of positions:

* that the term depression has a degree of validity
* it can be a useful means of signposting clients to appropriate therapies
* clients with a diagnosis of depression often experience common symptoms
* the experiences underlying these symptoms will always be personal, subjective and individual

In considering these points of view it is also important to appreciate contemporary critiques of diagnosis and its use.

Questions about the usefulness of psychodiagnosis have been raised from all quarters of the helping professions: psychology, psychotherapy, psychiatry, psychotherapy and not least by users of these services. Increasingly these critiques are launched from an evidence base which disputes both the validity and reliability of the diagnostic categories (e.g. Bentall, 2009; Boyle, 2007). Person-centred practitioners, however, have an arguably more serious quarrel with the interpersonal and intrapersonal dynamics of the very act of diagnosis, even if it were reliable and valid. In 1989, Angelo Boy's 'Psychodiagnosis: A person-centred perspective' in *The Person-Centered Review* opened a symposium on the contentious matter of psychodiagnosis in the person-centred therapy community. The topic had not received much attention in the literature since Rogers' early writings, although it was clear that Rogers and his theory were set against the medical model of mental illness. A number of highly respected person-centred theoreticians and practitioners responded to Boy's paper and the issues were comprehensively debated. The full symposium – Boy's opening paper and the responses – is available in Cain (2002).

The contentious nature of, and range of reactions to, psychodiagnosis amongst the individuals and 'tribes' of the person-centred approach presented in 1989 are largely unchanged in the early 21st century in the UK. In an interview with psychiatrist Anthony Clare for the BBC Radio Programme 'All in the Mind' in 1976, Carl Rogers said:

> We regard the medical model as an extremely inappropriate model for dealing with psychological disturbances. The model that makes more sense is a growth model or a developmental model. In other words we see people as having a potential for growth and development, and that that can be released under the right psychological climate. We don't see them as sick and needing a diagnosis, prescription and a cure. And that is a very fundamental difference with a good many implications. (Rogers, 1976)

In PCT theory terms, the iatrogenic nature of psychodiagnosis lies in the fact that the effort in PCT is to re-establish the internal locus of evaluation characteristic of good psychological health. The healthy individual determines their self-perceptions and puts their own values on them. Moreover, they do this in their own terms symbolically and linguistically. When vulnerable, the individual all too easily relinquishes this self-valuing process and accepts the perceptions, values, terms – the diagnoses – of others. This is not benign or neutral, it is both antitherapeutic and actively damaging to psychological good health.

Working within a clinical system that effectively runs on psychodiagnosis can be problematic for PCT practitioners, requiring them to evolve individual ways of reconciling themselves to this. We also understand that many counsellors from other orientations in primary care are behoven to find as comfortable position as possible with regard to the edifice of diagnosis. It is necessary because constant hand-wringing about diagnosis will divert precious energy away from the therapeutic endeavour, which is difficult enough without this extra burden.

Working with diagnosis – CfD good practice

We suggest the following to help practitioners navigate a course to effective practice whilst honouring their understanding of PCT theory.

First, it hardly bears repeating that Counselling for Depression is a therapeutic approach to depression. But that does not mean that practitioners have to accept the whole edifice of psychodiagnosis uncritically in order to be effective practitioners. Indeed, continual professional reflection – including questioning the framework of diagnosis on the basis of clinical experience – is a requirement of good practice.

Second, the *diagnosis* of clients is not the prime responsibility of CfD practitioners although they do have *assessment* of clients as part of their job. However, engaging with the diagnostic framework within which the client is positioned is necessary for a number of reasons:

- understanding basis for referral
- understanding and working within a stepped-care model of service delivery
- responding to clients who are reassured by diagnosis
- participating in outcome measurement

- engaging with clinical explanations for onward referral
- participating in case discussions
- accounting for recovery in therapy on the client's terms, the counsellor's terms and the terms of the service

Third, some practitioners are able creatively to use diagnosis as a starting point for the therapy process. It might be useful to begin by understanding who made the diagnosis and how the client now finds their experiences in relation to this, especially if it was made some time ago and the client has been waiting for counselling. Some clients will not recognise themselves in the diagnosis, whilst others will be relieved to have their distress named. Of course each client's experience of the diagnostic process and the diagnosis itself has implications in terms of person-centred theory and the locus of evaluation. However, practitioners are reminded that with diagnosis, along with all other aspects of the client's experience, it is the task of the therapist to follow, not lead. It is worth reminding ourselves to be flexible and non-judgementally accepting when it comes to listening to the client's narrative of their experiences, even when they enthusiastically embrace a diagnosis of depression as a life-saving event.

Finally, it is also worth remembering that at the very least, a diagnosis of depression is the client's access to treatment.

Assessment and stepped care – CfD good practice

Although pointing clients in the direction of particular services, diagnosis in itself is not sufficient to produce a good match of clients with therapies. Other factors need to be taken into consideration. Indeed in primary care psychological services in the UK, very few clients receive a formal diagnosis using a structured diagnostic tool. Instead their needs and preferences are taken on board in a process of assessment. Assessment is an integral part of CfD, in a way that it has not been in traditional person-centred and experiential practice. There are a number of reasons for this. NHS psychological services are multi-professional and CfD is just one form of therapy offered within these services. This inevitably raises the question of how clients can be directed to the therapy that will provide them with most benefit. A collaborative assessment process founded on the use of the core conditions of empathy, unconditional acceptance and authenticity, provides the best answer to this.

NHS psychological services are often organised around the principle of *stepped care*, where the recommended therapy is based on both the type of problem presented and the level of severity. Minimal interventions such as GP watchful waiting for about two weeks, followed by a limited number (usually about six) of guided self-help sessions from a psychological wellbeing practitioner (PWP) are offered for less severe presentations. If the client experiences sufficient recovery from these then they are no longer in need of further help. If clients do not respond to this level of treatment or it is obvious at assessment that their problems are of a severity that would warrant a more intensive therapy, they would access a high-intensity face-to-face talking therapy for 15–20 sessions. CBT tends to be the recommended frontline high-intensity therapy for most problems, however, CfD, interpersonal psychotherapy (IPT), dynamic interpersonal therapy (DIT) and behavioural couples therapy (BCT) are also recommended for depression. For anxiety, CBT is generally recommended, along with eye movement desensitisation and reprocessing (EMDR) for post-traumatic stress disorder (PTSD). It is important for CfD therapists to become familiar with the other interventions offered within the service in which they work and to be able to discuss with clients the options that are available.

While it is not possible here to discuss all these different therapies in detail, some simple examples would be:

- if the client's depression is leading to lots of conflict with their partner, who also wishes to engage in therapy, then BCT could be an option
- if the depression is experienced in interpersonal conflict without a partner's willingness to engage in therapy then IPT or DIT may be helpful
- if a client prefers a structured therapy and wishes to develop skills to manage their own behaviour and thought processes then CBT may be the best option

This stepped-care system is premised on the principles that less severe problems should not be *over*-treated, that clients should get the most effective therapy for their problems, and that clients should be able to exercise a degree of choice over the therapy they receive. Very straightforward information on some of the different therapies offered for depression is available in the NHS document *Which Talking Therapy for Depression?*[14] Working in this type of multi-disciplinary setting makes assessment skills a necessity for CfD practitioners. Generally the purpose of an assessment is:

- to gain an empathic understanding of the client's problem from the client's perspective
- to understand something of the client's past, including the development of the problem and past experiences that may have contributed to this
- to gain a sense of the client's current situation, including both ongoing stressors and supportive factors
- to gain an understanding of the clients' strengths and how they manage to cope with their difficulties
- to understand what the client may wish to gain from therapy
- to understand any risk factors relating to harm to self or harm to others
- to gain a sense of the client's level of motivation to resolve their problems
- to give information about types of therapy available, making sure the client understands the various options, and to get a sense of what their preferences might be
- to help the client engage in the therapeutic process

More specifically, CfD therapists would need to consider whether the client is both suited to and amenable to the approach they are offering. To benefit from CfD clients

---

[14] www.scribd.com/doc/51392570/Which-Therapy (retrieved 05/11/2013).

need to be able to engage psychologically, to work relationally and make good use of the therapeutic conditions. It cannot be assumed that this will always be the case: some clients find a warm and empathic relationship so acutely painful that they cannot derive benefit from it in the number of sessions available. It is also worth bearing in mind that a client's drug and/or alcohol use may also impair their ability to engage. Similarly the CfD approach is premised on the client's ability to contact and reflect upon emotional experience. If clients find it intensely difficult to express their feelings and reflect upon themselves psychologically, the CfD approach may not be best for them.

In an evidence-based system, the type of problem presented also has implications for whether a client is suited to CfD. Based on current evidence, CBT rather than CfD would be recommended where the primary problem is anxiety. However where anxiety and depression are comorbid, CfD may be an effective option, where a flexible rather than a structured therapy is indicated. Where clients struggle to adjust to adverse life events (such as bereavement, divorce, redundancy, long-term medical problems) CfD's phenomenological, empathic and experiential approach can provide significant benefits, helping clients make sense of their experience and develop new personal narratives which sustain their future development. A sound understanding of the theoretical profiles and recommended applications of other therapies is essential for the CfD therapist to carry out an effective assessment process, ensuring that clients are well informed and can engage in a therapy that is suited to their particular needs.

Medication and depression

We have included a short section on medication since many, if not most clients, will have direct or indirect experience (via relatives, friends or colleagues) of antidepressant medication, and GPs will prescribe antidepressants alongside psychological treatment. Other than the briefest of summaries, we do not intend to cover in detail the history of the use of medications for depression or the pharmacology of antidepressants. For more information on these subjects, readers are directed to Healy (2005) and we find the chapters on pharmacological and physical interventions in depression in *The NICE Guideline for the Treatment and Management of Depression in Adults: Updated Edition* (National Collaborating Centre for Mental Health, 2010) to be informative and helpful. Similarly, the NICE Depression Pathway[15] has general information, and on medication and associated clinical decisions in particular on the page describing antidepressant treatment in adults.[16]

There are three classes of antidepressant drugs: monoamine oxidase inhibitors (MAOIs), tricyclic antidepressants (TCAs) and selective serotonin reuptake inhibitors (SSRIs). Healy recounts that the 'original' antidepressants were discovered in the

---

[15] http://pathways.nice.org.uk/pathways/depression, retrieved 14/01/2013.

[16] http://pathways.nice.org.uk/pathways/depression/antidepressant-treatment-in-adults, retrieved 14/01/2013.

1950s during the search for neuroleptics or 'antipsychotics'. The first MAOIs and TCAs were developed in 1957 and during testing as antipsychotics were found to have mood-altering effects. Complex syndromes of side effects limited these medications to the treatment of what was then known as major, biological or endogenous depression.

SSRIs were discovered in the 1960s as a result of more detailed understanding of the action of TCAs in blocking the reuptake of certain neurotransmitters. Subsequently, it has been found that SSRIs have a noticeable anxiolytic (antianxiety) effect and that indeed this may be their main action. Whilst these findings are further examples of attending to the diversity of individual responses to medications, they also have some implications for psychological theories of distress which understand anxiety to be the underlying factor in the majority of psychological disturbance.

Choice of frontline treatment

Earlier in this chapter (p. 42) we briefly discussed the recent tendency to medicalise a growing number of aspects of what were hitherto thought of as everyday experiences. One feature of this tendency is the fact that antidepressant medication receives considerable media attention and SSRIs have been described as 'smart' drugs. These trends do nothing to highlight the fact that psychological treatments are also promoted as frontline treatments of choice by NICE. Furthermore, the evidence base for the effectiveness of antidepressant medication for mild to moderate depression has recently been critiqued, whilst the evidence base for certain psychological treatments of mild to moderate depression continues to strengthen. In a systematic review of counselling in primary care, Brettle, Hill and Jenkins (2008: 212) found 'clear evidence that among primary care patients, for the treatment of depression, there is a strong preference for counselling as opposed to medication'. They continue in the report of their findings 'The preference for counselling is unaffected by factors such as age, ethnicity, the presence of mental health problems, or problem severity' and 'The receipt of a preferred intervention improves treatment take-up and compliance but there is no clear evidence that the receipt of a preferred treatment improves clinical outcomes'. Clearly, patients prefer counselling and are more likely to complete the treatment when this preference is honoured.

The use of medication

The use of medications for experiences diagnosed as depression continues to excite vigorous debate. Although we will not engage with these debates here, some of the contentious areas will arise briefly or tangentially and we will provide signposts to relevant reading material. Four issues are worth highlighting:

Medication to match the diagnosis

The medical model of mental illness is predicated on the idea of a unique diagnosis providing clear indication of a unique treatment. We have seen how this ideal is confounded in real life, not least in the diverse diagnostic category of depression, with its subdivisions and flexible interpretations of experiences. Nevertheless, when it comes to the prescription of medication following NICE guidelines, very careful attention is paid to the severity and persistence of the symptoms.

Antidepressants are not recommended for people with simple first-onset subthreshold symptoms or mild depression. They may be considered if (i) the patient has a past history of moderate or severe depression, (ii) the subthreshold depressive symptoms have been present for two years or more, (iii) the symptoms have persisted following completion of other treatments, or (iv) the patient has a chronic physical condition, the treatment of which might be complicated by depression.

In all of the cases above, the prescription of antidepressants should be considered in comparison with or, in some cases alongside, approved psychological treatments, of which CfD is one. The treatment of severe and complex depression is the domain of specialist mental health services.

Side effects of medication

There is no disputing that antidepressants cause side effects, some of which are so objectionable and intolerable as to compromise treatment compliance and obviously this renders treatment useless. Whilst for many, side effects are minimal, for others they are only tolerable as an option in a desperate situation, but may be sufficiently debilitating and unpleasant that they can exacerbate low mood, hopelessness and other symptoms of depression. Prescribing clinicians are expected to monitor side effects, but it is also the case that clients might feel more comfortable disclosing problems with medication to counsellors.

All heathcare professionals working in primary care share responsibility in helping patients access appropriate medication, including responsibility to monitor the effects of medication, both positive and negative. It goes without saying that *hunting* for side effects has no place in CfD, and any mention of possible side effects by the client should be the basis of empowering the client to disclose appropriate symptoms to the prescribing clinician, rather than the counsellor immediately reporting the problems on behalf of the client. This is, however, always an option if the client's safety is thought to be in danger.

The NHS Choices website is a good resource for clients who want more information, giving a comprehensive list of side effects on the 'Antidepressants – side effects' page.[17]

---

[17] www.nhs.uk/Conditions/Antidepressant-drugs/Pages/Side-effects.aspx (retrieved 14/01/2013).

It is clear from the list that persistent severe side effects would make anyone feel low, let alone a person already suffering from the symptoms of depression. Finally, there is a small but significant increase in suicidal ideation in the early stages of antidepressant treatment. CfD practitioners should be alert to the implications of this.

Medication and talking therapies in tandem

NICE make it clear that it is acceptable to prescribe both frontline treatments – antidepressants and psychological treatment – simultaneously, although the evidence is mixed regarding the degree of improvement, if any, over either treatment prescribed individually. Some medical practitioners are persuaded that psychological treatment combined with antidepressant therapy is indeed associated with a higher improvement rate than drug treatment alone, but that the active contribution of the psychotherapy is to help keep patients in treatment. Furthermore, patient preference also has to be taken into consideration. It would be disappointing if the only rationale for combined treatment is to use psychotherapy as a compliance-enhancing factor.

CfD practitioners will have clients referred to them who have concomitant prescriptions for antidepressants. In the majority of cases, the medication will not have a deleterious effect upon counselling unless side effects are severe, whilst there is an equal chance that medication might energise a client sufficiently to be able to attend and benefit from the CfD sessions. So it is possible that the treatment compliance hypothesis might work both ways.

Withdrawal from medication and discontinuation effects

In the natural course of events, patients with mild to moderate depression come to the end of antidepressant treatment, most often due to the sustained remission of symptoms. When the cessation of medication occurs during CfD work, practitioners need to be aware of some of the issues which may become active. In particular, proper advice and support during discontinuation and the likelihood of relapse or discontinuation effects.

Stopping medication of any sort must be done under the guidance of the prescribing clinician. Withdrawal symptoms or discontinuation effects are common to all classes of antidepressant, however, CfD practitioners are most likely to be referred clients who are prescribed SSRIs. There is a well-documented discontinuation syndrome associated with SSRIs (Haddad and Anderson, 2007). The symptoms include dizziness, headache, nausea, lethargy, sleep disturbances and less commonly, mania and hypomania. The onset of symptoms is usually sudden and within hours or days of abrupt discontinuation of medication and highlights the need to discontinue SSRI medication carefully and slowly with full medical support. However, there are many reasons why clients might abruptly discontinue medication without consulting the prescribing clinician and the discontinuation effects can easily be mistaken for relapse or recurrence.

It is good practice for CfD therapists to be aware of the symptoms associated with SSRI discontinuation and alert to the possibilities of the client mistaking these symptoms for relapse. Even if discontinuation is conducted with medical support as part of a change in the profile of treatments for a particular client, the client should be made aware of possible withdrawal symptoms and supported appropriately. The duration of the symptoms is usually quite short, and often simply being aware of the likelihood of the symptoms and timely support from relatives, friends and therapist is sufficient.

Finally, CfD counsellors can have a role in supporting clients who have decided to discontinue medication under medical supervision. Regular counselling sessions can help sustain the client through the difficulties of discontinuation effects and counsellors can, if asked by the client, help monitor discontinuation effects and collaboratively develop coping strategies. However, it is worth stressing that these would not be the main focal points of the work, other than in relatively short episodes.

5

Person-Centred and Experiential Therapies

Competences covered in Chapter 5

B1-Knowledge of the philosophy and principles that inform the therapeutic approach
B2-Knowledge of person-centred theories of human growth and development and the origins of psychological distress
B3-Knowledge of the person-centred conditions for, and goals of, therapeutic change
B4-Knowledge of the PCE conceptualisation of depression
B7-Ability to experience and communicate empathy
B8-Ability to experience and communicate a fundamentally accepting attitude to clients
B9-Ability to maintain authenticity in the therapeutic relationship
S1.1-Ability to identify the ways in which clients manage and process their emotions, including the ability to recognise when clients are finding it difficult to access these
S1.6-Ability to help the client differentiate between feelings that are appropriate to (and hence useful for) dealing with a current situation and those that are less helpful to them, for example:

- because they are emotional responses relating to previous experiences rather than the present context
- because they are reactions to other, more fundamental, emotions

(Competences are listed in Appendix 1)

Philosophy and principles of PCE counselling

Person-centred and experiential therapy is, in the first instance, rooted in the work of Carl Rogers, particularly his books *Client-Centered Therapy* (Rogers, 1951), a paper 'The Necessary and Sufficient Conditions of Therapeutic Personality Change' (Rogers, 1957), his chapter (Rogers, 1959) in Koch (1959) and the new insights heralding the development of experiential approaches in Rogers (1961) and Rogers et al. (1967).

CfD is an evidence-based innovative integration of Rogers' work with the work of Leslie Greenberg, Robert Elliott, Jeanne Watson and colleagues. This group developed the work of Laura North Rice leading to the current iteration called *emotion-focused therapy*. This is most completely described in Elliott et al. (2004) and specifically with reference to depression in Greenberg and Watson (2006).

Some PCE practitioners preparing for CfD practice might think that this chapter can be skimmed over. We certainly don't want to be seen as trying to teach our grandmothers to suck eggs, but we do believe that periodically reminding ourselves of the founding principles of PCE therapies is a useful exercise, and is offered as much as a discussion starter as a refresher course. It might be that readers disagree with our selection and descriptions. We also assume that UK-trained therapists may be relatively unfamiliar with the EFT contributions to CfD. In this chapter we present CfD theory in terms of classical person-centred therapy and emotion-focused therapy as they tend towards, or approach each other, rather than discriminate their points of difference – especially where these points of difference do not impinge upon time-limited practice in the NHS.

Since EFT locates itself as an extension of person-centred theory, many of the points of theory covered in the following sections are common to both PCT and EFT. These similarities and overlaps will not be repeatedly highlighted – readers will be left to their own devices to integrate both theory and practice 'between the gaps'.

A perceptual theory

Rogers (1951) formally introduced his developing theory as 19 propositions in a chapter titled 'A Theory of Personality and Behavior'. The founding philosophy and principles of his work were rooted in phenomenology and the then new ideas of humanistic psychology. He began by emphasising the central role of lived experience and the perceptual field of the individual:

> Every individual exists in a continually changing world of experience of which he is the center. (1951: 483)

> The organism reacts to the field as it is experienced and perceived. This perceptual field is, for the individual, 'reality'. (1951: 484)

This emphasis on experience and perception helps locate client-centred therapy as a perceptual theory, i.e. changes in perception of the world (the world of experience) are effectively changes in reality for the individual. The influence of these propositions cannot be overstated when it comes to the nature of psychological health and processes of therapeutic change. They also pave the way for understanding the central role of experiencing introduced in Rogers' later work (Rogers, 1961) and the influence of the work of Eugene Gendlin (1998), leading eventually to the development of emotion-focused therapy.

These propositions also establish person-centred theory as phenomenological, i.e. our construction of reality is subjective. So, reality is the subjective experience of the individual, and includes our experience of intersubjectivity; specifically that others exist in relation to us and we in relation to them. These are the indices of consciousness. Of course perception, experience and the notion of consciousness cannot be completely understood quite so simply, but Rogers appeared keen to establish a set of principles uncluttered by esoteric philosophical discussion of the verifiability of reality. He stated his theory in very concrete, common-sense terms in comparison with, for example, the psychoanalytical theories of the time.

> For psychological purposes, reality is basically the private world of the individual percep-
> tions, though for social purposes reality consists of those perceptions which have a high
> degree of commonality among various individuals. (Rogers, 1951: 485)

By locating the creation of meaning and reality in the *perceptions* of the individual, Rogers lays the foundation of empathy as the preferred therapeutic method over observation and measurement. Behaviour can be observed and measured, whereas perceptions are best apprehended by trying to understand the world of the other as if it were your own.

The centrality of experience

During his work on the 'Wisconsin Project' Rogers became increasingly interested in the related concepts of therapy as a relationship (rather than the therapist as a simple provider of conditions), therapeutic change as a process (rather than an event) and self-experiencing as the core internal process. These developments in his thinking came about, as always, from his work with clients – in this case the project was providing psychotherapy for hospitalised patients with a diagnosis of schizophrenia. The work with people having such unusual psychological processes provided such rich qualitative data that Rogers and his colleague Gendlin began to develop new theory. Rogers retired from academic life to California before the full project report was published, but Gendlin continued developing some of these ideas into focusing-oriented therapy.

Looking back from the 21st century, it might not seem so remarkable to think that therapy is a relationship, that change is a process and that self-experience is a key psychological event, but in the late 1950s these were revolutionary concepts. Later in this chapter we will look at the therapeutic relationship and the process of therapeutic change, but for now we turn our attention to the notion of experiencing.

Rogers noticed that clients seemed to be able to tap into an internal process of experiencing in the moment, often having a physical, visceral quality:

> I mostly want to call attention to this part we just played [where the client says] 'I'm just
> a pleading little boy' and here again he used kinesthetic means. In trying to get at what
> he was feeling he put his hands in supplication. … Here it seems to me that he's really
> *experiencing* himself as pleading … in the immediate moment. (Rogers, 1958, cited in
> Kirschenbaum, 2007: 288)

The 'experiential' in PCE psychotherapy comes from this understanding of the immediate felt awareness (or in Gendlin's terms, the 'felt sense') that lies at the centre of human psychological functioning. A felt sense is sometimes spontaneously in awareness, sometimes at the edge of awareness, and sometimes out of awareness yet can be accessed deliberately and mindfully. This dipping into the constantly flowing stream of experience in the therapeutic relationship provides the substrate for moments of change.

The content of experiencing is limitless and might take the form of bodily sensations, urges, feelings, memories, sensations, thoughts and so on. Sometimes such awarenesses come with clear meanings associated with them, but many times they do not. The awareness might be puzzling, disconnected from other experiences or fuzzy and imprecise. What is clear is that the effort in pursuit of meaning can be extremely therapeutic. Even this statement requires qualification, though, since sometimes simple apprehension of the felt sense is all that is required. It does not *require* understanding the meaning and connections of the felt sense in order for resolution, integration or therapeutic movement to take place. In short the client (and by extension the therapist) does not *need* to understand the meaning of experiences in order to feel therapeutic movement, but in most cases it is fulfilling for a client to have access to a complete narrative. We will look at specific methods for working with felt sense and similar experiences associated with depression in later chapters.

The role of emotion

The terms 'feeling' and 'emotion' are often used interchangeably and there is a plethora of accounts of differences between emotions and feelings, with little agreement. So we will use the terms interchangeably unless a specific case forces a definition upon either term.

In classical client-centred theory, opinion can differ regarding the particular role of emotion in psychological health and therapy. In the first instance, Rogers (1951: 492–3) explained the role of emotions thus:

> Emotion accompanies and in general facilitates ... goal-directed behavior, the kind of emotion being related to the seeking versus the consummatory aspects of the behavior and the intensity of the emotion being related to the perceived significance of the behavior to the maintenance and enhancement of the organism.

So Rogers describes two types of emotion (anticipatory, excited, possibly unpleasant, and satisfied, pleasant, calm). He doesn't debate the possibility of emotions having a motivational or reinforcing effect, simply saying that they both accompany and facilitate behaviour – nor does he cast them as either a requirement or a consequence. Yet it is clear from his writings that the experience and processing of emotions is important to psychological health.

In what many consider to be his most comprehensive theory statement, Rogers (1959: 198) writes that the:

> experiencing of a feeling ... denotes an emotionally tinged experience, together with its personal meaning. Thus it includes the emotion but also the cognitive content of the meaning of that emotion in its cognitive context. It thus refers to the unity of emotion and cognition as they are experienced inseparably in the moment.

So, according to Rogers, feelings do not enjoy special status as ways of processing sensations or intrapersonal energies. Rather they depend for their meaning and relevance upon the context, both internal and external and then are experiences in tandem with, inseparable from, thoughts. They are important elements of the internal landscape of experience.

All PCE theoreticians would concur that fluidity in the self-structure is a sign of psychological health. Importantly this includes feelings in that the unrestricted experience of a complete range of feelings, matched by the unfettered expression of these feelings, is part of the basis for a healthy self-structure, free from anxiety and tension. Poor psychological health involves hardly recognising experiencing or expressing feelings at all, possibly being frightened of or by them. And to revisit the previous paragraph, Rogers (1961) explains that for best psychological health, cognitions, constructs and ideas – particularly self-related cognitions – are also best held flexibly, rather than as rigid thought patterns and stereotypical responses.

EFT holds emotions at the centre of human psychology – the clue is in the title. Indeed, Elliott et al. (2004) devote 12 pages to *emotion theory*,[1] and the importance and centrality of emotions in psychological health is the substantial contribution that EFT makes to Counselling for Depression.

EFT emotion theory

Readers will notice that this theory overlaps with Rogers' work in several places, both extending and elaborating the detail of the importance of emotions. The first position is that experienced reality always includes emotion and:

- emotion precedes language-based symbolisation
- as infants develop they fuse emotion and cognition
- emotions signal the importance of experiences (see Rogers, 1951, above)
- they add meaning, value and direction to experiences (see Rogers, 1951; 1959, above)
- emotions contribute to motivation:
  - they help generate wishes and needs, in turn provoking and amplifying goal-directed behaviour (we bond because we feel afraid or attracted, flee danger when frightened, care for others when we feel compassion, and so on)
- emotions facilitate survival by providing automatic or rapid responses as necessary

---

[1] For a brief account of EFT emotion theory, see Elliott, 2012.

Three further elements of emotion theory are useful to incorporate into CfD.

First, the internal experiential landscape is populated by *emotion schemes*: idiosyncratic processes which are continuously constructed and reconstructed, only available to consciousness upon active self-reflection, acting as foci for all kinds of self-related intra- and interpersonal activities. They can be thought of as operating as a network wherein activation of one scheme spreads to adjoining schemes.

Second, experienced emotional responses can be grouped into four types (adapted from Elliott, 2012: 110–12):

- Primary adaptive emotion responses – first, natural reactions to a situation that would help us take appropriate action
- Maladaptive emotion responses – initial reactions, but ones learned from previous experience, e.g. a person who has been sexually abused may respond to warmth and caring with anger and hostility because of what they have learned to associate with these
- Secondary reactive emotion responses – emotional reactions to either primary adaptive emotions or maladaptive emotions which *replace* the initial responses, e.g. a person who feels anger rather than vulnerability: the anger disguises the vulnerability
- Instrumental emotion responses – strategic displays of an emotion for an intended effect, e.g. crying in order to get sympathy, rather than as authentic upset

Third, EFT introduces the importance of emotional regulation. This refers to a person's ability to experience emotions within what we might think of as an acceptable or useful range. In this sense, 'useful' means for the benefit of the individual in question, e.g. to experience distress in a regulated, rather than overwhelming way, or to be sufficiently aroused to pursue and achieve a goal. So in real life, it is not sufficient to simply experience emotion. Given the centrality of emotion in both motivation and creating contexts, it is better to experience emotions within a range that is accessible and useful – being overwhelmed by or being out of touch with emotion is incapacitating as both prevent people acting in order to get needs met.

These understandings of the role of emotion have implications both for the creation and maintenance of psychological tension and disturbance, and the process of therapeutic change.

Human beings are relational

This principle should hardly need stating, such is its ubiquity in psychological theory. The important extension of this central quality of human nature is that, in PCE theory, the relationship is the principle location for therapeutic change. Not simply as a conduit through which treatments are delivered – as might be the case in, for example, cognitive behavioural therapies – but that the relationship per se is the active therapeutic factor. Relationships are powerful vectors for influence and change – both positive and negative – and in PCE theory it is held that the right type of relationship (comprising Rogers' therapeutic conditions (1959)) is intrinsically therapeutic.

Empathy, for example, is not 'used' in PCT simply as a method of collecting information in order to make an accurate assessment or diagnosis (of course it is necessary in order to make an assessment, but not brought out as a tool, just for this purpose). It is offered for two related reasons: first it is the primary way in which interpersonal connection, accompaniment and companionship is communicated. To paraphrase John Shlien (1997/2001/2003), through empathy we establish interpersonal confirmation and self-affirmation. Through this relational moment clients discover that they can be known, understood and can reciprocate in kind. Through this *knowing* there is a confirmation of being, the recognition of another's humanity and confirmation of one's own. Obviously, this process requires some degree of self-with-other encounter, or relationship. Second, when we say that clients may discover that they can reciprocate in kind, we mean that the client's ability to empathise is a sign of higher levels of process or psychological functioning. It could be hypothesised that this initially might be achieved through simple modelling in the therapy hour – even so, it can be a breakthrough for many clients and herald significant progress.

We will explore the complete set of qualities necessary to constitute a therapeutic relationship in PCE terms later in this chapter.

Human motivation

Theories of motivation are fundamental to psychology – motivation being the term used to describe the reason or push behind behaviour. It is argued that organisms need a reason to do something, and then a reason to do the next thing, and in some theories, the organism without motivation is dormant. These reasons or motives direct, drive and sustain the organism in its effort towards a goal. Some theories posit levels and types of drive and since the drives are the precursors of behaviour, any change in behaviour (often the client's intention in therapy) is clearly linked to motivation.

The actualising tendency

Rogers' (1951: 487) proposition IV states 'The organism has one basic tendency and striving – to actualise, maintain and enhance the experiencing organism'. This simple statement of a single motivating drive is testimony to Rogers' uncomplicated view of human psychology. Of course, to call this uncomplicated does not mean that when revealed in the lives of individual humans, the statement does not allow ample room for infinitely nuanced expression. Rogers saw no need for over-complicated systems of drives and needs: '... it seems entirely possible that all organic and psychological needs may be described as partial aspects of this one fundamental need' (1951: 487–8). Here he dispenses with both the Freudian and behaviourist systems of motivation: understanding behaviour based on a complex of unresolved hypothesised psychological tasks in infancy on the one hand, and primary needs for food, water and sex on the other.

The statement describes a directional force which pushes all behaviour, the direction being towards survival, maintenance and enhancement of the individual. Maslow's hierarchy of needs can be pressed into service to contextualise the more precise meaning of any behaviour alongside the testimony of the client. Clearly, some behaviour is simple survival, whilst some might be reaching for a peak experience. Indeed, there is nothing to suggest that both cannot be evident simultaneously, since the individual might perceive their self to be under threat in one area of life, whilst striving for a more esoteric sense of fulfilment in another.

Note the absence of any self- or other-destructive tendencies in the PCE model of motivation – in colloquial terms, the organism is always doing the best it can to survive, maintain and enhance itself. Furthermore, Rogers sees the individual always acting as a unified being, not fragmented, meaning that although a person might superficially appear to have parts pulling in different directions, when the meaning of the person's world is understood, it will be seen that as a whole, the person still moves towards survival and growth.

This point is important when working with people diagnosed with depression, since their behaviour can be easily interpreted in some models as self-destructive. The PCE therapist does not interpret the client's behaviour, but, with an open mind seeks to unfold its meaning by empathic understanding. This is core practice for CfD, though it may be difficult for non-PCE trained therapists to eschew interpretation or loaded questioning.

This position of open-minded, naïve seeking of meaning is essential in CfD since it also is the precursor of being non-judgemental – another of Rogers' necessary therapeutic conditions (1959). We would argue that if the therapist begins with the idea that some self-destructive primal urge within the client is bound to be fulfilled, then this is what they will find. If they begin each session in each relationship as a naïve traveller in a foreign world, they stand a better chance of discovering the true meanings there, and if any part of the client's self-structure appears to be pulling against growth, they will be best placed to find out why it seems this way on the surface. In CfD counsellors empathise with all configurations while ensuring that they are not judged. It is the conflicting nature of the dialectic created between opposing aspects of the self that creates a distressing, sometimes incomprehensible impasse or disturbance, rather than anything inherent in the aspects themselves. We will look at specific theoretical constructions and therapeutic interventions dedicated to these aspects of self later in the book (see Chapters 6 and 8), and in the section on uniqueness and diversity below we find further resonance with Mearns' (Mearns and Thorne, 2000: 114–16) injunction to accept and indeed prize these 'not-for-growth' elements.

Emotions and motivation

In what might be called *actualisation theory* (above), motivation is undifferentiated until we empathically engage with the internal world of an individual client. Then the matrix of needs and drives which push and pull that particular individual are revealed. Although EFT provides a somewhat more elaborate framework for the links between emotion and motivation, in practice the motivational matrix of the client can only be discovered by engaging with them empathically. The extension of PCT understanding of motivation is contained in the way EFT links emotions and motivation. On pp. 72–3 above, we explained how EFT theory places emotions at the centre of the human psychological landscape. In that section we noted that emotions contribute to motivation in three ways:

- they initiate goal-directed behaviour
- they amplify goal-directed behaviour
- they become associated with goal-directed behaviour and by this association, can come to represent goal-directed behaviours

Emotions are involved in (i) the origination and production of the needs and wishes which push behaviour; (ii) the intensity of these needs and wishes, which determine the strength and resilience of the behaviour; (iii) emotions can be very strongly associated with behaviour. This framework within which to understand the importance of emotions does not require special practice in CfD – it simply outlines why emotions are important and how they can directly and indirectly affect behaviour.

Human beings are self-determining

Allied with the single directional motivational force of the actualising tendency and the notion of the personal power of the fully functioning person is the idea that human beings are autonomous and capable of self-determination. By this we mean that in life in general, as well as the therapeutic relationship in particular, person-centred theory understands the individual as *agentic*. In other words, humans have *agency*, the autonomous ability to make choices and act upon them in their lives – intrapersonally, interpersonally and in relation to the material world. In the realm of therapy, it means that PCE theory and practice expects the client to be the best expert on their own lives, to have a natural tendency to self-heal and to have a palette of coping strategies. Both classical client-centred therapy and emotion-focused therapy have autonomy and agency at the centre of being human. EFT theorists have it as a headline feature of human beings in their declaration of EFT as a neo-humanistic theory – human beings are free to choose what to do and how to construct their worlds (Elliott, 2012: 106).

Recently, agency, rather than autonomy, has been emphasised by Art Bohart, and the importance of agency to therapeutic practice is at the forefront in his work with Karen Tallman (Bohart and Tallman, 1998) who detail the various *self-righting* mechanisms that clients use when in distress. They claim that clients often progress in therapy in spite of the therapist – even crass errors on the part of the therapist are creatively surmounted by the client and sometimes even turned into opportunities for growth. We take this as evidence of the power of clients' self-agency, not a licence for therapists to make mistakes.

This capacity for self-determination has consequences. It militates against infantilising the client and overprotecting them. It militates against seeing the client as resistant or avoidant. It requires therapists to see clients as autonomous, responsible adults,

capable of making growth-oriented choices. It means that CfD therapists will be comfortable knowing that clients' self-directing choices can be trusted. Possibly most
importantly, it means that clients can fully own the changes they make in their lives and
take credit for them. This last consequence makes it more likely that clients will internalise their sense of self-agency – a sense that is often missing in people with a diagnosis of depression who feel that they have little or no control over their lives.

[margin handwritten notes: // , NB.]

Rogers did not take a position on the thorny subject of free will, except to say that the
psychologically mature person may have a feeling of personal freedom, and the power
to be self-determining, and will take responsibility for their choices.

Uniqueness and diversity are to be valued

Although this principle might be unspoken or assumed in many therapeutic models or
practices, it is not only a central virtue in PCE therapies, but also another active therapeutic factor and, lest it be overlooked, is repeatedly stated.

To begin with, this basic statement is the foundation of the non-pathologising stance
of PCE therapies. The entire range of different selves, idiosyncratic desires, unusual
experiences, are all valued expressions of human diversity. PCE theory does not seek to
label or constrain difference, but to celebrate it. Many readers will think that this is such
an obvious central tenet as to be not worth repeating, but in work with people experiencing the negative self-critical and self-damaging thoughts and feelings so common in
depression, it is important to be able to accept these experiences as expressions of diversity (albeit extremely distressing ones) without automatically understanding them as
symptoms to be blocked, extinguished, supressed or avoided.

As a general principle, the entire world of the client's experience is to be embraced
equally. Within this, considering the experiences of clients with a diagnosis of depression in particular, EFT views some elements of this world as standing out as specific,
useful targets for empathy. It remains the case however, in the practice of both EFT and
Counselling for Depression, that these experiences are welcomed, not pathologised. The
skilled CfD practitioner must develop the competences to offer both the general acceptance of the whole world of the client, whilst attending to the specific depression-related
targets of empathy. Put another way, therapists must simultaneously a) approach, understand and accept the internal frame of reference of a client as complete, integrated and
actualising and b) notice, when presented with cues, any specific signposts pointing
towards areas which might be specifically relevant to the client's presenting problem.

Growth and development

The development of personality structure is again a matter of clear and simple principles
in person-centred theory. EFT adds a further layer of understanding without conflicting
with the fundamental principles outlined by Rogers (1951, 1959, 1961). Unlike some

other theories, PCE theory posits that the processes underpinning personality development are active throughout life, albeit in possibly attenuated forms. So there are no critical periods as there are in some theories of attachment, nor special categories of primary caretaker. That does not mean that special relationships are not key in infant development, simply that there is no absolute formulaic specification for child-rearing. Children are unique actualising organisms, making the best of the circumstances available, striving to survive, maintain and enhance themselves.

Although the developing infant is thought to be particularly vulnerable, the processes which powerfully influence personality development are evident throughout life. Their potency lies in the vulnerability of the individual at the time of crisis. So, for example, when a person changes their job, they will be feeling not only excitement and anticipation, but also a sense of vulnerability, of not knowing the rules of the new workplace. Approval (positive regard) will be conditional – that is to say that new work colleagues will give their approval when the new person learns, and abides by, the rules: they behave acceptably. And the concept of 'acceptable behaviour' encapsulates the process by which conditional acceptance is bestowed in the new workplace. Most readers will be familiar with the sense of vulnerability, the struggle to discover the new ethos and rules, and the effort to be accepted, approved of and, frankly, liked. So CfD theory states that life events triggering inter- and intrapersonal tension experienced as depression can occur at any time in life, not exclusively during childhood.

Development of self

Person-centred theory of personality development is no different from others in some respects. Initially all elements of macro-culture are understood to be 'delivered' to the growing person through what, for convenience, we will call the family. The culture of the immediate family environment is, itself, also understood to contribute a powerful set of personality attributes and processes. Finally, the relationships with the 'significant others' in the growing person's life have a particular leverage on personality formation both in terms of content and internal transactional dynamics.

The question is what are the particular dynamics in caretaker and family relationships which shape personality development for good and bad and how do they operate?

Rogers (1959: 222) postulates the following characteristics of the human infant:

- She perceives her experience as reality
- She has greater awareness of that reality than anyone else
- She has an inherent actualising tendency
- Her behaviour is basically an attempt to satisfy her needs as perceived or experienced
- She interacts as an organised whole
- She uses her actualising tendency as a yardstick to evaluate experiences – those that maintain or enhance her are positively valued, those working against maintenance and enhancement are valued negatively. This is her *organismic valuing process*.
- She has a tendency to move towards positively valued experiences and avoid negatively valued experiences

Note that the infant has an inherent motivational system (the actualising tendency, as previously explored), an inherent regulatory/evaluatory system and these are directional – the infant moves towards growth-oriented experiences, and by extension, growth-oriented situations and stimuli. This sets the infant on a permanently exploratory course, not one governed by homeostatic balance, but one with inherent permanent tension, seeking enhancing experiences. These experiences are assimilated into the growing matrix of experiences, along with the values attached to them. The organismic valuing process builds up a resource by which the infant can navigate their world.

In classical PC theory (Rogers' early writings) the infant initially exists in an undifferentiated world of experience, with no form or structure. Psychologist William James referred to this state as follows: 'The baby, assailed by eyes, ears, nose, skin, and entrails at once, feels it all as one great blooming, buzzing confusion' (James 1890/1983: 488). The infant has not yet developed the mental structures to experience these sensations separately or in any categories. With time, this accumulation of experiences becomes increasingly differentiated, as perceptions and the values associated with them are refined. The world of experience of the infant becomes an increasingly detailed picture. At a certain point, not specified by theory, occurring as a result of maturation (i.e. a natural consequence of physical development), the process of discrimination of experiences leads to the infant distinguishing experiences related to the environment from those related closer to the locus of the experience, i.e., the infant's emerging sense of self – the difference between 'me' and 'not me' experiences. This means that, in classical PC theory, before this developmental landmark, the infant is unavailable for social interaction and incapable of benefitting from positive (or negative for that matter) parental offerings, such as positive regard.

The self then becomes a differentiated part of, an object in, the perceptual field. Now the self is an object, the infant develops a concept of self, or self-concept. The self-concept then develops as the accumulated experiences of the 'I' or 'me' along with the values attached to them, in the same manner as described above in the general matrix of experiences, or whole perceptual field. The self-concept becomes a special, particular part of it.

More contemporary writers differ from Rogers in that they have the infant socially connected and therefore requiring positive regard from birth (Biermann-Ratjen, 1998). Margaret Warner (2005: 93) explains that a strong relationship from birth with a caregiving adult is required for healthy development and claims a special place for empathy, rather than positive regard, as the pivotal developmental condition.

Self-processes and configurations

The self, whilst ultimately adhering to the holistic imperative in person-centred psychology (that the organism acts as an organised whole), is understood by theorists to not be a homogenous structure.

In mainstream person-centred psychology, Mearns' (1999) notion of plurality of the self-structure, 'configurations of self', is helpful. Here Mearns proposes what might be called 'subpersonalities' or more simply, parts of the self, each with its own distinct characteristics. It is common for people to talk about parts or bits of themselves each with different needs and proclivities. Some people talk about these parts as though they have different personalities to the extent that they might give them names. Mearns gives a detailed account of the phenomenon and ways of working with configurations in Mearns and Thorne (2000). An important feature of configurations is that they can relate to each other within the self-structure, i.e. intrapersonal dialogue between these discrete parts is possible. This is also a common experience with people describing conversations, or parts of themselves issuing instructions, apologies, commentaries or criticisms. These dialogues are subvocal, not voices in the head, although some theorists maintain that these intrapersonal dialogues are precursors to voice-hearing (e.g. Romme et al., 2009).

Emotion-focused therapy, drawing on focusing-oriented psychotherapy theory, sees the self as a dynamic structure comprising many elements in continuous interaction. From the start EFT hypothesises many voices and self-processes which may be expressed as one self at any moment, but with no implication that the voice speaking in any moment – indeed any voice or self-element – holds any authority or executive status. This (as indeed is the notion of configurations) challenges the idea of the true self, or a 'self that one truly is'. Along with focusing/experiential theory, EFT has developed terms for some typical self-elements that could almost be considered generic, such as the 'inner-critic', and names for typical intrapersonal processes, such as 'self-evaluative split' or self-criticism.

The origin of these parts of the self is thought to be introjections – explored on pp. 81–2 later in this chapter. We have seen how Rogers' writings describe the introjection of values and it is easy to see how the process of introjection of whole elements of the world can take place, including relational elements or persons. So the experience of a critical voice or set of unrealistic or unwanted expectations which take on a shape, personality or become more psychologically embodied is the result of introjection due to conditions of worth. Of course, introjected elements are not necessarily negative. Family culture, however 'positive', is still an unwelcome prescription for living; 'We are a family of winners, so you are expected to be a winner', 'All the women in our family have had several children', 'You come from a line of miners/steelworkers/doctors/lawyers'. Such prescriptions may be experienced as a threat to the self-structure and be perceived to be either separate within or, in the case of hearing voices, separate from, the self-structure. Some of these self-configurations keep a relentless commentary on life, and when critical, can be completely defeating.

The need for positive regard and the development of conditions of worth

Rogers (1959: 223) goes on to assert that humans have a universal 'pervasive and persistent' need for positive regard. He did not believe it was important to his theory whether this need was inborn or learned. He charts the development of a matrix of regard and its dynamics thus (ibid.: 223–4):

- The infant satisfies this need by guessing what other people want and so the positive regard is often ambiguous (because people expect different behaviours at different times, and different people want different behaviours).
- It is reciprocal, i.e. when the infant discovers that she can satisfy another person's need for positive regard, she experiences satisfaction of her own need for positive regard. In this way it is rewarding for both parties, or in the case of infants, for both parent and child.
- Positive regard is particularly potent when it is associated with significant others since it is more likely to be associated with survival and maintenance of the individual.
- This positive regard can become more compelling than the organismic valuing process.
- The infant separates some of the self-related reciprocal positive regard experiences and experiences them as existing independently of any other person. This is *self-regard* and can be positive or negative.

As the regard complex develops, with both negative and positive values attached to the perceptions of both others and the infant herself, a set of conditions become identified as being attached to positive regard. In other words, if the infant wants to experience love and affirmation, they must behave in a particular way. These conditions under which positive regard is dispensed (most potently by a significant other – a parent), are known as 'conditions of worth'. Conditions of worth provide the leverage for the internalisation of values and perceptions of the infant from outside the self – Rogers calls these elements 'introjected values'.

Introjection and incongruence between self and experience

If a child experiences pleasure whilst playing with their body, they will be drawn towards this experience and explore their body more. They may experience sexual pleasure when exploring their genitals and, again, be drawn to and indulge in more play of this sort. If left to their own devices, their organismic valuing process will install the experience and the positive value associated with it (pleasure) in her matrix of growth- or enhancement-oriented experiences. This describes the natural development of the self-related experience of genital pleasure and we would expect it to be naturally self-regulated. However, if a parent notices the genital play and, through their verbal admonishment or non-verbal behaviour, lets the infant know that they will withdraw love, affirmation and approval (positive regard) if the child continues, then a condition of worth has been set up. Positive regard from this parent is conditional on not indulging in genital play, and in order to obtain positive regard the infant must stop.

This is not the end of the matter, however, since the infant is likely to then internalise the experience of genital pleasure alongside the value attached to it; a negative one, possibly including disgust and the idea that it is 'dirty'. This is an introjected value and the implications for adolescent and adult sexuality are obvious. Sometimes the introjections are literal and instrumental, or they can be creatively introjected, sometimes in figurative or symbolic ways, depending upon how the infant creatively maintains the integrity of their self-structure. And, as we explained above, they can be ambiguous. The final twist is that introjected values are indistinguishable from elements of the self-structure gained by the organismic evaluating process.

Potential problems are compounded by the fact that introjects are often in contraposition to organismically valued experiences. So an internal conflict is embedded in the self-structure, waiting to confuse and distress the individual in the face of lived experience later in life. These conflicts and confusions will range from the momentary and inconsequential to deeply seated, enduring and intensely anxiety-provoking.

One of the creative ways in which individuals can introject experiences and values is in the form of an aggregated set of critical experiences and negative values. These may take the form of a person, or voice or entity – an 'internal critic' or a part of the self. This can be upsetting when the critical part is experienced as a separate entity from the self, or the person experiences the distressing consequences of self-critical dialogue and feels low about themselves as a result. It is often through therapy that the critical part of the self becomes more differentiated and this is often a step towards psychological health.

In people with a diagnosis of depression, it can be common to experience a part of the self as split off, making a sometimes relentless critical commentary on everyday thoughts, feelings and behaviour.

Psychological tension

Incongruence

In classical person-centred theory Rogers proposes that this internal conflict – incongruence between organismically valued experience and introjected values – leads to potential or actual psychological tension. 'Potential' because unless deliberately and specifically addressed, these conflicting introjects are always present, albeit most of the time out of awareness, and ready to cast their effect on present experiencing. They are kept out of awareness in three ways:

1. They are irrelevant to our everyday life *at the moment*. The words in italics are key – what is irrelevant today might become relevant at any point. Something positive, e.g. a promotion at work or the start of a new relationship, or something distressing, e.g. a family bereavement or suffering a trauma – *any* change can bring an introject into action.
2. Denial: experiences which might conflict with an introject and cause psychological tension are ignored or, in Rogers' terms, *denied*. That is, we arrange our perceptions so that threatening events simply don't register in our awareness, but since this is an active process it creates tension.
3. Distortion: experiences which might conflict with the introjected self-structure are distorted so that they can be assimilated into the self-structure without threat. In this case we rearrange the experience to fit, and this creates tension.

Tension between experience and self-structure – the 'real or potential' psychological tension of Rogers' early writings – may manifest itself in a number of ways. In fact, it might sound odd to those not familiar with person-centred psychology, it is manifested in more ways than there are people, since each person can manifest real psychological tension in a number of ways. Really getting to grips with this is central to understanding person-centred psychology, since it puts a positive shape to the 21st century slogans regarding the uniqueness of each person. We understand that a core developmental process (introjection) can be expressed in an infinite number of ways in practice. Furthermore, this explains why empathy is the essential road to therapeutic effectiveness, rather than comparing behaviour to objective symptomatologies and diagnostic categories.

Having said that, most readers will also know that many people express this tension in ways that are sufficiently similar for us to be able to think constructively about these similarities, hopefully without crushing the uniqueness of each person's experience. Included in the various expressions of psychological tension will be those which we will look at in Chapter 6, 'Conceptualising depression from a PCE perspective'.

It is not difficult to imagine introjects which are based on, for example, parents' expectations that are in conflict with the infant's organismic valuing process. 'You are only lovable if you are a success – everyone in our family is a success', 'You are only lovable if you are like your brother/sister', 'You are only lovable as a daughter if you are useless at mathematics', and so on. When the processes of denial and distortion buckle under the relentless drip-drip pressure of experience, or conflicts are thrust into one's face as a result of, e.g. redundancy, the resulting psychological tension can be extremely distressing. Men from the communities steeped in mining and steel work reported their whole identity crumbling when their work was taken away. The expression of this crumbling self-structure was more often than not diagnosed as depression.

Other distressing or unhealthy intrapersonal conflicts

Whilst EFT embraces the fundamental importance of introjection and incongruence at the heart of a more classical understanding of psychological tension, it supplies a more highly elaborated framework for understanding psychological tension, and several processes have been identified and described in some detail (Elliott et al., 2004). There are some processes described in EFT theory which require consideration in CfD.

We have already considered the notion of self subcomponents called self-splits. These can be evaluative introjects that are highly critical or repeatedly perform other intrapersonal self-structure functions such as blocking feelings, getting unreasonably angry, resigning and so on. While these self-splits are all manifestations of the care-taking activity of the actualising tendency, they are distressing and unwelcome in the experience of many clients.

The fact of trauma in a person's life needs no explanation. It can be the focal point of evaluative introjects, problematic reaction points and meaning protests (see below).

Problematic reaction points are puzzling over-reactions to a situation. Once again, based in responses under threat to life experiences, they can be repeatedly triggered and clients might say, 'I don't know why I feel so helpless/sad/defeated when that happens' as they express their confusion over the strength of a particular emotional reaction.

When one of a client's cherished beliefs is violated, it is called a meaning protest. 'A job is for life' can be violated by redundancy, 'true love overcomes all' can be violated by relationship breakdown, and so on. These cherished beliefs might be introjected or be an authentically held belief. When challenged by experience, though, they are another example of tension between experience and self-structure, sometimes going to the very centre of a person's identity.

These processes are essentially ways of talking about common human experiences. We must remind ourselves that they must arise from the client's experience, not be forced onto a client by the therapist like a cookie-cutter, discarding the experiences that don't fit. Importantly, once installed as self-structure dynamics, they can be more than stand-alone moments. They can form the substrate for an unremitting, nagging psychological tension – a defeating repetitive dynamic from which it is difficult to escape. They help provide the co-ordinates for depression.

Child development and adult psychological health

Many theories of personality imply that it is practically impossible to reach adulthood without hidden reefs and faults lurking below the surface of even the calmest waters. Psychological distress is an inevitable outcome of human child-rearing – the human condition. We are sure it is possible to pick up this impression from literature describing person-centred psychology – given a 'typical' upbringing, we can assume that most people reach adulthood with varying degrees of self-estrangement. However, Carl Rogers wrote prolifically and optimistically on the subject of good psychological health in a number places. Person-centred psychology is essentially a psychology of healthy environments – the therapeutic conditions describe the relationship variables required to constitute a healthy, restorative, environment. Restorative change is largely obviated if the individual is reared and lives in a healthy environment. We will turn to the idea of what constitutes a healthy environment for child-rearing in a moment.

We say *largely* obviated above, because regardless of how psychologically strong, autonomous and personally resilient someone is, life still happens. Regardless of other favourable circumstances of protection and privilege, there will be substantially hurtful events, bereavements, traumas and so on. These events will cause long-held perceptions and elements in the self-structure to change even though they may be there as a result of the organismic valuing process. Few childhood environments and parenting practices would prepare us for the death of a parent or child, or witnessing a murder, without experiencing pain, confusion and other distress. Therapy provides the supportive environment comprising the necessary conditions to support a person whilst their actualising tendency helps them restore and move on.

Child development – the foundation of psychological health – does not enjoy an extensive literature in PC psychology. Rogers' writings on the subject were rather sparse, but since that lean start, contemporary theorists have taken up the subject with increasing enthusiasm. From the paragraphs above we learn that, in Rogers' view, the infant is incapable of registering the effects of a significant 'other' (parent or caretaker) until they have developed a sense of self. Before then, the infant cannot differentiate themselves and their self-related experiences from the rest of their perceptual field. Other writers (e.g. Mearns and Cooper, 2005) propose a self- and other-aware infant from birth, and advocate a dialogical, relational self, suggesting that the infant has a requirement to *interact*, rather than *simply receive* positive regard, empathy or any other parental psychological provision for that matter. Mearns and Cooper contend that the infant needs to experience giving as well as receiving interpersonal communications. Writing in the context of relational depth, they suggest that resilience against interpersonal injuries and other life-trauma in adulthood is constructed out of the satisfaction of the infant's relational needs from birth.

Regardless of the theoretical structure of self and network of early-life relationships required, the image of the psychologically healthy adult is almost identical. Based mainly on Rogers' writings collated in *On Becoming a Person* (Rogers, 1961), extended slightly by his writing on 'The person of tomorrow' (Rogers, 1980: 348–52), the following picture emerges. Firstly, Rogers emphasised some overall features of human psychology, most importantly that personality should be understood as a process or number of processes, not a state or building-block structure. This permits fluidity, adaptability and responseability rather than simple, mechanical stimulus–response relationships, both intra- and interpersonally. Furthermore, this view insists that human beings are always *in process* – never a 'state', always travelling – never arrived, always a work in progress – never completed. The psychologically healthy adult has the following characteristics:

- Openness to experience: this is best understood in contrast to having experience limited by distortion and denial. The person is open to the full range of their experience, not simply without fear, but with a sense of relishing new experiences. It also means that the individual does not impose a structure on experience, but apprehends life in all its richness.
- Trust in the nature of their organism: similar to the above, this highlights trusting one's needs and tendencies as a living organism.
- Internal locus of evaluation: the individual feels that their ability to evaluate their experiences lies within themselves. They do not have to refer to an external authority, but can trust their own valuing system.
- Comfort in experiencing self as process: the individual is untroubled by and rejoices in sensing themselves as a fluid, ever-changing process.
- Fluid and adaptable: rather than stuck or rigid, the psychologically healthy and resilient person is able to adapt, and fluidly respond, to the world – they 'go with the flow' rather than resist change.
- Existential living: Rogers defines this as the tendency to 'live life fully in each moment' (1961: 188), and that each moment would be responded to as new, free from historical patterns and habitual responses. The individual apprehends life just as it happens.
- Becoming more fully functioning: Rogers introduced the concept of the 'fully functioning person' (1961: 183) meaning a person able to fully utilise all human capabilities to

maintain and enhance the organism. Rather than ticking over, the person 'is more able to permit his total organism to function freely in all its complexity' (1961: 191).

- Creativity: this should need no amplification, except to say that Rogers considered human beings inherently creative, and that the fully functioning person would simply express their creativity as a natural part of living as a whole person. He does not mean tutored, formal creativity, e.g. in painting, music etc.

These 'specifications' for psychological health are detailed, but not complete or exclusive. Person-centred theory is continually revised to keep abreast of human ingenuity and achievements. Furthermore they express a number of elements central to more general humanistic psychology, provide a matrix which dovetails with a number of contemporary spiritual forms and can be recognised as the template for a very commonly held contemporary image of humanity, in Rogers' own terms, the 'person of tomorrow'.

To complement this catalogue of features of good psychological health, we would add the contribution from EFT outlining how the inherent healthy multiplicity of the self flourishes in a self-structure fluidly 'organised' as described above. Elliott et al. (2004: 37) use similar terms to Rogers:

[we] view the person as a complex, ever-changing, organised collection of various part aspects of self …

… there are no permanent, fixed emotion schemes, the same is true of self-aspects, and each part continuously constructs itself by integrating many inputs, including 'silent' or disowned parts.

They go on to compare the self-structure with a choir of singers performing a complicated jazz piece – sometimes in unison, sometimes in deliberate counterpoint, momentarily in discord, but always singing the same piece. This open, fluid, creative, permanently moving, endlessly constructing and reconstructing in response to the world is a close approximation to the more classical person-centred view of psychological health.

Therapeutic processes

In this section we will look at the roots of classical person-centred theory and practice, followed by the extensions contributed by the newer experiential strand of theory and practice development, particularly that of emotion-focused therapy.

We begin by revisiting Rogers' widely cited propositions regarding the active constituents of a therapeutic relationship and the additional methods devised by EFT theorists. We follow this with the less well-reported work on the proposed mechanisms of exactly how therapeutic change takes place.

Classical client-centred therapy – the therapeutic conditions

For the majority of readers the next few paragraphs will be very familiar territory. Rogers 'Necessary and sufficient conditions for therapeutic change' (1957) paper, and chapter (1959) detailing the same conditions must be two of the most widely read and cited works on counselling and psychotherapy in history. Rogers boldly proposed that six conditions were needed in a clinical (or other) relationship before therapeutic change could take place, and most contentiously, that *no other conditions* were needed. It is classical person-centred theorists' claim for the sufficiency of the conditions that has been most widely critiqued since, and Counselling for Depression deviates from classical person-centred theory and practice at this point. When specifically working with clients whose experiences match the diagnostic requirements for depression, CfD insists, based on evidence (see Chapter 2, p. 15) that a subset of insights and practices from EFT increase effectiveness without compromising the core person-centred position.

Wyatt (2001: iii) combined Rogers' 1957 and 1959 versions[2] of the therapeutic conditions with the 1957 variations in italics:

1. That two persons are in *(psychological)* contact
2. That the first person, whom we shall term the client, is in a state of incongruence, being vulnerable, or anxious.
3. That the second person, whom we shall term the therapist, is congruent *(or integrated)* in the relationship.
4. That the therapist is experiencing unconditional positive regard toward the client.
5. That the therapist is experiencing an empathic understanding of the client's internal frame of reference *(and endeavours to communicate this to the client)*.
6. That the client perceives, at least to a minimal degree, conditions 4 and 5, the unconditional positive regard of the therapist for him, and the empathic understanding of the therapist. *(The communication to the client of the therapist's empathic understanding and unconditional positive regard is to a minimal degree achieved.)*

Some accounts of PC theory talk about 'core' conditions of empathy, unconditional positive regard and congruence, and others refer to these as the 'therapist-provided conditions'. Whilst this might appear to make some sense, it is both unnecessary and problematic since it gives the impression that PC therapy is something the therapist does to the client. However, the six conditions must be taken as a whole because the relationship is central to therapeutic change, with both client *and* counsellor bringing

---

[2] In a quirk of history, it is worth noting that Rogers wrote the 1957 version *after* the 1959 version, but the 1959 chapter was delayed in the production schedule of the book edited by Sigmund Koch (1959) *Psychology: A Study of a Science*. Thus, the 1957 paper represented Rogers' revisions of the conditions.

essential elements. So the client and counsellor *together* make the change happen: together they contribute the necessary principal ingredients to make the active therapeutic moment possible.

This forces practitioners to think about helping as a relationship from the start and is different from those therapeutic approaches in which the client is seen as someone in receipt of *treatment* by an *expert*: the therapist. It can also lead to the client not being seen as a person, but rather as a thing, a machine or computer to be fixed in a step-by-step procedure. These ways of thinking about counselling do not fit in with the fundamental principles of PCT or EFT and hence, by extension, to CfD. When it comes to the practical activity of Counselling for Depression, it makes more sense to see the counsellor as bringing these qualities as one complete helping relationship, not a collection of separate conditions.

Psychological contact

Rogers' first condition states that therapy requires two people to be in psychological contact. Person-centred theorists are not the only ones nor the first to locate contact at the centre of human psychology and although Whelton and Greenberg (2002: 107) declare: 'The type of contact that is called "psychological" is the type of contact that a human self has with another human self', this must not be taken for granted.

In circumstances of extreme acute or chronic distress, some clients withdraw from psychological contact, and indeed contact with the world. Although most frequently connected to anxiety attacks, some clients diagnosed with depression might experience episodes of dissociation or depersonalisation. Clients whose depression is linked to trauma might experience dissociation as a fugue state within a therapy session. Rather than assume that the client is permanently in psychological contact, it is better for therapists to keep this first condition in mind and be ready to use techniques to help the client reconnect and maintain contact.

Client incongruence

This second condition identifies the client as a person in need of help and is the simplest expression of person-centred psychopathology. Earlier in this chapter we explained how classical person-centred theory understands the root of psychological tension as a discrepancy between self and experience. In the classical literature (Rogers, 1951; 1959) this is referred to as 'incongruence' between the introjected elements of the self-structure and the self-related experiences of the individual. It is the single, universal source of anxiety, depression and all symptoms of distress which are uniquely expressed by each person. In classical person-centred practice it provides the rationale for empathy – the method for understanding the narrative of the world of experience of the client.

We will see later in this subsection how EFT extends person-centred psychopathology beyond this notion of incongruence in both general and specific terms.

Therapist congruence

The third condition is one which demands we read carefully the phrase that the therapist is congruent 'in the relationship'. In classical theory, this means that in relation to the client the therapist is more integrated as regards the (inevitable) discrepancy between self-structure and experience. In this relationship at least, the counsellor has to be more congruent or integrated than the client. In simple terms Rogers means that whilst the client *in this moment* may be feeling distressed and in need of help, the counsellor *in this moment* is not and is prepared to help.

Thus in a structured helping relationship, the counsellor needs to be prepared to be the counsellor, and there are several ways of understanding 'be prepared to be'. This condition refers, at least in part, to the counsellor's *fitness* to help, and in contemporary professional helping this includes:

* that they have appropriate training, qualifications and supervision
* that they have not done anything which might impair the carrying out of their professional responsibilities
* that they feel psychologically prepared and able to be the therapist (i.e. congruent as the therapist) with that client, and this includes having sufficient personal therapy

In Counselling for Depression, we expect this to comply with Rogers' statement:

> [T]he therapist should be, within the confines of this relationship, a congruent, genuine integrated person. It means that within the relationship he is freely and deeply himself, with his actual experience accurately represented by his awareness of himself. (1957: 97)

Gill Wyatt (2001: 84–5) elaborates the concept further and identifies the following features of therapist congruence:

* Being authentic and 'real' rather than putting on a professional facade
* Psychological maturity, indicating the degree to which the therapist is open to their experience

These clearly are restatements of some of the qualities of being psychologically healthy, confirming the concept of congruence as a statement of the therapist's fitness to practise, *with that client, at that time.* She further *explains that being authentic takes into account the personal style of the therapist* – referring not to *what* the therapist does, but *how* they do it. Requiring them to interpret the ground rules of being a person-centred therapist in their own way, whilst remaining ethical and adhering to (in this case) CfD competences.

Unconditional positive regard

To the annoyance of classical person-centred therapists, this condition is sometimes called 'acceptance'. However, the term itself clearly indicates that here are two components to the concept, unconditionality and the positivity of regard, both of which have raised criticisms from various quarters in the psychotherapy community over the years.

The positive regard element of this condition is not the same as 'liking' or 'being nice to' (Mearns, 2003: 3–5). Nor does it have anything to do with having similar values or beliefs to the client. In some texts, Rogers described positive regard as 'prizing' and warmth and respect also convey the positive nature of the attitude. These terms all convey something about the depth or genuineness of the attitude that, as Tony Merry explained, 'can't be turned on and off like a tap' (Merry, 2002: 80). It's virtually impossible to affect a display of prizing or respect towards someone without appearing false.

There can be no *guarantee* that the therapist will feel warm towards a particular client but it can help if we invoke the cliché 'love the sinner, not the sin'. This permits, or possibly even *instructs* the therapist to prize the client as a human being worthy of their warm attention without having to condone their behaviour. The key to prizing clients lies in the self-awareness of the therapist. The more self-aware the therapist is, the more they will know their own prejudices, based as they are on fear. The fewer prejudices the counsellor has, the less judgemental they will be.

Few areas of person-centred theory have attracted more criticism than the idea of the *unconditionality* of positive regard, to the point that many critics confidently assert that it is both philosophically flawed and impossible to practise. Rogers writes:

> It is the fact that he feels and shows unconditional positive regard toward the experiences of which the client is frightened or ashamed, as well as toward the experiences with which the client is pleased or satisfied, that seems effective in bringing about change. (Rogers, 1959: 208)

Of interest to CfD practice is the idea of 'configurations of self' (Mearns, 1999; Mearns and Thorne, 2000). Mearns notes that a client might have different internal selves or configurations, each with its own distinct characteristics. A client might say they have different selves within them: a 'depressed loser', 'controlling careerist' and an 'optimist'. The person-centred therapist must display UPR towards all of these, or put another way, create a level playing field for the configurations within the client's self-structure. However, it is easy to see how a therapist, even without intending to, could tilt the playing field and favour one configuration at the expense of the other two. This might be good practice in some therapies where the configuration with, e.g., the rational resolution to a difficulty might be favoured. However in PCT the therapist is creating the conditions in which the client's actualising tendency can resolve the tension and move forward regardless of which internal facet of self might hold the key. For this to take place, inviting 'dialogue' between any or all configurations is desirable and may even be necessary. It is clear then, that each must be equally valued, and indeed prized, since in person-centred theory terms, all configurations must be acting for at least survival, and possibly maintenance and enhancement of the organism, even though one or more might appear to be acting against growth, when viewed from the external frame of reference.

Empathic understanding

The relational nature of therapy consists mainly in this condition – a unilateral experiencing of empathy is almost certainly impossible, since implicit in the experience of empathy is the idea of checking that you are accurate. Thus experiencing empathic understanding is the experience of checking that your understanding is accurate. Communication is, therefore, an essential ingredient, as attested by Rogers explanation of the conditions: 'and endeavours to communicate this to the client' (Rogers, 1957, in Kirschenbaum and Henderson, 1990: 221). Empathy experienced by the therapist, without communicating it to the client, is of little or no use.

'Internal frame of reference' is a term used to describe the client's private world of perceptions, experiences and meanings and is only available to the therapist via empathy. According to Rogers, 'It can never be known to another except through empathic inference and then can never be perfectly known' (Rogers, 1959: 210).

Rogers continues:

> … being empathic is to *perceive* the internal frame of reference of another with *accuracy*, and with the emotional components and meanings … *as if* one were the other person, but without ever losing the 'as if' condition. (Rogers, 1959: 210, our italics)

Rogers' last major statement about empathy 'Empathic: An Unappreciated Way of Being', available in his book *A Way of Being* (Rogers, 1980), was a defence against the critics who called it 'wooden' and 'parroting'. Here he writes about the *process* of empathy, rather than the *state* of empathy as 'being sensitive, moment by moment, to the changing felt meanings which flow in this other person' (p. 142) and that we have to 'lay aside your own views and values in order to enter another's world without prejudice' (p. 143).

Sanders (2006: 69–72) summarised the developments and extensions of definitions of empathy since Rogers' death:

> *Godfrey 'Goff' Barrett-Lennard* summarised the traditional idea that counsellor empathy facilitates self-empathy or 'listening within' in the client. Self-understanding in a non-judgemental atmosphere begets self-acceptance which facilitates integration of previously difficult areas of experience (Barrett-Lennard, 2003: 34–50).

> *Eugene Gendlin* proposed that empathy moves the client's experience forward by allowing the client to monitor their experience through the repeated reflections and checking of the counsellor (see Purton, 2004).

> *Fred Zimring* proposed that empathy helps us shift our way of processing from an objective 'me' self-state to an inward-looking subjective 'I' self-state, making internal self-structure change more possible (Zimring, 2000/2001).

> *Margaret Warner* in a similar vein to Gendlin, writes of how empathy fosters the ability to hold experiences in attention in ways that stimulate personal growth (self-understanding depends on our ability to stay with or 'hold' an experience for long enough for us to engage with it). This is particularly important in infancy (and parenting) and has a crucial role in healthy personality development (Warner, 1997).

Jerold Bozarth (1984/2001: 138) stated unequivocally that 'reflection is not empathy' – that empathy is the *state* of *effort-to-accurately-understand* that the therapist is trying to communicate to the client. Reflection is just one of the responses, according to Bozarth, through which empathy may be communicated and he goes on to make a case for a very wide set of responses such as using metaphor, personal reactions, mimicry and jokes.

Peter Schmid explains the dialogical definition of empathy as the art of naïve not-knowing. Empathy as a human attribute comes without a particular intention but always as an expression of the personal quality of solidarity. We are empathic because we *must be* in order to be human and relate to others. Thus empathy in a therapy relationship is an expression of flourishing human being, and restores this quality in others.

These various understandings of empathy reveal some common themes:

1. Therapist-provided empathy facilitates the development of self-empathy, self-monitoring, or self-reflection. This is seen as an essential prerequisite for perceiving and accepting previously 'difficult' experiences.
2. Empathy is not only achievable through reflection, but by creatively communicating in any and all possible ways.
3. Empathy is not a one-way event, tool or instrument. It is a two-way relational process.

These principles are central to the practice of Counselling for Depression.

Client perception

This subheading is an attempt to summarise the final condition which underlines the relational nature of person-centred psychology. In Rogers' (1957; 1959) words, cited in Wyatt (2001: iii) with Rogers' 1957 variation in italics:

> That the client perceives, at least to a minimal degree, conditions 4 and 5, the unconditional positive regard of the therapist for him, and the empathic understanding of the therapist. (*The communication to the client of the therapist's empathic understanding and unconditional positive regard is to a minimal degree achieved.*)

The intent of this condition is clear – to clearly state the importance of communication in therapy. The client must actually experience empathy as being accurately understood, and must feel prized and not judged. That the therapist intends to offer these conditions is not sufficient. The conditions cannot be seen to be fulfilled unless the client experiences these conditions, therefore the therapeutic outcome cannot properly be judged.

Godfrey Barrett-Lennard realised that the 'conditions theory' hinged upon the client's experience of the therapist in the counselling relationship. In 1962 (Barrett-Lennard, 1962) he devised a questionnaire instrument which would reliably measure the client's perceptions of the therapist. This resulted in the Barrett-Lennard Relationship Inventory, and following subsequent work he concluded that there was a plausible causal connection between the client's perception of the therapist-provided conditions and change in the client. It is clear that successful communication of the therapist-provided conditions is a precursor to being able to evaluate the effectiveness of therapy.

This condition also points to the importance of the evaluation of skills and micro-skills in training. Debates amongst counsellor trainers regarding the role of microskills training and assessment will not be rehearsed here, but suffice to say that communication skills figure as central to being a competent therapist. It is also worth noting that Rogers does not mention the communication mode through which these conditions are transmitted and received. Bozarth (1984/2001) makes the case for idiosyncratic empathy, but we are certain that *all* of the therapeutic conditions will be offered idiosyncratically[3] in a counselling relationship with any life in it. This is also explicitly addressed above in Wyatt's (2001) understanding of congruence as comprising authenticity which is dependent on the personal style of the therapist – *how* the therapist says or does things as well as *what* they say or do. Naturally, this includes non-verbal communication, and can be as varied as the creativity of the counsellor will allow.

Emotion-focused therapy

The EFT model of therapeutic change is much more structured in comparison with non-directive CCT. In EFT, therapeutic change could be loosely defined as developing new, personally productive ways of integrating experience. This is achieved by action in two interrelated domains – client therapeutic tasks and therapist responses – set against any obstacles to emotional expression which may be experienced by the client. An important underpinning notion to remember from the section on adult psychological health, above, is that the client's emotional and task landscape is continually adapting and changing in life and within the therapy session. This means that the therapist must have empathic responses as their fall-back position and to hold micro-diagnoses of therapeutic task accomplishment very lightly – being ready at all times to abandon any process-guiding ideas they may have and return to empathic responding. This is the default position of the CfD practitioner (see Chapter 8). In this book we abridge EFT theory and practice to those elements mainly, but not exclusively, relevant to CfD competences.

Therapeutic tasks, their identification and therapist responses

The structured nature of EFT comes to the fore when looking at the process of therapeutic change. The client comes to therapy because they are experiencing psychological distress. The therapist's starting position is to help the client elaborate their experience

---

[3] By this we mean the way the counsellor must respond personally and authentically to the unique experiences of the client – idiomatically, colloquially, and in a way that is congruent with the emerging micro-culture of the relationship. It is not possible to specify this as a series of mechanistic call-and-answer interventions. This way of being is covered in the metacompetences.

of distress in their own words – to tell their story. The way the client talks about their distress (including the notion that this distress might morph into something else in the telling) contains clues (called markers) which help the therapist and the client identify *the things that need to be done* in order to resolve the distress. These are called *therapeutic tasks*. Only a subset of EFT theory and practice is integrated into Counselling for Depression, so the entire catalogue of markers, tasks and responses is not required, but interested readers are directed to, e.g., Elliott (2012) for a brief introduction, and Elliott et al. (2004) for a complete account. The therapeutic rationale in EFT can be stated as:

1. task identification
2. appropriate therapeutic response by therapist
3. reprocessing work by client
4. resolution

It is important to note that this is an idealised scheme which might be looped through repeatedly at any stage and in any combination of stages. It is not intended to be a prescription or rigid procedure. It is a guideline to assist understanding and practice.

EFT elements are of particular use in brief work, since they give focus and bring a pace to the work whilst still placing control with the client. Task work is best seen as an offering made by the therapist to the client – one which the client may reject. The skill of the therapist is located in their ability to enable the client to freely reject their offerings as easily as they can be accepted. Therapeutic tasks of interest to CfD therapists can be grouped into three types:

- Relational tasks

  o Telling the story and engaging with vulnerability – empathy-based tasks: empathic exploration and affirmation
  o Establishing the therapeutic relationship – empathic exploration and alliance dialogue: exploring the roles of client and therapist

- Experiencing tasks

  o Symbolising unclear feelings – experiential focusing
  o Locating and paying attention to difficult feelings – clearing a space and establishing a working distance to the feelings

- Reprocessing tasks

  o The need to retell difficult or traumatic experiences – empathically supported narration
  o Dealing with puzzling over-reactions to specific situations – systematic evocative unfolding (see Chapter 8, p. 147 for a description), empathically supported narration
  o Resolving tension when a life event violates a cherished belief – containing and clarifying discrepancies between a belief and an experience

These tasks and the associated therapist responses, adapted from EFT for Counselling for Depression practice, clearly overlap in the large part with PCT practice. On one level it is simply using a different vocabulary for the things that person-centred therapists would do when following the client, since the tasks represent the client's agenda. The task-focused language used in EFT does draw attention to the goals of therapy which are the centrepiece of the collaboration between the client and the counsellor. In Counselling for Depression, the communication skills expected of a good person-centred counsellor are necessary and sufficient.

The nature of the process of change

For the purposes of Counselling for Depression, we will look at the change process in two sections – person-centred therapy and emotion-focused therapy – to identify the nuanced differences. This might be seen as irrelevant in practice and nit-picking in theory terms, but it does have implications for how individual practitioners think about the work they do.

The nature of change in person-centred therapy

In 1961 Rogers shifted understanding of personality from a state to a process and similarly moved from an events-based understanding of therapeutic change; from a *mechanism* (a pre-morbid state to a resolved state, or a from a 'sick' state to a 'healthy' state) to a continuous *process*. This process is best understood as one of development or unfolding – continuous assimilation of unfolding experience and adaptation to new situations.

Rogers describes the process of change in a completely arbitrary array of seven stages. There is nothing in Rogers' description of the process of change that implies stages or the number seven – he simply gives a structure to what would otherwise be a rather difficult description of a fluid process. Rogers condenses the six therapeutic conditions into one process, 'that the client experiences himself as being fully *received*', calling this the 'basic condition' (Rogers, 1961: 130):

> By this I mean that whatever his feelings – fear, despair, insecurity, anger, whatever his mode of expression – silence, gestures, tears, or words; whatever he finds himself being in this moment, he senses that he is psychologically *received*, just as he is, by the therapist. (Ibid.: 130–1, original emphasis)

It is the totality of the continually changing therapeutic relationship comprising this 'basic condition' that ensures the client feels *fully received*. Here again, the relational nature of therapy, dependent upon the communication skills of the counsellor, is stressed, in Rogers' words: 'it is the client's experience of this condition which makes it optimal, not merely the fact of its existence in the therapist' (1961: 131). The change process continuum is arranged by Rogers between two polarised positions, one in which process is stuck, rigid and fixed, and the other in which it is appropriately and completely fluid, flowing and adaptable.

Stage 1	Stage 2	Stage 3	Stage 4	Stage 5	Stage 6	Stage 7
process is so fixed and stuck that the person is unlikely to come for therapy – they think everyone else has a problem		⟹ process of change ⟹				process is so spontaneous and fluid that almost continuous change happens outside the session as much as in the session

Figure 5.1   Rogers' seven stages of process

(Sanders, 2006: 88, adapted from Rogers, 1961)]

Within the continuum, Rogers marks thresholds in the seven stages which are important in our understanding of what may or may not be achieved in the counselling and may require subtle nuances in the counsellor's behaviour.

In stage 1, Rogers describes the person as not likely to come for therapy because their self-structure is so rigid, their self-perceptions so controlled through denial and distortion that they do not perceive themselves to have any problems – all problems are external. Rogers concedes that traditional therapy has little to offer the person in Stage 1, not least because they do not present themselves for therapy.

In Stage 2, the client will notice patterns of experiences in their life, but are likely to see no significant connection to themselves, saying, for example, 'Chaos just follows me around' or 'The boss always had it in for me, that's why I was sacked this time'. Any self-perceptions are experienced as immutable facts, e.g. 'I'm a depressive' or 'I can never get anything right, it's all my fault'.

From Stage 3 onwards we find a general loosening of process, so that once-rigid perceptions are more likely to change as a result of being fully received. Now therapeutic change has a foothold and all manner of characteristics and self-perceptions become more fluid. However, this more fluid process is fragile and clients may experience a high degree of anxiety as they approach the possibility of change. A key moment in Stage 3 is when the client realises that their self-perceptions are constructs or ideas, rather than facts about themselves. This signals the client's further realisation that ideas can be changed, and personal change becomes at least a possibility, albeit one which may seem frightening.

The remaining stages see the client able to increase the sophistication of their self-reflection and the flexibility of their self-structure. Rogers documented this continuum of change in a number of dimensions of processing. Here we have summarised the most important – for our purposes – dimensions and the changes predicted by Rogers.

Feelings: The person moves from hardly recognising feelings at all, to describing feelings as objects in the past ('I was feeling desperate'), then tentatively acknowledging feelings but being frightened of them, to fully experiencing feelings in the present. Feelings no longer are feared, nor do they feel 'stuck'. In the later stages, Rogers (1961) says that feelings flow to their full result, meaning that they don't get strangled or halted before the full expression leads to a feeling of being cleansed.

Personal constructs: In Stage 1, ideas about the self are not even entertained. The person gradually becomes aware of personal constructs but only thinking of them as facts. Then at a key moment in Stage 3, they are recognised, albeit rigidly, as ideas not facts, and therefore potentially changeable – so the client can now believe that change is possible. As self-related ideas become increasingly acknowledged and flexible, the whole self-structure becomes fluid and eventually open to being revised frequently.

Internal dialogue: The person starts off having little or no internal dialogue and being largely fearful of paying too much attention to him/herself ('you think too much'). As their fear of looking inside at themselves lessens they slowly experiment until they are able to have almost constant, mostly comfortable, internal dialogue as a matter of course in daily life.

Expression: People in the early stages of process are largely inexpressive. They don't talk about themselves much and are embarrassed or nervous when doing so, thinking it is pointless. Loosening of their process leads to free expression, including expression of feelings. In addition, in the final stages, individuals welcome and trust this flow of expression.

Differentiation and elaboration of experience: People in the early stages of process see things (their experiences of others and themselves, moral issues, etc.) in highly contrasting, right/wrong categories – there are almost no 'grey areas'. As they begin to differentiate and elaborate an increasing proportion of their experiences of themselves, others and the world, they begin to see the complexity in experience. This leads to discovering diversity and plurality *in themselves*, amongst others and in the world. Eventually they not only experience this diversity and plurality without fear, they welcome it.

Perception of problems: People start off believing that they couldn't possibly have any problems. Everyone else has the problem, not them. They gradually begin to be able to look at and understand themselves (see personal constructs above) with less and less fear, eventually being comfortable with the idea that they are a mixture of lived possibilities, some of which they experience as positive, some as negative. None of which necessarily generate feelings of great fear.

Attitude to change: Where it was once denied even as a possibility, change becomes an accepted, welcome part of the process of living. Clients might start with a 'if it ain't broke, don't fix it' or 'a leopard can't change its spots' attitude, but end up relishing change as a challenge. Along the way, the client will move through times of being afraid of change to varying degrees, depending upon how central the focus of change is to their self-concept. The client remains open to change in the future as a result of getting to the later stages of this process.

Bodily changes: The psychological changes described above run alongside what Rogers (1961) described as 'physiological' changes. What he described included the increasing tendency to suffer from fewer bodily (embodied) symptoms of anxiety (headaches, irritability, digestive problems, etc.) on the one hand, and more physical manifestations of ease, contentedness and feeling at one with things and happy with oneself (muscular relaxation, bright eyes, free breathing, physical responsiveness).

It should be remembered that these stages or phases don't exist and never have done in any real person's change process – they are completely arbitrary signposts to help us put some structure to the abstract theory. In the lived experience of real people, the process of change is unique. It has an irregular, halting trajectory not always appearing to move forward when observed from the external frame of reference. Furthermore it is quite likely to proceed at different rates in different areas of a person's life. It is useful as a theoretical construct but we caution against the temptation to think about these stages when with a client.

The nature of change in emotion-focused therapy

Founded on *dialectical constructivism* (Elliott, 2012; Elliott et al., 2004), EFT proposes a change process in which the individual both assimilates experience and may adapt to it. The primary active sources of change experiences are relationships. The self-structure is seen as a network of parts (configurations of self), self-processes and emotion schemes all in perpetual dynamic interaction. This dynamic interaction takes the form of internal dialogue, which if flexible (rather than rigid patterns), open and flowing (rather than constrained by threat), can generate new more adaptive and satisfying processes and emotion schemes. For all the structure we have described thus far in EFT theory, we must remember that the keystone of the theory remains – the living human being weaves a completely unpredictable cloth of internal processes, emotional framework and subsequent experience. The therapist must follow, never lead in the unfolding of this landscape.

Having described the nature of the change process thus, we can see how this can be applied to the dimensions highlighted by Rogers in person-centred therapy above. In many respects, insofar as Counselling for Depression takes a limited sample of EFT theory, we are dealing with similar processes of change separated by vocabulary and structure, rather than the essence of the change process.

6

Conceptualising Depression from a Person-Centred and Experiential Therapies Perspective

> Competences covered in Chapter 6
>
> B1-Knowledge of the philosophy and principles that inform the therapeutic approach
> B2-Knowledge of person-centred theories of human growth and development and the origins of psychological distress
> B4-Knowledge of the PCE conceptualisation of depression
> S3-Ability to help clients reflect on and develop emotional meanings
> S4-Ability to help clients make sense of experiences that are confusing and distressing
>
> (Competences are listed in Appendix 1)

Introduction

The previous chapter gave a general grounding in the PCT theory and the elements of EFT theory that go to make up Counselling for Depression. In this chapter we assemble and examine the particular aspects of these theories which relate to the experience of depression.

Before we look at the theoretical underpinning of the experience of depression, we must remind ourselves that although PCT theory of personality and psychological distress is a universal theory, this does not prevent us selecting a set of client experiences (experiences of depression) and turning our attention to examining the specific elements of theory which help us understand those experiences. EFT, on the other hand is a more structured and technical approach, with a substantial literature on specific applications to client experiences of depression.

This chapter then, describes the integrated theoretical substrate of Counselling for Depression as it is drawn from the theories of person-centred and emotion-focused therapy. The four cornerstones of this coherent approach to the experience of depression are i) *the nature of the self,* ii) *self-discrepancy,* iii) *self-configuration dialogue* and iv) *the nature of emotions.*

The nature of the self

The term 'self', as used widely in psychology and everyday life, has many meanings. It has been pointed out by many writers that the self is an ethnocentric construct originally accepted uncritically by western psychology (see Cushman, 1995). Non-person-centred psychologies view the self in various ways with varying degrees of overlap in understanding, and self-psychology, developed by psychoanalyst Heinz Kohut in the 1960s, whilst of peripheral interest, is too firmly rooted in the 'deficiency' model of psychoanalysis to be helpful in an explication of CfD theory (Kohut, 1971). Tudor and Merry (2002/2006: 125–6) identify three ways in which the term is used in person-centred psychology and over 30 entries with 'self' as part of the entry, and Tudor and Worrall (2006: 101–135) comprehensively explore the wide range of meanings of the term and their implications in person-centred and experiential psychologies. Here we present descriptions and discussions of the self only so far as to lay out the foundations of the CfD conceptualisation of depression.

The self as a concept

Rogers (1951: 497) described the self in developmental terms as a portion of the perceptual field of the infant which is concerned with awareness of being, the pattern of perceptions of the 'I' or 'me', plus the values attached to the emerging concepts and perceptions. In 1959 (1959: 200) he reinforces the perceptual nature of the self with important consequences for personality and change: the self is i) a concept, a stable, consistent,[1] durable set of I/me-related perceptions, ii) a perception, a concept, a *process,* primarily an experiential response to the world,[2] including the internal world (so it is reflexive) and iii) therefore amenable to change, since its 'natural' state is adaptation. This is the basis of Counselling for Depression as an integrated PCE therapy.

---

[1] It is important to explain that the self is both permanently fluid and adaptable, yet consistent and stable. That is to say that I experience myself as being the same person this morning as I was when I went to bed last night. There is a day-to-day, week-to-week, year-to-year consistency in the self. The self, is fluid *and* stable.

[2] Note: whenever we use the term 'world' in this chapter, we will be meaning both the external environment (including relationships) and the internal world of meanings of the person.

CfD Theory of Depression #1: Symptoms of depression can result from rigidity as a result of threat.

Since a well-functioning self is a fluid and adaptive process, assimilating and accommodating experiences and organising responses to them, any rigidity will restrict the potential range of experiences and consequent responses to the world. This rigidity will affect both the range of possible perceptions which can be admitted to awareness and the range of responses which might be made as a result. The structure of the self may become rigid as a result of threat. This can arise in a number of ways, not only in sudden intense moments of threat, such as accidental trauma or deliberate abuse, but also by the drip-drip of low-level negative comments. Threat can also arise from within the self-structure, as we suggested in Chapter 5. The self as a reflexive process can and will turn experiences back upon itself, so healthy, fluid self-processes can be impeded and curtailed by other impaired self-processes, such as intrusive thoughts, anxiety, and so on, especially when these specifically target elements of the self, e.g., when intrusive critical thoughts recur whenever the individual experiences pleasure.

At a very simple and straightforward level, these threats (both intense and repetitive) can result in patterned restrictions of perception and response which become configured as depression. We will go on to detail particular problematic psychological factors, but at a general level, threat can result in the following processes which can create a fertile psychological substrate for depression:

- limited and limiting outlook, leading to a feeling of loss of agency and helplessness
- reduced range of responses which can be experienced as restricted capacity for experiencing emotions
- pervasive feelings of negativity, e.g. self-blame, when experiences are variously selectively filtered and targeted
- social and experiential withdrawal resulting from these restrictions on experiencing

The self as organism

Rogers also uses the term self in relation to the organism, indeed Tudor and Worrall (2006: 125–6) assert that Rogers conflates the concepts of self and organism. Some writers (although not Rogers himself) use the term 'organismic self' (originally Seeman (1983) in his work describing organismic integration as the epitome of health) and it is often popularly used to mean the true self, one that is inherent or originating in the organism. The problems associated with this cluster of concepts are carefully dissected by Tudor and Worrall (2006: 125–6), however, for the purposes of laying down the theoretical foundation of CfD, we do not need to reproduce them here.

The notion of self as part of an integrated organism does allow us to establish the importance to CfD of the internal, or in this case we might say 'integrated' wisdom of the client.

CfD Theory of Depression #2: Symptoms of depression can result from the embodied self.

Locating the self as an organismic phenomenon allows us to emphasise the *embodied* nature of the self. As a result we can see two processes important to the understanding of the genesis of depression.

First is the inclusion of bodily feelings in the palette of experiences available for work in therapy. Since the individual is an integrated organism, with all domains acting in concert (whether this is clear to an observer or not), psychological tension can be embodied. Elements of experience are embodied with a psychological referent, a tag, clue or handle, which points to the meaning of the bodily sensation. There is no formula or taxonomy of embodied feelings in CfD. Each is unique and is even likely to change from moment to moment. Given the commonality in the descriptive vocabulary, figurative language and metaphor used by clients when asked to describe the feelings of 'depression', we might speculate that when people talk of 'pain', 'heaviness', 'lack of energy' or 'feeling dead inside' they are expressing their undifferentiated awareness of embodied experience. It is also the case that the experience of depression can include more direct, concrete somatisation of distress, such as weight loss or weight gain. This is explained in CfD as the human organism acting as an organised whole; clients and their experiences are best understood as an indivisible entity. Somatisation such as weight gain or loss can itself add secondarily to the distress experienced, and we find people experiencing a downward spiral of helplessness and feeling out of control.

This embodied self-related experience brings the technique of going inside and 'clearing a space' – originating in focusing and focusing-oriented therapy (Gendlin, 1978/2003) – to the Counselling for Depression repertoire of skills. We will look in more detail at this in Chapter 8.

Second is the straightforward notion that experiential elements of the self-structure can involve embodied feelings. So, for example, there might be an alignment of distressing elements, some of which might be embodied. In some cases, people ascribe more weight, importance or even 'wisdom' to embodied feelings. A client might feel unable to get out of bed because they have no physical energy and their feelings of helplessness would be redoubled if they believe there is nothing to get out of bed for. Of course some people give bodily sensations less importance or are likely to dismiss them altogether, thus reinforcing the injunction to empathically follow the client in question, not take ready-made recipes for understanding into the therapy session.

As easy as it is to see the reinforcement of distressing self-related experiences, there is also the possibility of discrepancy between a bodily sensation and a thought. So, in contrast to the example above, a client might feel unable to get out of bed because they have no physical energy, whilst becoming further distressed by thinking 'this is not like me, I am never like this, I don't feel like myself any more, why can't I do the simplest of things like getting out of bed?' This most basic example of a discrepancy between parts of the self is used here simply to illustrate a possible dynamic involving an embodied element of the self.[3] It is also an example of a much larger category of intrapersonal events which we call 'self-discrepancies' and will be detailed below.

We can see how these most simple of individual intrapersonal processes might aggregate to form an experience specific enough to be labelled as depression and severe enough to bring a person to their GP. Since a very high proportion of people experiencing depression have suicidal thoughts, the aggregation of more 'simple' processes clearly is sufficiently severe to make people think about killing themselves.

The pluralistic self

Although not explicitly addressed in Rogers' original work, the notion of the self as a pluralistic system or matrix rather than unitary entity is of central importance not only to CfD theory, but also to the developing PCE theory of the 21st century. There are several strands of PCE theory which rest upon understanding the self as comprising subselves, parts, configurations, voices, schemas and so on. There are both similarities and differences between the PCE understandings of what Mearns (Mearns, 1999; Mearns and Thorne, 2000) calls 'configurations', and, for example, constructs such as 'objects' in object relations theory and 'ego states' in transactional analysis, but we make no comparisons here, limiting ourselves to the range of PCE understandings. For the purposes of simplicity and unifying vocabulary in CfD we will use the term 'configurations' to describe this phenomenon. Although this is Mearns' term, concepts very similar if not identical to configurations of self have been developed in parallel over many years in different strands of PCE psychology.

We need go no further than an everyday conversation to seek validity for the construct, since there can be few conversations in which a person does not spontaneously say something like 'I can't decide: a part of me wants to and a part of me doesn't', 'Sometimes I enjoy it and other times I don't, I'm like two different people', or 'When asked to do it, I always have this debate inside: one me says "do it", another me says "don't do it", and the me that often wins is the one that says "wait and see, it'll blow over".'

The experience of several parts of the self, or even several selves, is a common one with which almost everyone can identify, as is the experience of these parts in conversation or dialogue, often representing different points of view, different options or different aims.

---

[3] Client statements can be understood to be *signposts* to specific intra- and interpersonal problems, in this case pointing to embodied self-discrepancies.

CfD Theory of Depression #3: Symptoms of depression can result from the dialogue between parts of the self.

This general statement about everyday experience of parts of the self is necessary to draw attention to the differences between Counselling for Depression and more classical person-centred theory. CfD deliberately posits the notion of a pluralistic self, and takes elements of emotion-focused theory to explain the symptoms of depression, as we shall describe below. From classical person-centred theory, CfD takes the notion of discrepancy between self and experience sometimes written about as the discrepancy between the real and ideal self. We believe these elements of theory are consonant to the extent that it is easy to present this as a coherent theoretical position requiring little adjustment for most counsellors encountering CfD practice for the first time. We will explore this in more detail in the section on 'self-discrepancy' below.

From the broader tradition of experiential therapies and EFT in particular, we take the notion of dialogue between different self-configurations, with a special focus on tensions between self-configurations. There is a variety of dialogue dynamics between the aims or modus operandi of different self-configurations other than simple conflicts. Discussions, arguments and disagreements are commonplace and whilst possibly less immediately disruptive than discrepancies, they can set a distressing, tedious or hopeless backdrop to day-to-day life, or aggregate feelings in a drip-drip fashion which eventually and dramatically break when the load gets too great. These are explored in detail in the 'other self-configuration dialogues' section on pp. 107–11.

On the other hand we note that psychotherapy has little concern for *agreements* between self-configurations. It could be argued that subselves develop by necessity in order to provide us with psychological balance, e.g. an individual needs a balance of self-criticism and self-belief to stop themselves from becoming narcissistic. This would be a natural expression of a well-developed holistically functioning organism. Problems arise when subselves get out of balance or become polarised in their positions.

This discussion of the nature of the self gives us the general platform from which to understand the detail of the CfD conceptualisation of depression. It also contributes the basic intrapersonal architecture within which distress can arise in the form of symptoms of depression. We now proceed to look inside this structure to the more detailed intrapersonal dynamics which may lead to depression.

Self-discrepancy

We have appropriated this term from the work of Neill Watson (Watson et al., 2010), who in turn took the term from 'self-discrepancy theory' developed by Edward Tory Higgins (Higgins, 1987). Watson and his colleagues further developed the notion by integrating the ideas of Rogers and Higgins.

Self-discrepancy is a succinct phrase under which to gather the various – sometimes subtly different – expressions of discrepancies within the self-structure which lead to psychological tension as outlined originally by Rogers (1951) and later elaborated by others in PCE theory. Rogers used the term 'incongruence' to describe the single source of psychological tension (see Chapter 5), but in CfD we acknowledge a more broadly based palette of self-discrepancies which are considered to be precursors for experiences which might be diagnosed as depression. Watson and his colleagues particularly aligned self-discrepancy with depression and developed instruments to measure how levels of self-discrepancy might be associated with depression.

The CfD conceptualisation of depression embraces the self-discrepancy definitions used by Watson et al. (2010) at a conceptual level. Watson and his colleagues first restate Rogers' theory – introjection of conditions of worth leads to undifferentiated psychological tension (anxiety and/or depression) generated by a real–ideal discrepancy.

Higgins' self-discrepancy theory

Higgins (1987) distinguishes between domains of self and standpoints on the self to create a complex matrix of possible self-objects and their interactions. Domains of the self are:

- the actual self: representations or experiences of the attributes you (or someone else, another) thinks that you possess
- the ideal self: experiences of the attributes that you (or another) would like you, ideally, to possess (hopes and aspirations for you)
- the ought self: experiences of the attributes that you (or another) believes you ought to possess (a representation of your duty and responsibilities)

The standpoints on the self are:

- experiences from your own standpoint
- the standpoints of another or others

So the domains of the self (actual, idea and ought) can be seen from either of the two standpoints (own and other). Importantly, we can translate both the domains and standpoints into Rogers' personality theory by understanding that all 'own' representations are authentic experiences, while all 'other' representations are possible introjects.

Thus Higgins' self-discrepancy theory uses a matrix of self-objects based on the experiences of the owner of the self (authentic experience) versus the perceptions or demands of a significant other (introjected values). The matrix of possible interactions is a more detailed, systematic elaboration of Rogers' notions of congruence.

Higgins' self-discrepancy theory and depression

Within the matrix Higgins proposes two types of discrepancy important to CfD: i) actual or real self vs. the *ideal* self: the self you or others *want* you to be (real–ideal: RI); and ii) actual or real self vs. the self you think (or have been told) you *ought* to be (real–ought: RO).

He then goes on to propose a link between sets of discrepancies and concomitant outcomes, for example:

- own ideal self/other ideal self is associated with depression
- own ought self/other ought self is associated with shame and anxiety

Higgins' contribution of the RO discrepancy and discriminating the differences between the discrepancies and the experience of anxiety or depression is an interesting and useful elaboration of theory. Furthermore, both RI and RO discrepancies have been measured in, and validated by, a number of studies (see Watson et al., 2010).

Finally, and parenthetically, it is acknowledged in theory literature, diagnostic manuals and clinical settings that many clients receive mixed anxiety and depression diagnoses and report overlapping symptoms and experiences of depression and anxiety. This is entirely concordant with CfD explanations of idiosyncratic combinations of client experiences being due to unique elaborate patterns of introjected values discrepant with authentic experiences.

The entire edifice of Higgins' self-discrepancy theory is unnecessary for understanding the CfD conceptualisation. As a perceptual theory, CfD takes the key notion that conflict between the way we experience ourselves and the way we ideally want to be is an important archetypal self-discrepancy in the genesis of depression and that there is some evidence to establish the validity of this (Watson et al., 2010). As a phenomenological theory, CfD does not adopt Higgins' discrepancy theory as a diagnostic or treatment tool. The experience of the client is paramount, and the therapist follows the client in order to understand the unique network of associations and meanings that go to make up their lived experience of depression and works with that, even though it might contradict any and all theories.

In summary, CfD theory proposes that self-discrepancy is one starting point, a template from which to build possible understanding, or a signpost from which to explore the client's world. The signpost points to a theoretical starting point from which we consider the idea that personality is composed of many self-aspects in relation to each other. That starting point in theory leads to a number of possibilities, including distressing intrapersonal processes where one aspect is, for example, excessively critical of another, constantly suppresses another, regularly interrupts another, or experiences the absence of another.

> CfD Theory of Depression #4: Symptoms of depression can uniquely result from the discrepancy between a person's real or actual self and their introjected ideal self.

Discrepancies or incongruence between parts of the self can be experienced by the individual person as a fixed state, in the same way that some people describe depression as a global and permanent state. CfD practice accepts the client's fatalistic apprehension of their world, whilst understanding that these global, totalising experiences are often maintained by micro-processes that can fix our general mood or sense of who we are. In Chapter 8, we explore how this translates into the CfD therapeutic stance.

The purpose of identifying and working with self-discrepancies of this type is to reduce the tension by any one or combination of means – many of which will be managed by clients themselves. Sometimes awareness alone is sufficient, sometimes the origin of the ideal self or ought self can be uncovered, revisited and revised, effectively removing the tyranny of who the client wants to be, or thinks they ought to be. We will explore the practice issues involved and look at examples in Chapters 8 and 9.

There are other types of discrepant dialogue between configurations of self that make significant contributions to the CfD conceptualisation of depression, and we group these under the heading 'other self-configuration dialogues'.

Other self-configuration dialogues

As we have shown there is a commonsense basis for understanding dialogues between two or more configurations of self. These configurations are not 'multiple personalities' in the clinically accepted sense of the term (for detailed analysis of the difference, see *DSM-IV* compared with a discussion in terms of EFT, see Elliott et al., 2004) but they can be experienced as distinct entities with their own agendas, aims and characteristics. Nor are they 'voices' as in the commonly used term 'hearing voices' describing a symptom of psychosis, but they are often experienced as having a voice, and they might even generate subvocal expressions, particularly negative ones. It does not require a leap of imagination to appreciate the reality of dialogue between these elements, since i) practitioners with scant experience will have encountered clients describing such experiences, and ii) most people with a modicum of self-awareness will share the experience.

In some psychotherapeutic approaches we find a taxonomy of configurations of self. The most basic of these is to sort them into 'pathological' and 'healthy', 'adaptive' and 'maladaptive' or, in PCE terms, those that are 'for growth' and those that are 'not for growth'. Counselling for Depression does not assign a value to self-configurations from an external frame of reference. In CfD, the 'problem' resides in the lived distress which follows from the level of tension and nature of the incongruence itself and any further value is attached by the client, i.e., the client decides on the importance and meaning of the tension. Many, if not most people live with some level of tension due to discrepancy or incongruence. The *degree* and *type* of conflict and the resultant amount of disturbance is what brings people to seek help.

As a phenomenological approach, the first position in CfD – both in theory and in practice – is to let the description of the nature and explanation of the function reside with the client in question. Furthermore, in the context of the in-session practice of CfD, 'off the shelf' psychiatric diagnoses are regarded as potentially stigmatising and antitherapeutic. However, it *is* instructive to understand that there are some well-defined, commonly experienced patterns of self-configuration and resultant dialogue which are associated with the experience of the symptoms of depression. Hence CfD incorporates the concepts of conflict splits and self–inner-critic dialogue derived from EFT (Elliott et al., 2004).

Conflict splits

To acknowledge the origin – emotion-focused therapy – of the importance of this cluster of processes, we retain the vocabulary and use the term 'conflict-splits', and it is almost self-explanatory. Some theorists and approaches understand the dynamics between differing aspects of the self as 'splits', and when two elements of the self are in opposition, this is known as a 'conflict-split'. CfD theory does not identify any self-elements as maladaptive or adaptive, per se. Rather, it is the emotional responses to conflict between self-elements that produce distress, or can be 'maladaptive' in terms of EFT theory.

In CfD, a conflict split is most simply expressed as an oppositional clash between two aspects or elements of the self. Rather than look for specific self-elements (ideal self, ought self and real self), in a conflict split, we just acknowledge and accept that two aspects are in conflict without naming or valuing either of them. Conflict splits are often out of, or barely on the edge of, the client's awareness so the first step is to help bring them into full awareness if possible. Sometimes the client is readily able to do this themselves when offered empathic attunement and clarification. However, simply becoming aware of the conflicting configurations is often not sufficient to resolve the conflict. The therapeutic task is to clarify and differentiate the oppositional configurations and then encourage contact and dialogue between them. In Chapter 8 we describe interventions to more actively help clients resolve these conflicts.

> CfD Theory of Depression #5: Symptoms of depression can result from conflicts between parts of the self that result in shutting down of experiencing, withdrawal, and feelings of guilt, unworthiness, hopelessness, helplessness, blame, etc.

Some conflict splits are more characteristic of depression, particularly those which result in the client shutting down experiencing, or feeling guilty, blameworthy, unworthy, helpless or any of the other long list of symptoms of depression. For example, the critical self can beat down on the experiencing self to the point where the latter feels defeated and hopeless. Under these circumstances, the critical self can be experienced as the part that verbalises the 'shoulds', 'oughts' and evaluations of the self. This is one way Rogers' constructs of introjections and conditions of worth plays out in the pluralist self.

This is a continuing process which maintains depression, not a static state. Again we see a relentless process of both wearing down resistance of adaptive parts of the self and aggregation of psychological tension over a long period. The following are highly stylised examples, but for illustration, conflict splits expressed in everyday language might include:

- I am ambitious and want to apply for the job – you're too useless to get anywhere or do anything.
- I feel bullied by her – you're not a real man – a real man can't be bullied by a woman.
- I am being suffocated in this relationship – you are no good on your own.

And the mechanics of the links between conflict splits and depression can work like this, for example:

- I am ambitious and want to apply for the job – you're too useless to get anywhere or do anything.

  Can lead to paralysis, fear of rejection and a feeling of hopelessness: 'It's useless applying for jobs, I'll never get one.'

- I feel bullied by her – you're not a real man – a real man can't be bullied by a woman.

  Can lead to a feeling of self-loathing: 'If I can't stand up to her I'm not a real man, I'm a useless feeble, excuse of a man.'

- I am being suffocated in this relationship – you are no good on your own.

  Can lead to a feeling of helplessness: 'I have stopped thinking about the future because I know I'll not be able to change anything for the better.'

So CfD holds that depression may result when the relationship between different aspects of the self is hostile (e.g. where a person experiences a punitive 'inner-critic') or oppressive (e.g. where an aspect of the self is suppressed or silenced). And to all of these possible outcomes, we can add the feeling of failure. It is not uncommon for people to have more than one conflict split and for these to have been persistent and pervasive – seeping into everyday life over many months.

Self-critical dialogues

A self-configuration that is relentlessly negatively evaluative is a common experience. Taking terms from experiential therapies, CfD calls this the 'inner-critic' or 'critical-self'. It is highlighted because, although several therapeutic approaches consider it a simple matter to 'reframe' the criticism as concern, exaggerated protection, etc., in CfD we acknowledge that the unyielding, universal taint that can be brought by a critical-self can be a foundation for depression. Such a foundation can be long-standing and particularly stubborn. Even when brought into full awareness it can persist as an obstacle to fulfilled living unless actively worked with employing specific interventions.

Most experienced therapists will have encountered clients with vigorous inner-critics, and might have wrestled with their own in personal therapy. It is a common experience and one that is occasionally alluded to in everyday conversation: 'Stop beating yourself up', and so on.

Examples of self-critical dialogue include:

- I know I passed my exams – but it was only just a pass, that's not good enough.

  A double-edged sword and can lead to a pervasive feeling of being not good enough. This can lead to perfectionism – useful up to a point, but beyond this can lead to a self-destructive spiral.

- My boyfriend says he loves me but I'm not attractive. In fact when I look in the mirror I wince, I'm so ugly. He must be blind or stupid.

  The client's inner-critic puts down the client and, importantly, significant others in order to maintain the logic of the negative self-image. This invalidates positive messages from outside as well as inside – represented in theory by Rogers' processes of denial and distortion of experience (Rogers, 1959: 205).

- I just can't get that voice that says 'you are a failure' out of my head.

  A stubborn and relentless feeling of failure will wear the client down and lead to feelings of hopelessness and helplessness, preventing them from being able to move on and self-heal.

- I wanted to be a dancer but wasn't disciplined enough. I'll never be really happy, but it's my fault.

  Self-blame can be generalised to taint the future as well as explain past failures. It also sets up failures in the present.

A common feature of these critical-self messages is their totalising nature. They put a negative, unpleasant spin on the past, present and future, defeating hope and agency, and limiting the range of experiences – not only are positive experiences made less likely, but the palette of experience is reduced from vivid colours to plain grey. They invalidate all sources of affirmation from inside the person and from others. Having such an overactive inner-critic can also be a lonely, isolating experience, especially if the critic is shaming.

Some (Shafran et al., 2002) suggest that a degree of self-criticism provides essential balance to the personality, a basis for self-improvement and prevents the individual becoming complacent. From a CfD perspective the problem is the *imbalance* between elements of self-structure, not the *fact* that there are several self-configurations: an inner-critic configuration balanced by a resilient and self-believing configuration would not necessarily lead to psychological tension and distress. On the other hand, classical person-centred theory has it that people with little incongruence in the self-structure have a natural balance between the individual and the social and are inherently 'more understanding of others and … more accepting of others as separate individuals' (Rogers, 1951: 520). This understanding of Rogers' original work renders the notion of the adaptive, or balancing, inner-critic unnecessary.

Either version of theory is supported by CfD practice in which the client's lived experience of psychological tension, their self-generated therapeutic tasks and collaborative, creative work with the counsellor are the drivers for therapeutic processes.

Other problematic psychological processes related to depression

In drawing from person-centred and experiential therapies and EFT, CfD embraces a range of techniques marshalled into a coherent theoretical framework. A further group, taken mostly from EFT, do not obviously spring from dialogues or discrepancies between self-configurations. In CfD most of these are best thought of simply as problematic psychological processes which have been identified through client observation and research (Elliott et al., 2004). They range from uncomplicated psychological processes which can block progress and suggest a simple method of resolution, to more fundamental processes requiring more extensive work.

These processes are listed here in order to give theory coordinates for specific potential features which commonly occur in experiences of depression. This will then allow us to map the theory territory on to practice in later chapters.

Emotional overwhelm

> CfD Theory of Depression #6: Depression can be the result of, or exacerbated by emotions that are too overwhelming to be faced or worked with in therapy.

Starting at the more theoretically elementary end of the continuum, CfD specifically acknowledges that people can get stuck, in life and therapy, in the face of overwhelming emotion, for example as result of grief or a reaction to trauma, etc.

This overwhelm can present problems in two ways. First, the person may get frozen like a rabbit in headlights, unable to engage with an emotion because they sense the sheer scale of the emotional response that awaits them and then, quite reasonably, avoid it at all costs or simply come to an emotional standstill. In CfD theory and practice we do not cast an individual's behaviour as 'avoidant' or 'resistant'. We understand that we are all doing the best we can in order to survive and maintain ourselves in the face of difficult experiences. From Rogers' (1961: 125–59) 'process conception of psychotherapy' we know that until Stage 5 (out of seven) the immediate, present experience of feelings is mistrusted and feared.

This gives the first set of theory coordinates for which CfD practice must have a strategy.

Second, we know that sometimes people do try to engage with their emotions. They *know* that feelings are important and somehow represent a road to health if only they were not so scary, dark and simply huge. They make repeated attempts to let their feelings flow, and indeed they might spend hours weeping, but seem unable to move on – on each attempt they experience the full depth of their feelings, only to feel brief relief and return to square one.

The difficulty here is that whilst they have *experienced* their emotions, they have not *worked* with them, no change has taken place, no realignment or other adjustments in the self-structure have spontaneously occurred. In CfD theory *experience itself* is not necessarily a change process – it might be for a few people, but for many more, some other change process must be engaged. One problem is that the sheer depth and size of the emotions involved mean that they are too big to be worked with – they need to be cut down to a digestible size.

Another problem can be the masking of a helpful, adaptive emotion by a more intense unhelpful maladaptive emotion. What is 'helpful' or 'unhelpful' is uniquely determined by the context and personal responses of the client in question. CfD practice provides appropriate ways of working with both of these scenarios of emotional overwhelm which will be explored in Chapter 8.

Problematic reaction points

> CfD Theory of Depression #7: Some symptoms of depression can be the result of, or exacerbated by, puzzling, unexplained experiences which feel exaggerated or out of character.

Next we explore the tendency for clients to get stuck in the experience of having an unexplainable, uncharacteristic reaction to a situation. This experience can be understood at two levels. First is when the client feels a deep sense of their reaction being *absolutely* uncharacteristic, behaviourally or emotionally, indeed so out-of-character that the reaction doesn't seem to belong to them. Such experiences can be frightening to the extent that the person will avoid them, often at great cost in terms of shutting off areas of experience, avoiding activities and situations. Feeling inauthentic, incongruent and having the immediate sense that everyone can see that you are not who you say you are, may lead to intrapersonal, interpersonal and social withdrawal. This simply adds to the common experience of feeling that they are watching their lives from a third-person position. Problematic reaction points can also result in self-criticism, possibly adding further fuel to an already active internal inner-critic (above). The problem is that when the client is not inhabiting their experience, not agentically in touch with it, the client cannot gain any purchase on the problematic behaviour in order to change it.

Rogers (1951) connects this kind of experience with a self-structure based on the introjection of values and the subsequent denial of 'organic experiences and needs which have not been symbolized' (p. 509). This links to the CfD understanding of the embodied self – organic needs and experiences can be thought of as bodily needs and experiences. In the case of problematic reaction points, the client is unable to inhabit their experience. There is such dissonance between the bodily needs and the lived sense of introjected self that the bodily experiences seem so alien as to be 'not me', and the shock of this can stop a client in their tracks. This raises an immediate anxiety and a sustained shadow is cast over the trustworthiness of experience, leading to withdrawal on many levels, as explained above.

Second is a much more superficial experience where the reaction may be puzzling, nagging or unclear, feel somewhat uncharacteristic, over-exaggerated, and can cause a persistent anxiety or cast a dark shadow of doubt on a situation, relationship or any life event, causing the person to avoid thinking about, or otherwise engaging with the experience. In EFT these are called 'problematic reaction points'. Not only are they a driver of some symptoms of depression, they can also be an obstacle to progress in therapy or a presenting problem, i.e. the client begins therapy by bringing this puzzle, possibly one that has been nagging at them for some time, making them feel low.

Meaning protests

> CfD Theory of Depression #8: Some symptoms of depression can be the result of having a cherished belief about the world destroyed.

Many readers will recognise that moment in our lives when something challenges or destroys a cherished belief about the world or life. The more central the belief is to our sense of self or identity, the greater will the reaction be. The feelings of shock, surprise, injustice, outrage, violation and anger can feel overwhelming and disabling. Sometimes it is such a violation of our understanding of life, the feelings can persevere for a long time, taint almost all experiences and shake our faith. The resultant constellation of feelings is called a 'meaning protest'. Nothing short of the meaning for living has been shaken.

In terms of personality theory, it might be that such a belief has been incorporated into the self-structure by a process of authentic organismic evaluation. In such cases the belief would be expected to be flexible and therefore reviewable in the light of subsequent changes in circumstance. Alternatively beliefs can be *introjected*, that is taken in under threat, whole, from the experience of significant others, along with the values put on them by others. With regard to meaning protests the key point is not whether the belief is introjected or the result of organismic evaluation. The problem arises simply because the belief is 'cherished', i.e. central to the self-structure. Whilst we might expect authentically incorporated experiences to remain reviewable, up to a point, we also know that the whole self-structure can become rigid as a result of threat, so we must expect a reaction of distress when any cherished belief is destroyed. How flexible the self-structure is at the time of the challenge is the important matter.

Beliefs that provide a foundation against which the unfolding narrative of our lives is set might be something like: true love lasts forever, a job is for life, good people do not get ill and die, the world is a safe place, parents die before their children. A belief about the world that is central to our identity might be: every man in this town has worked in the widget-making trade, or a woman is only fulfilled when she has children. Redundancy, bereavement, illness, disability, trauma and so on are the typical triggers for challenging such beliefs.

If such a belief is at the centre of our self, then the whole self-structure can feel shaken and collapse, and although we might refer to the result generically as 'psychological tension', it often leads to the symptoms of depression. For many people the symptoms are also intractable. The psychological balance engendered by a cherished belief central to our understanding of justice, relationships, life itself, is not easily restored once destroyed. Even if the meaning protest is not a keystone in the self-structure, essential to its structure, it can still unleash a temporary tsunami of outrage. At the peak of this tidal wave of feelings, there can be a collapse, resulting in symptoms of depression which can outlast the outrage. Other clients may not be aware of exactly what the cherished belief is that has been violated. They just have a dull sense that something is wrong. Naming the meaning protest then expressing outrage and upset are often sufficient for the client to experience release and resolution, facilitated by empathic following. Meaning protests often leave lasting impressions, and sometimes these are sufficiently distressing to be a cause of depression which needs attention in therapy.

Unfinished business

CfD Theory of Depression #9: Some symptoms of depression can be the result of particular types of incompletely processed life events.

Unfinished business is used to describe any issue which remains unresolved, coupled with associated unresolved emotions. Clients often report symptoms of depression beginning after distressing life events which have not been processed sufficiently to render them benign and allow the person to move on, e.g., redundancy, neglect, abandonment, bullying or other abuse, relationship breakdown, bereavement, etc.

Many unfinished business scenarios involve another person, such as a deceased friend, partner or relative; a work colleague, manager; friend; current or ex-partner; parent or authority figure such as a past teacher.

Some therapeutic approaches, including EFT, propose that unfinished business in adult life is a replayed archaic dynamic, a vestige of a past relationship, most likely a poor care-giving relationship in infancy that resulted in an attachment injury. In CfD theory it is unnecessary to ascribe any particular cause to unfinished business since when offered the therapeutic conditions, some clients will be able to describe the circumstances surrounding unfinished business and let any meaning unfold. Resolution can follow spontaneously. For those whose experience remains unresolved and painful, more active techniques can be offered. These are explained in Chapter 8 and examples of them in action given in Chapter 9.

The nature of emotions

> CfD Theory of Depression #10: Some symptoms of depression can be the result of inappropriate and unhelpful learned emotions.

Taken from both PCT and EFT theory, Counselling for Depression conceptualises depression as resulting from particular types of emotional experience and emotional processes. This means that in practice the therapeutic focus should be on the client's feelings and emotions.

The relationship between emotion and psychological growth and wellbeing has been carefully established in Chapter 5 from a theoretical point of view, and is worth briefly reprising here in our discussion of depression and PCE concepts. Regardless of the depressive processes experienced by clients (self-discrepancy, self-critical dialogues, unfinished business, etc.) a core issue is how clients relate to their emotional experience. From the CfD point of view, greater openness to feelings is associated with lower levels of depression and better psychological health, but in supporting clients, counsellors should be alert to the nuances and subtleties of how feelings are expressed. For example, to regularly experience core maladaptive feelings of worthlessness is likely to result in unsatisfying, unpleasant responses and behaviour sets that will beget further unfulfilling, uncomfortable and noxious cycles of experience, reinforcing depressive symptoms. Similarly, to express unhelpful secondary reactive emotions, such as guilt as opposed to helpful, adaptive anger, can deprive clients of the resources necessary to assert themselves and get their needs met. Using emotional expression to manipulate others can also have negative consequences such as the type of unhappy interpersonal relationships that are often associated with depression.

In Chapter 5 we also explained that there is an optimal level of emotional arousal for processing emotion and difficulties in achieving this are often associated with anxiety and depression. These elaborations of understanding of emotions are of interest as the background to CfD theory and practice. It is important for CfD practitioners to understand that *being emotional in itself* does not necessarily have any particular therapeutic benefit for clients: the quality and the kind of emotional arousal is important. The CfD definition of emotional wellbeing is a client restored to open, authentic processing of fluid adaptive emotions – a life facilitated by fit-for-purpose emotions which change according to circumstances. CfD puts the definitions of such value-laden terms as 'maladaptive', 'satisfying' and 'fulfilling' firmly in the control of the client. In terms of emotion, the prime therapeutic task of the CfD practitioner is to try to enter the client's world of emotions and their meanings without any hint of judgement.

7

Working Briefly

Competences covered in Chapter 7

G6-Ability to engage client
G7-Ability to foster and maintain a good therapeutic alliance, and to grasp the client's perspective and 'world view'
G9-Ability to manage endings
G10-Ability to undertake a generic assessment
G12-Ability to use measures to guide therapy and to monitor outcomes
B5-Ability to explain and demonstrate the rationale for counselling
B6-Ability to work with the client to establish a therapeutic aim
B10-Ability to conclude the therapeutic relationship
M1-Capacity to implement CfD in a flexible but coherent manner
M2-Capacity to adapt interventions in response to client feedback
M4.1-An ability to balance any tensions between the maintenance of the therapeutic relationship and the achievement of therapeutic tasks
M4.2-An ability to maintain a balance between directive and non-directive dimensions of the therapeutic process

(Competences are listed in Appendix 1)

Introduction

'Working briefly' immediately raises two parameters in therapy which all approaches have to negotiate in both theory and practice – time and limits – and these issues have generated much debate across all approaches and modalities in counselling and psychotherapy. In recent years, the accountability zeitgeist has drawn counsellors into reflecting upon and understanding therapy praxis in terms of financial, personal, social and legal accountability. The outcome of counselling cannot be understood as independent of, for example, the cost. This is the reality of 21st-century state-funded healthcare in which Counselling for Depression is provided and this book rests upon accepting this professional context while developing strategies of best practice. The debates provoked by the social and professional context will not be conducted at length here, not because we think they are not important, but simply because first there is not the space and second, they have been covered thoughtfully elsewhere (e.g. King and Moutsou, 2010).

In Chapter 3 we explained that counselling is recommended by NICE for the treatment of persistent subthreshold depressive symptoms or mild to moderate depression in episodes of 6-to-10 sessions delivered over 8-to-12 weeks. Although research evidence for the effectiveness of counselling with more severe forms of depression over a longer period of time is currently not strong, in developing CfD within the UK IAPT programme, there was consensus that CfD should be offered in episodes of up to 20 sessions depending on the needs of the client and the severity of their problems. Although therapy offered in this approximate number of sessions is generally considered brief, it is worth bearing in mind that based on weekly contact and taking into account holidays, natural breaks and individual arrangements, this could represent a therapeutic relationship of six months duration.

There might be a tendency for therapists to believe that clients invariably actively like coming for therapy and are at least disappointed – with possibly severe negative therapeutic consequences, arresting or upsetting the client's progress – when therapy comes to an end. For quite some time there have been strong indications, however, that clients' experiences do not always bear this out – they themselves may think otherwise. For example, given the choice of finishing therapy when they wish, Budman and Gurman (1988) found that a majority of users of outpatient mental health services chose to end therapy after relatively few sessions, suggesting that on many occasions, clients may prefer brief to long-term therapy. Well-established evidence from other sources likewise suggests that the greatest improvements in therapy are experienced in the early, as opposed to the later phases of therapy. For example, in a large-scale dose-effect analysis Howard et al. (1986) found that by 8 sessions approximately 50% of patients were measurably improved, and approximately 75% were improved by 26 sessions, lending further support to the case for therapy, in most cases, being kept fairly brief.

So despite there being a compelling case that working briefly makes best use of resources and is effective and acceptable to clients, in PCE therapies it is frequently presented as problematic, from being benignly obstructive up to the point of being actively antitherapeutic. For the thoughtful and comprehensive presentation and discussion of the issues, we recommend the collection edited by Keith Tudor (Tudor, 2008) and many of the points carefully elaborated by Tudor and his contributors are briefly sketched here.

The parameters of time and limits bring several theoretical and practical matters into sharp relief. Tudor (2008: 19–20) asserts that structure, focus and direction in therapy are frequently conflated in our understanding and need to be looked at separately. He then discusses the degree to which certain types of structure, focus and direction of the therapeutic project, and/or each session, are *encouraged* by limits. Consideration of time and limits also requires counsellors to develop a contextual awareness of the notions of goals, accurate, ongoing, collaborative assessment of the client's needs and an understanding of when therapy is 'happening' and when it is 'finished' or completed. These words are put in quotes to indicate that each term signals a somewhat contentious idea. PCE therapies' identification of the client as the 'owner', and therefore driver and manager of the therapy process means that understandings of both progress in therapy, and when the client has achieved sufficient movement to feel able to discontinue therapy, are held by the client. This chapter will explore some of these issues a little further.

When relaxed service limits apply, in classical, non-directive forms of PCE therapies, where the client is put at the centre of the entire process, the counsellor will follow the client in all respects – content, pace (including getting stuck), direction, limits (including duration of relationship, within ethical and safety boundaries) and so on. Whilst an idealised position and unattainable for many, this is an important theoretical therapeutic position, validating the client's agency and encouraging the client's internal locus of evaluation. With the client in control, the classical person-centred therapist would not diagnose 'resistance', 'denial' or 'avoidance' as client devices, nor would they have any strategy save congruent reflection. There would be nothing pressing the therapist to, e.g., proceed at a pace any quicker than that set by the client's actualising tendency or ask why the client is not (in the view of the therapist) attending to the salient problematic issues. The therapist would understand the client's actualising tendency to be directing the process for the maintenance and enhancement of the client. The therapist's strategy, if they cannot understand the client's process, would be to be more fully empathic.

It is worth remembering that Rogers' main theory development took place at a time and in a culture when psychotherapy theory and practice was dominated by psychoanalysis. A complete analysis would normally take years and be prescribed by the analyst. Psychotherapy was almost universally thought of as being a major life commitment in terms of time, effort and money. Rogers' early thinking was influenced by the work of Jessie Taft, women's advocate, social worker and academic in the renowned Philadelphia School of Social Work. Her book *The Dynamics of Therapy in a Controlled Relationship* was a seminal work, the first section of which examined the understanding and use of time in therapy. In it she critiqued long-term psychoanalysis and stated:

> If there is no therapeutic understanding … many interviews equally barren will not help. In the single interview, if that is all I allow myself to count upon, if I am willing to take that hour in and for itself … I myself am the remedy at this moment if there is any … Here is one hour to be lived through as it goes, one hour of present and immediate relationship, however limited, with another human being who has brought himself to the point of asking for help. (Taft, 1937: 11)

This quote requires no explanation. It does not advocate time limits, but challenges therapists to provide an active 'present and immediate relationship'. This challenge is felt all the more keenly when the relationship is *of necessity*, brief, and therefore provides the foundation of CfD practice.

PCE therapists practising brief forms, including Counselling for Depression, approach the notions introduced above – when therapy is 'happening' and when it is 'finished' – first by following the client and second by processes of collaboration and negotiation.

A number of generic principles which underpin CfD as a brief model are worth bearing in mind:

- Counsellors should be responsible for holding the therapeutic frame. That is contractual issues should be clearly negotiated in the early stages and thoughtfully adhered to: the duration and number of sessions would obviously form a part of this.
- The importance of collaboration cannot be over-emphasised, to ensure the client can exercise the highest levels of autonomy and agency in both shaping the frame and engaging in the process of therapy.
- Remember that the client has come to therapy for a reason, something has prompted them. In exploring this, the counsellor should work with the client to agree a focus for the therapeutic work and if this shifts during the process of therapy, this should be discussed and made explicit. This creates shared clarity about what counsellor and client are trying to achieve in therapy, maximising the likelihood of a meaningful outcome for the client.
- Session-by-session feedback should be used to review progress and to make collaborative decisions about any changes to the therapy and when the therapeutic relationship should come to an end.
- Due to external circumstances, therapy may sometimes have to come to an end before the client is ready to finish. In such circumstances counsellors should discuss with the client alternative sources of support that can be accessed post-therapy and work to make the ending as constructive an experience as possible for the client.

Working positively – structuring the brief relationship

As counsellor educators, both of us were enthusiastic advocates of routine audio-recording of client sessions on placement. Most students had one of two experiences – some had a reasonable number of clients refuse to be recorded, whilst others had few or none. The difference was that in order to introduce taping to clients and gain their permission, the first group would say something like 'I'm sorry to ask you about this, but my college wants me to tape record these sessions. I'll understand if you say no, because it can be a bit scary, and because of the confidentiality issues. My lecturer and supervisor will listen to the tapes. If you don't want me to tape the sessions, just say so now.' The second group said something like 'I am a trainee therapist and it would help me become a better counsellor if I could tape record these sessions. The tape will only be listened to by my college lecture and supervisor in order to give me feedback. Is that OK? If you have any objections you can stop the tape at any time or just say now and I will not tape any of these sessions with you.'

This example illustrates how easily the therapists' anxieties and agendas can be brought into the relationship in the first session. A confident, hopeful, positive attitude will be communicated and is more likely to elicit a positive response, and conversely an anxious, negative attitude is more likely to elicit a refusal. And so it is with the therapist's attitude to time-limited work. CfD counsellors should be confident that working in contracts of up to 20 sessions is both an effective and acceptable way to deliver therapy, which also makes careful use of resources, i.e. it ensures access to therapy is offered to the maximum number of clients. We earnestly hope that CfD counsellors will not feel apologetic about working within this framework.

Structuring

Communicating the ethos of CfD, setting the scene, establishing expectations, parameters and ground rules all describe a task called *structuring* the relationship. It includes contracting, but extends far beyond and is a much richer and more comprehensive relationship-building activity than that which is usually understood by professional contracting. Structuring actually begins before the start of the first session. Client's expectations about the nature of therapy are initiated by, for example, media representations, what their GP or mental health professional has told them, what they have read in leaflets and self-help books, the location of the service and the welcome given by the receptionist. Structuring is then picked up by the counsellor and is set by their manner and what they say in the first minutes of the first session and includes not only the establishment of a positive tone, but also how many sessions are available, lines of accountability (e.g. reporting, supervision, availability of ethical guidelines), any measurement protocols that might be used, attendance expectations, and ongoing assessment and review processes. The majority of these will be second nature to experienced practitioners in the NHS.

Structuring lays a positive foundation for engaging with elements of therapy that might otherwise be problematic or disruptive to the therapy process, such as establishing the client's goals, reviewing progress, using outcome measures, making referral suggestions and negotiating the ending. In classical person-centred therapy, where all such moments are *entirely* dictated by the client's needs, these events can be left to the natural unfolding of therapy. There is rarely any need for the therapist to instigate them. In contrast, when working briefly in CfD it is the counsellor who must raise, and sometimes return these issues to the client's attention. The beginning of the first session is both relationally and professionally the most appropriate time to introduce the client to the inevitability of establishing realistic goals, reviewing progress, use of outcome measures and endings. It would be unprofessional and potentially disruptive to therapeutic progress if any of these issues were to suddenly arise without warning. Strategies for managing these elements of therapy sessions are discussed throughout this chapter and in Chapters 8 and 9.

How brief is briefly?

Time-limited work is presented as an effort to meet the efficiency and effectiveness targets required by limited funding. Government, employers, insurance companies and individual clients all want to pay no more than is necessary to ensure successful outcome.

Developers of services might hope that clear time limits will helpfully focus the minds of all concerned, leading to a more efficient use of time and resources. However, time-limited protocols often press the number of sessions available into the awareness of both therapist and the client in ways that can be problematic. Some therapists and clients turn to the unsatisfying and possibly distressing game of guessing how many sessions might be required by the client in question. Announcing that CfD is typically limited to a 20-session treatment might lead to situations which could bring potential difficulties, and the same situations could also present a therapeutic opportunity. For example:

- clients might wonder whether they are 'typical' and if they don't sense improvement in, e.g., 8 sessions, are likely to become anxious that the treatment is not working

   o this anxiety may be an obstacle to recovery
   o once declared, this anxiety can be worked on

- clients might be encouraged to think that 'depression' is a unitary diagnosis

   o clients may believe it will be completely resolved or 'cured' in 20 or fewer sessions and that since NICE approved treatments are evidence-based, that this is a scientifically proven 'dosage'
   o brief explanation and discussion of the nature of diagnosis can bring client's lived experiences to the fore, rather than, e.g., media representations of depression

- clients think that *exactly*, e.g., 15 sessions are *required* for recovery

   o clients view CfD as if it were analogous to a prescribed course of medication – take the right number of pills and you're cured
   o again, the counsellor can discuss the real nature of CfD and possible realistic trajectories of improvement

Agencies, services and individual therapists must have publicity, reception and assessment protocols and ways of working which effectively disarm these problems. As we insisted in the previous sections, CfD *must* be presented as a positive, flexible treatment which is *always* tailored to the needs of the individual client, even though there is an upper limit of sessions available in the majority of cases. The way the individual practitioner structures the relationship (above) is key to the manner in which the client approaches the work, notwithstanding that clients experiencing the symptoms of depression are already likely to feel hopeless, isolated and lacking agency in the world.

Practitioners might have experience of services using assessment protocols which attempt to estimate the number of sessions which might be required for a particular client and those that don't do this number are seen as 'non-completers'. CfD doesn't have this conception. Endings are negotiated between client and counsellor, based on the client's progress, up to a maximum of 20 sessions, and this is an important feature of CfD practice.

Assumptions might be based on different understandings of PCE theory – for instance, that more complex problems require longer therapeutic relationships. There are difficulties with this assumption, e.g. 'complexity', used in this context, conflates two elements of psychological distress: difficulty and severity.

'Severity' is a descriptor of the client experience of symptoms, whereas 'difficulty' is a descriptor of the tractability of the problem. From a person-centred perspective it is neither possible nor sensible to estimate the level of 'difficulty' of a person's problems. However, it might be possible to assess the 'severity' of a person's symptoms fairly simply as part of a diagnostic or assessment procedure – the intensity of desperate feelings, the number of suicidal thoughts per day, and so on. Severity of symptoms might help decide on the type of treatment offered to a particular client or flag concerns about safety, but as we explain below, we do not think it is a major factor in determining the length of the therapeutic relationship. There are trends in treatment outcome – e.g., as noted above, 75% of clients improve within 26 sessions – but these are based on averages and so cannot predict what will happen in an individual case. Counsellors should interpret such data cautiously.

It is also worth pointing out that there is no absolutely clear relationship between symptoms and distress. Some clients experience many symptoms but may not be extremely depressed, and conversely, others may experience few symptoms, but be practically disabled by them. The full picture of the client's experience and nature of their psychological tension cannot be gained from looking at studies of co-related factors. Empathic following is the central method specified in PCE – and consequently CfD – therapy practice to gain an understanding of the client's distress.

Regarding 'difficulty', some clients quickly move to a point of resolution by making what to outside observers appear to be frankly breathtaking changes in their lives or ways of perceiving the world. Others seem to dwell interminably on what might appear to be minor blips in life. We do not apologise for repeating the simple mantra of the fundamental position of the Counselling for Depression practitioner – empathic attunement with the client is the entry-point to their world of complex associations and meanings. Only then will the therapist understand what is truly 'difficult' and, in sensitive consultation with the client, how long they might need to take in therapy to achieve their goals.

Naturally, we also expect the counsellor and client to collaborate in agreeing the ending to therapy. Similarly, counsellors will understand that clients make improvements in wellbeing outside of therapy and strategies for maintaining wellbeing after therapy has ended can be discussed prior to ending. Finally, an ending is often indicated even though a client may still have distressing symptoms but increased sense of autonomy. In such cases, the client simply feels capable to manage their own difficult processes without the assistance of a therapist.

It might also be the case that counsellors' attitudes towards working briefly are affected by the interaction of personal and professional issues. For example, they may resent or feel intimidated by having therapy restricted to a limited number of sessions. People choose to train in a particular therapeutic orientation for a complex mix of reasons: personal values, understanding of the nature of being human, a model of change, personal experience in therapy, job vacancies and career prospects, and so on. Few would choose a training solely based on how it performed in terms of contemporaneous outcome evidence. Whilst personal therapy is recommended preparation for competent practice, many practitioners continue to hold the principles of change as close personal values – and this makes a positive contribution to their practice as an authentically lived experience. However, it can also make responding to restrictions on the freedom to practise extremely difficult. If continued employment is contingent upon changes to established ways of practising, in the first instance, supervision is the place to work with and resolve such issues, one way or the other.

Working briefly and the client's internal wisdom

Throughout this book we emphasise and return to an important pivotal element of PCE therapies theory, the notion of the internal wisdom of the client, or in Rogers' terms, the actualising tendency. This proposition is the basis on which PCE therapists understand that the client has the resources to make positive changes in their lives without expert psychotechnological interventions (Bohart and Tallman, 2010). We began this chapter by dissecting the notion of brief work into time and limits and, particularly in PCE approaches, the idea of externally applied limits is anathema to the freedom and emancipation implied by putting the client at the centre of the therapeutic hour. There is a close fit between trust in the internal wisdom of the client, taking a hopeful view of potential change, and being as non-directive as possible in the circumstances. CfD as an IAPT therapy in statutory healthcare necessarily works in circumstances that moderate the degree of non-directivity that is possible. But CfD remains a 'potentiality model' rather than a 'deficiency model' of human psychology. This is manifest throughout, like the name of the seaside resort in a stick of rock.

Working briefly and the needs of the client

The needs of the client are paramount in any kind of psychological treatment but not all clients are able to make best use of all kinds of helping. Accessible information, client choice and assessment are at the heart of matching clients to the most suitable helping formats and approaches. Setting aside the matter of formal assessment which we discussed in Chapter 4, we will briefly acknowledge the need for ongoing apprehension of the client's needs as therapy unfolds in relation to working briefly.

It should go without saying that certain limits must be declared and checked at the beginning of the helping relationship. CfD is a time-limited therapy, initially with the expectation of offering up to 20 sessions. All CfD practitioners will be routinely collecting outcome data at intervals during the therapy relationship. Scott D. Miller, an advocate of feedback-informed treatment (FIT), suggests counsellors routinely ask clients how things are going and what, if anything, is helping. Miller (2010) suggests three steps to implement FIT – the first two of interest to CfD counsellors are i) create a culture of feedback, and ii) integrate feedback into the relationship. Creating a culture of feedback starts in the first session according to Miller. When woven in to the natural rhythm of the session, such requests for feedback empower the client and help the CfD practitioner understand the unique links between practice and outcome for each client. They simply help each therapist become more effective for each client.

As counselling proceeds, both the client and the therapist will become aware of what number of sessions are likely to be sufficient to enable the client to achieve their goals. When working positively with limits, this is unlikely to catch either the client or the counsellor by surprise. An ongoing awareness of the limits can help give early warning of the few cases where extra sessions might be required and conversely, it is more likely that fewer sessions will be needed than have been allowed for. In both cases the CfD practitioner follows the client.

Of course, significant improvement on outcome measures can prompt useful discussion of whether and when an ending is indicated. Similarly when a client is not improving this may be a prompt to stop therapy and try something else. Lack of improvement isn't a reason to prolong therapy; it may be a good reason to stop doing it.

The number of sessions is not a prescription which *must* be followed, it is an allocation which may be taken as required with the proviso that the extent of therapy is adjusted as a matter of client need and clinical judgement. CfD best practice suggests that the number of sessions should neither be added to or shortened on the basis of uninformed protocol or local rules, since CfD best practice is flexible and client-led as supported by both research evidence and NICE guidelines. CfD provides a theoretically coherent and practically consistent method for establishing the length of the therapeutic relationship in each individual case.

Working briefly and assessment

In psychological helping, practitioners have three ways of apprehending the clients' needs for treatment – diagnosis, formulation and assessment. Whilst these procedures appear to share a general aim, they tackle the issue from very different philosophical positions.

Diagnosis is the most formal of these procedures, and is also the term most popularly used by the public at large. Some clients can find a diagnosis something of a relief, as they find it reassuring to have a name for, and validation of, their distress, and furthermore diagnosis gives access to treatment. It implies a level of medicalisation and categorisation that makes it a contentious notion for probably the majority of PCE therapists. Bayne et al. (1999) list the main PCE objections to diagnosis and these help us tease out the differences between diagnosis and assessment. Then, incorporating Jerold Bozarth's comments on assessment, we take some opportunities to assemble an approach to assessment suitable for CfD. Bayne's criticisms of diagnosis and labels are comprehensive and include:

- diagnostic labels are often poorly defined and meaningless
- labels can become self-fulfilling prophesies
- labels beget formulaic treatments
- labels focus on history rather than present experience and potential for future change

- practitioners can become preoccupied with pathology and underestimate a client's strengths
- diagnosis can lead clients to become dependent upon experts
- diagnostic labels have a superficial appearance of scientific objectivity

However formidable these objections appear, they do help us understand that assessment does not equal diagnosis – assessment can be a process which facilitates therapeutic engagement rather than stifling it. Indeed, research shows that assessment interviews can have a therapeutic effect in and of themselves (Poston and Hanson, 2010). Appropriate explanations from the therapist set in a genuinely collaborative way of working, the therapist as companion rather than expert, and emphasis on the client's experience and narrative rather than diagnostic manual language, all contribute to constructing assessment positively as an assistance to therapy, not an obstacle.

In classical person-centred practice, the status of assessment is not clear-cut, since Jerold Bozarth (1998: 127) on the one hand declares that 'Psychological assessment as generally conceived is incongruent with the basic assumptions of client-centered theory', yet on the other hand goes on to discuss situations in which assessment may be considered by person-centred therapists, in the service of the client's 'self-authority' (ibid.: 128). He lists three circumstances where person-centred therapists could engage in assessment by the use of measures, as follows:

- the client requests assessment or the use of measures
- the agency or professional setting may require assessment
- the client and therapist might have to make a decision regarding future treatment suggested by such mediators of therapeutic possibilities as agency protocols, funding or the law. Assessment or diagnostic tools might afford an 'objective' view which could inform the client's and therapist's decision (ibid.: 128–31)

We can also adapt Bozarth's (ibid.: 130) axioms for a model of person-centred careers counselling to Counselling for Depression, to be applicable to assessment thus:

- the CfD practitioner has attitudes and behaviours which focus on promoting the inherent wisdom of the client
- there is an initial emphasis on a particular area of client concern, in this case, depression
- there are opportunities for the client to test their emerging concept of self with outcome measures
- the CfD practitioner has certain information and skills available to the client through which the goal of ameliorating depression can be implemented

So, in psychological therapy services associated with CfD, assessment involves getting a sense of the problem from the client's own point of view, looking at the history and development of the problem(s), getting a sense of the client's resilience and vulnerabilities and collaboratively agreeing a course of therapy. We hope that this short section does more than render assessment barely acceptable: something that practitioners do – only because they *must* – whilst holding their noses. Our intention is to lay the foundation for assessment to be creatively developed and implemented by CfD practitioners within their local service framework. It is an important element of good practice when working briefly in NHS settings. In Chapter 4 we explore both formal and informal assessment in more detail.

Working briefly with the experience of depression

Counselling for Depression necessarily presses the client and therapist to work with the primary presenting symptoms – the experience of depression. It appears to impose a limit, a focus on the *entire therapeutic endeavour* – namely to work with depression. However, we have seen in Chapter 4 how varied the experiences of depression can be, both between clients and from moment-to-moment in the same client. Depression is a complex set of experiences within a complex matrix of life experiences. The client's experiences are described as *symptoms* and the client will most likely be seeking relief from them, but the prime task of CfD is to identify and understand the experiences underlying the symptoms and seek resolution, rather than simply ameliorate the symptoms at a relatively superficial level.

CfD may begin with the focus of 'working with depression', but with its modus operandi of following the client, the counsellor will, together with the client, discover the salient intra- and interpersonal factors which are implicated in the psychological distress and there is no telling where this will lead. We must remind ourselves that the client's internal wisdom – on which therapeutic movement in CfD is predicated – will most likely not absolutely follow diagnostic categories or theoretical systems, even though CfD does propose some tentative conceptualisations (see Chapter 6). Therapists must not be distracted by the nature of, e.g., time limits, focusing the therapeutic relationship on the limits themselves, rather than the experiences and therapeutic process of the client. Appreciating the internal wisdom of the client includes appreciating the client's ability creatively to engage with the world – specifically, creatively to engage with the limits of the current therapeutic relationship. Following the client is not simply the first position in CfD, it must be an enlightening omnipresence, even when practice becomes task-focused and specific. Following the client and trusting their actualising process will remind therapists just how creatively 'self-righting' (Bohart and Tallman, 2010) clients can be.

Working briefly and structure[1]

Keith Tudor (Tudor, 2008) discusses how the imposition of time limits might lead the counsellor to think that it is necessary to impose some or more structure (in the sense

---

[1] Here we are using 'structure' to mean the framework of content and process (what happens next), rather than the setting out and aligning of expectations.

of framework) on therapy sessions, i.e. that formatting or sequencing the work makes it more time-efficient. Tudor makes it clear that he does not think that increasing structure necessarily follows from working in a time-limited way. We note that the term 'structure' is ill-defined, even in Tudor's discussion, but he uses classical non-directive person-centred therapy as his baseline. With this as the baseline, *any* structure would be seen as an iatrogenic imposition, drawing power and control to the therapist and away from the client.

Discussion regarding the degree of structure that is acceptable always returns to drawing a line, creating a limit or prescribing a degree. It is difficult to maintain a discussion of the possibility of *no* structure without stretching the feasibility of practice beyond what most would consider practicable in anything other than private practice. What is clear though, is that neither PCT, EFT nor CfD has a required implicit processional framework or works in ordered stages, so the mindful application of any such framework by the therapist would be a definite and deliberate change in the architecture of the therapeutic relationship. The first task of a therapist so minded would be to explain the theoretical basis for the introduction of structure and how it would improve the therapy. Within existing PCE and CfD theory, there is little to suggest that structure would make a positive contribution. The imperative to work with the client's idiosyncratic structure, or lack of it, remains intact.

The only construction implicit in CfD is that imposed by the limited number of sessions. The therapist's first imperative is to structure the relationship positively and hopefully (above). Next the therapist is advised to keep the fact of the limited number of sessions on the table, so to speak. This requires a degree of sensitive awareness which should be well within the skills set of a good therapist. One extension to the practice of a more classical therapist would be to review the therapy in as non-intrusive a way as possible at reasonably regular intervals. Miller (2010), for example, calls this 'feedback-informed treatment' (FIT) and makes concrete suggestions for integrating into practice gentle enquiries such as 'How is this going?', 'Are you finding these sessions helpful' and 'Has anything been especially helpful?'

Working briefly and direction

Directivity is a contentious issue in the context of working briefly. Whereas Tudor (2008) cautions against letting time limits push the therapist to be more directive, Gibbard (2004; 2007) explains how an increase in directivity *is* necessary to help the client achieve their goals within a limited number of sessions. The degree to which the counsellor directs elements of the therapeutic hour is a matter of significance for PCE therapies. An aim of therapy is for the client to develop a greater internal locus of evaluation and a key factor in this process is letting control of the therapeutic process rest with the client. The therapist taking control of aspects of therapy or being the expert is considered antitherapeutic – simply adding to any possible feelings of helplessness and loss of agency felt by the client. In CfD, the therapist seeks to restore the client's sense of self-agency by arranging the helping relationship around the central pillar of trust in the client's experience, internal wisdom and personal power, however fragile the client might initially feel it to be. This control can be taken from or given back to the client in many ways and by many degrees. CfD practice is based on a non-categorising, non-judgemental attitude; establishing a collaborative relationship; following the client's experience and respecting their preferences and choices as wise; not leading them to 'expert' solutions; sharing knowledge when requested; making tentative offers of ways of working in a cooperative relationship. With these characteristics the CfD practitioner constructs the level of non-directivity in the helping relationship in sharp contrast to one where the counsellor is a consultant, diagnostician, advisor or expert administrator of psychotechnology.

Later in this book we examine how CfD offers the client a range of possible task-oriented ways of working derived from emotion-focused therapy. In CfD practice this involves noticing issues and processes that the client finds problematic, checking with the client that these are areas of significant importance and offering to focus empathically on what is important for the client at their own pace, rather than *introducing* techniques. We outline the theoretical basis of these interventions in Chapter 8 and give examples of their use in practice in Chapter 9. They are offered in CfD as a matter of clinical judgement on the understanding that they are part of the collaborative venture of therapy – one person making suggestions informed by experience in the moment-to-moment relationship in the service of helping the other. They should be offered in such a way as to make it equally possible for the client to consider them, take them up, refuse them or put them aside to be tried later – so it is entirely possible that the client will eschew any offers of task-oriented elements, negotiated or otherwise. In this case, the counsellor proceeds with person-centred therapy as usual, since for some clients, freedom from direction and external loci of control is the very key to removing the threat which is locking the self-structure in incongruence. The counsellor continues to trust the client's internal wisdom to choose or refuse offers, whichever feels most helpful.

This 'default position' of trusting the client's internal wisdom is in contrast to approaches which might require counsellors to interpret the client's behaviour as 'resistant' or 'avoidant' and implement designated interventions. When we suggest counsellors work with limits positively, this is no more than a manifestation of the theory-derived obligation to understand all of the client's behaviour as being the best they can do at the time and that they know their own experiences better than the therapist. In Rogers' terms, the client behaves at all times 'as an organised whole' with 'one basic tendency ... to maintain and enhance ...' themselves (1951: 486), or, put even more simply: 'It is the *client* who knows what hurts, what directions to go, what problems are crucial, what experiences have been deeply buried' (Rogers, 1961: 11–12).

PCE theorists and practitioners identify two important domains of direction in therapy – the direction of content and the direction of process (see Sanders, 2012). These continue to be vigorously debated, and we briefly describe each and their implications now.

Directing content

The content of a session literally means the topics of conversation, client narrative or what the client talks about. It is easy for a counsellor to influence this content, and this can happen in a number of ways, for example:

- by choosing which elements of the client's narrative to reflect
- by being simply and atheoretically curious about certain elements, or saying 'tell me more about …'
- by believing that certain topics are more germane (e.g. to the issue of depression) and asking the client to follow them – a counsellor might have an idiosyncratic theory regarding the importance of, for example, certain feelings or past experiences

It hardly bears repeating the elements of PCE theory which assert that there is nothing in PCE theory to suggest that directing the content of the session is a good thing. Indeed, as alluded to above, content direction establishes the therapist as more of an expert in the client's experience than the client themselves and this is seen as antitherapeutic. The difficulty is that in extremis or when under pressure due to time limits, the therapist might feel pushed to be more active and 'do something'. This urge can be assuaged by taking control of the content of the session and directing the client to areas of experience that the therapist thinks more useful. However in CfD there is no evidence base to back up such direction of content and the basic CfD therapeutic stance is to avoid content direction in general and to certainly not resort to it in desperation if either the client, or worse still, the counsellor is anxious about time limits.

Directing process

Process direction is altogether a more contentious issue. Classical person-centred practitioners will understand process direction to be as absolutely antitherapeutic as content direction and for those who wish to resolutely pursue a classical non-directive practice, it will be at least *difficult* to incorporate any interventions into a therapy session. In Chapter 2 we explain how some of the evidence base of CfD is provided by the more active elements of emotion-focused therapy and it is in approaching these interventions that the counsellor will be directing the therapeutic process. In Chapter 8 we explore the CfD stance and how these interventions are integrated, and in Chapter 9 we offer examples of how they might be incorporated into practice.

In CfD, we expect many clients to identify specific therapeutic aims in collaboration with the counsellor. These general aims are likely to point to more specific therapeutic tasks which in turn suggest particular process interventions. These will be described in Chapter 8 and demonstrated in Chapter 9. Some of these process interventions have the effect of helping the client move more quickly to a nexus of energy, stuckness or opportunity in their experiential landscape. The rationale for making such an offer would be therapeutic, but the intervention might well have the secondary – hopefully welcome – effect of moving the process along more quickly towards a satisfactory resolution, hence mentioning them here in the chapter on working briefly.

As we have explained previously, process direction interventions are offers, not instructions. They are made as part of a collaborative stance, the nuances of which depend upon the attitudes and skill set of the counsellor. CfD good practice dictates that the offer of appropriate interventions is seen by the client as a facilitative opportunity to achieve their self-identified goals, not expert prescriptions which must be followed to meet externally set outcome criteria.

The end of working briefly

As we have explained above, the actuality of having to work briefly presses the counsellor to reconsider many aspects of therapy, making them more likely to think that processes should be brought under the management of the therapist, rather than be left to unfold as natural, co-created experiences. The ending of the therapeutic relationship is another such event.

Given that in classical PCE practice the ending of therapy is left in the control of the client, it is perhaps understandable that some CfD counsellors will believe that they have to take control of the ending of therapy when a time limit is imposed. However, this is a misunderstanding of the CfD relationship as a co-created helping episode. Clients approach and enter the Counselling for Depression relationship in the full knowledge of the number of sessions available. It is somewhat infantilising of the client to suggest that if control of the ending does not reside with the client, it then automatically passes to the counsellor. In fact, the timing of the ending is always, and remains a moment of creative negotiation taking into account a number of factors, but now mindfully including the number of sessions available.

In the section on structuring (p. 120), we point out how many aspects of the relationship are introduced at the very beginning, and it will be a matter of routine for the typical number of sessions available in CfD to be announced in literature, at reception and then by the therapist in the first session. It is then that the die is cast in terms of how the ending will be dealt with. As a matter of good practice, counsellors must always be prepared for an ending which *does* remain under the client's control, either a negotiated natural ending because the client has achieved their goals in fewer than 20 sessions, or when the client terminates therapy unexpectedly. The latter case will provide material for supervision and other forms of professional review.

In any other circumstance, the approaching ending of the relationship should not come as a surprise. The opportunity for periodic consideration of it will be possible and is recommended as a process of constant, session-by-session monitoring of progress. This will allow the client and counsellor to negotiate further sessions if necessary or prepare to complete the therapeutic tasks planned in the earlier interviews. It also allows time for the client to prepare for life without therapy, since for some clients, the sessions will have become woven into their routine. Consideration of the transition to life without therapy needs be no more complicated than checking how prepared the client is for the end of counselling and working with their responses. Their readiness for moving on in their lives can be gauged by the degree to which they look forward, make plans, and talk about future events and ways of coping.

Counselling for Depression has no one-size-fits-all prescription for the maintenance of wellbeing after the end of counselling, neither do we expect counsellors to make suggestions from a CfD approved list, yet we do encourage counsellors to raise this issue with clients. Such exploration can open up discussion of what works for them in their individual circumstances and gives clients an opportunity to evaluate any changes in lifestyle they may have made during the course of therapy. It should go without saying that the counsellor empathically follows and explores options with the client rather than making judgements about lifestyle changes. As the sessions unfold, the client might develop therapeutic tasks which specifically relate to life after counselling. Working towards the end of a counselling relationship should give opportunities for such themes to develop and be addressed.

Some clients' level of need is such that they are distinctly fearful of ending. For those few clients who approach the ending of the therapeutic relationship with some trepidation, time must be allowed for appropriate therapeutic tasks to emerge, be worked with and hopefully resolved. This is easier to achieve if it is prepared for during structuring early in the relationship and the topic will often arise naturally if a client has real concerns. As always, CfD best practice is to allow sufficient time for non-judgemental empathic exploration, collaboratively identifying the relevant therapeutic tasks and working to resolve them.

Clearly signalled during structuring, and properly included in progress reviews, the end of counselling has the potential to be a positive, realistic review of goals achieved and tasks set for everyday life in the future.

Epilogue

There can be no doubt that working briefly presents PCE therapists with considerable challenges, yet CfD does not make a virtue out of working to a time schedule. The aim is to achieve therapeutic change in the most respectful and sustainable way possible, given that research tells us that a significant number of clients choose therapy lasting fewer than 20 sessions and that the most therapeutic gain is made in the first few sessions of a counselling relationship. This research illustrates how fruitful it can be to make the client the driver of the therapeutic process, rather than working through a set system of interventions. The realities of 21st century statutory healthcare may well demand that limits be set and that therapeutic relationships last only so long, and Counselling for Depression asks therapists and clients to respond both positively and creatively to this challenge whilst putting the needs of the client first and last. CfD therapists are encouraged to develop their own idiosyncratic creative responses to working briefly in the service of each client with whom they work.

8

The Counselling for Depression Therapeutic Stance and Auxiliary Techniques

> Competences covered in Chapter 8
>
> **The CfD therapeutic stance**
>
> G12-Ability to use measures to guide therapy and to monitor outcomes
> B7-Ability to experience and communicate empathy
> B8-Ability to experience and to communicate a fundamentally accepting attitude to clients
> B9-Ability to maintain authenticity in the therapeutic relationship
> B6-Ability to work with the client to establish a therapeutic aim
>
> **CfD auxiliary techniques**
>
> S1-Ability to help clients to access and express emotions
> S2-Ability to help clients articulate emotions
> S3-Ability to help clients reflect on and develop emotional meanings
> S4-Ability to help clients make sense of experiences that are confusing and distressing
>
> (Competences are listed in Appendix 1)

Introduction

Counselling for Depression is an integrated time-limited approach comprising person-centred therapy and elements of emotion-focused therapy. CfD practice is underpinned by a competence framework introduced and explained in detail in Chapter 3. In brief, the CfD-related competences are divided into *basic* CfD competences and *specific* CfD competencies.[1] The current volume presents this competence framework in terms of a basic CfD therapeutic stance and auxiliary CfD techniques. The basic therapeutic stance may be sufficient for many clients in and of itself. The auxiliary techniques are offered as acknowledgement of the particular needs of clients experiencing depression.

CfD is a collaborative approach, engaging with and employing the agency of the client from the first moment of the first session. It is relational, not formulaic or prescriptive, and an important active therapeutic factor is the self of the counsellor. How therapy unfolds – specifically the integration of the basic therapeutic stance and the auxiliary techniques – will be different in each case, determined by a number of interacting factors, including:

- the self of the counsellor
- the counsellor's personal reading of basic therapeutic stance
- the client's level of processing
- the client's therapeutic goals
- the client's unfolding lived experience: including their symptoms
- specific techniques offered by the counsellor and negotiated with the client
- the counsellor's clinical judgement

In this chapter we outline the basic therapeutic stance and the auxiliary techniques which, in collaboration with the client, can be offered in a coherent, integrated framework in response to the client's goals and developing process in therapy. In Chapter 9 we will present examples and annotated vignettes of fictional therapy sessions to illustrate Counselling for Depression in practice.

The CfD basic therapeutic stance

The basic therapeutic stance is described in the basic CfD competences (see Chapter 3) which build upon the core professional competences described in the generic therapeutic competences. Since CfD is a therapeutic approach intended to be provided by experienced counsellors, this volume assumes readers will have an established understanding of, and skills in, the generic therapeutic competences. This section, therefore, elaborates the CfD basic therapeutic stance with this assumption in mind. The basic therapeutic stance of the Counselling for Depression therapist is simply stated:

- establish the person-centred therapeutic conditions
- emphasise collaboration (in contrast to more classical person-centred therapy)
- formulate the client's therapeutic goals by negotiation
- initiate regular review of progress and client's goals
- positively engage with the time limited-nature of CfD

---

[1] *Counselling for Depression Competency Framework*, Improving Access to Psychological Therapies, www.iapt.nhs.uk/silo/files/counselling-for-depression-competency-framework.pdf (retrieved 20/05/13).

Since experienced person-centred therapists will have a clear understanding of the first of these elements, we will cover the therapeutic conditions in an abbreviated form, but with references for further reading regarding recent developments where appropriate. The remaining elements were introduced in Chapter 5 and will be further elaborated below on pp. 139–45.

It is important to understand that in CfD, the person-centred therapeutic conditions are offered in a time-limited context. This affects the offer and how they might be used by the client. It will be the case that the conditions themselves will be sufficient for a proportion of clients, bearing in mind that in CfD they are offered in the context of a collaborative style, formulating the client's goals and engaging with the time-limited nature of the work. This is the 'first position' in CfD. Other CfD techniques, extensions and therapeutic offers, based on the client's unfolding goals and needs, will be offered according to the counsellor's clinical judgement negotiated in collaboration with the client.

The person-centred therapeutic conditions

This section concerns the three therapist-provided conditions from Rogers' six therapeutic conditions (Rogers, 1959), congruence, or authenticity; unconditional positive regard, or acceptance; and empathy. We also note that Rogers' original sixth condition is that the client must experience the qualities of empathy and acceptance. These conditions offered by the therapist are best thought of as attitudes held, rather than skills practised. Grant (1990/2002) differentiates between principled and instrumental directivity in classical client-centred therapy – here we wish to make a similar, more generalised, distinction between holding all of the therapeutic conditions with deep conviction as *attitudes*, in contrast to performing, dispensing or acting out the conditions as *skills*. The aims of these two ways of being are completely different. In the first way of being, the conditions are provided as the very fabric of the therapeutic relationship – therapeutic offers in themselves. They are not being used as instruments, but provided for their own sake in the understanding that they are healing relational moments in and of themselves in concert with the client's own internal wisdom. This is the basic Counselling for Depression stance. Other therapeutic approaches might use empathy, for example, as an instrument or tool in order to gather information for diagnosis or formulation, or to establish trust or treatment compliance.

Empathy

The utility of empathy as a therapeutic condition is built upon the fact that Counselling for Depression is a phenomenological approach. It puts the client's reality, their narrative or story at the centre of the therapeutic endeavour and the only way into this story is by being empathic.

In Chapter 5, pp. 91–2, we pointed out the importance of understanding empathy as a *process* (Rogers, 1980), whereby the counsellor attempts to '*perceive* the internal frame of reference of another with *accuracy*, and with the emotional components and meanings … *as if* one were the other person, but without ever losing the "as if" condition' (Rogers, 1959: 210).

Thus the 'internal frame of reference' is a person's unique viewpoint, their private world of perceptions, experiences and meanings, which according to Rogers, 'can never be known to another except through empathic inference and then can never be perfectly known' (Rogers, 1959: 210). So, the empathic counsellor perceives the world of the other person, but does not experience it.

Rogers (1959: 213) makes an interesting point when he says that it is not *essential* that the therapist *communicates* the conditions – he asserts that what is essential is that the client *receives* or experiences empathy. To give an idea of how the client might experience empathy, Rogers quoted an item from Godfrey Barrett-Lennard's Relationship Inventory (Barrett-Lennard, 1962) as follows: 'He understands what my experience feels like to me' (Rogers, 1980: 143). The idea that it is not essential for the counsellor to communicate empathy in order for the client to receive it also makes way for Bozarth's concept of 'idiosyncratic empathy' (Bozarth, 1984/2001), or in Rogers' (1959: 213) own terms, 'often it is by some casual remark, or involuntary facial expression' that empathy is communicated, rather than the deliberate intent of the counsellor.

There are a number of ways of communicating empathy including:

- reflection
- paraphrasing
- the 'empathic following response' (see Brodley, 2002 for an account of the wide range of possible empathic following responses)
- evocative empathy (Rice, 1974/2001)
- embodied empathy (Cooper, 2001)
- 'subtle' empathy – Rose Cameron extends understanding of empathy beyond the cognitive and affective to include it in spiritual or transpersonal terms, sensing the client through 'energetic contact' (Cameron, 2003)

One thing that all methods of communicating empathy share is the use of a tentative tone and frequent checking to make sure that the counsellor has understood the client correctly. The frequency of this checking is a finely judged art – sufficient to ensure that the therapist is accurate and that the client senses the therapist's effort, but not a constant series of interruptions, interfering with the client's telling of their story. The use of reflection as the single empathic tool has been criticised as 'parroting' or 'wooden', but in a letter to Carl Rogers, John Shlien strikes the right note for describing empathy in CfD practice when he says:

> Reflection is unfairly damned … It is an instrument of artistic virtuosity in the hands of a sincere, intelligent, empathic listener. (Shlien, cited in Rogers, 1986/2002: 13)

In 1974, Laura North Rice talked about being empathic in a way which went beyond the immediate expressions of the client. The responses she described are intended to attend to what is implicit in the client's communications and extrapolate from the actual utterances of the client to open up potential experiences rather than simply to follow by paraphrasing and reflection. Rice (1974/2001) described this as 'unfolding' the client's experience and called it *evocative empathy*. The aim is both to 'bring to life what it is like to be the client in that situation' (Rice, 1974/2001: 121) and enable the client to progressively deepen and enrich their experience through increasingly accurate constructions and expressions. Rice's work is important to CfD since it comes via EFT and surfaces here as *systematic evocative unfolding*.

Systematic evocative unfolding is a recent iteration of Rice's evocative empathy, so named to emphasise the unfolding, elaborative effect on the client's experience. Here empathy not only uncovers the client's experience but allows it to develop new, more elaborate, forms. This acknowledges the way human experience itself is continuously moving 'forward' carrying all past experience at its edge. Experience, even memory, is not fixed in a state, does not stand still, but is being continuously constructed and (in the case of memory) reconstructed. Systematic evocative unfolding facilitates this process in the understanding that it is in the continuous construction of experience that new understandings are born and resolution can take place. There are sufficient differences between reflection and empathic following responses and systematic evocative unfolding for the latter to be considered a technique in its own right. We will describe it in more detail along with the client issues with which it best offered later in this chapter on p. 147.

Embodied empathy (Cooper, 2001) deserves a special mention since we have been careful to point out the importance of the embodied nature of the self and embodied experience in Counselling for Depression theory. Cooper describes the requirement to attend to the embodied nature of experiencing by drawing attention to the ways that the therapist may empathise and resonate with the client's physical presence. It is easy for counsellors to confine themselves to the verbal in therapeutic relationships – focusing on listening at the expense of looking. Regardless of the emphasis on listening in the literature, we remember that empathy is all the more powerful when we use our full range of senses in being with the client and entering their world.

Rose Cameron's descriptions of 'subtle contact' (Cameron, 2003) both echo Cooper's reminder to use all of our senses, and also points out that for some clients, their experience goes beyond that which is tangible to the counsellor. Rather than dismiss such experiences, Cameron urges us to consider the transpersonal and also the cultural context of individual clients' experiences of themselves and the world. It is easy to be complacent and not stretch ourselves to apprehend the almost unimaginable range of experiences that a client will describe.

Importantly, for the purposes of understanding the CfD therapeutic stance, we do more than take it as read that the therapist is skilled in communicating these therapist-provided conditions. Measuring adherence to the competences of CfD employs a method of rating similar to that pioneered by Barrett-Lennard (Barrett-Lennard, 1962), except it is not clients who evaluate the counsellor's communication, but independent raters trained to use the PCEPS, presented in more detail in Chapter 10.

Acceptance and positive regard

Rogers' original term 'unconditional positive regard' pointed to two elements, non-judgemental, unconditional acceptance and prizing or warmth. In Counselling for Depression, both elements are viewed as actively therapeutic and essential. In PCE theory, acceptance and positive regard are a necessary condition of therapeutic change because rigidity, stuck process and defensiveness in the personality are a result of threat in various forms. Revisiting Proposition XVII from Rogers' (1951: 517) writing we find the simple recipe for revision of the self-structure and reintegration of incongruent experience where he says: 'Under certain conditions, involving primarily complete absence of any threat to the self-structure ...' the self-structure can be revised. One of the best ways of removing threat is to be non-judgementally acceptant, or as Jerold Bozarth puts it: 'unconditional positive regard is the curative factor in client-centred theory' (Bozarth, 1998: 83).

The basic therapeutic stance in CfD is to create as threat-free an environment as possible *and* simultaneously warmly affirmative, positively valuing, or 'prizing' the client. The provision of this safe, prizing relationship over a period of time will help the client spontaneously recover or develop for the first time, *positive self-regard* – an important process in balancing, or preventing the conditions of development for, self-critical elements within the self-structure. A safe, warm environment is one in which hope and sufficient freedom to experiment with new ways of thinking, feeling and acting are all more likely. And, sometimes, such an environment, in and of itself, can be a welcome oasis for people whose lives are blighted by the relentless experience of the symptoms of depression. Remember that this condition is not offered in isolation – along with being understood and accompanied by a counsellor who is transparently genuine, the basic CfD therapeutic stance presents a powerful opportunity for positive change.

However, the provision of a warm, accepting environment can be a challenge for many clients as well. Some people come from a family where the infant's need for love was responded to with neglect, violence or abuse. For them, warm unconditional acceptance could be puzzling or untrustworthy. For other clients with particularly active inner-critics a warm accepting environment might cause their critical selves to bombard them with thoughts suggesting they are undeserving and not worthy of respect. These are just a couple of examples of the fantastic variety of ways people will react to acceptance and positive regard. Indeed there is no way of predicting how clients will experience the basic therapeutic stance in CfD, which is why empathy, the effort to see the world from the client's viewpoint, is such an important constituent of this stance. It enables the counsellor to encounter, and work with from moment to moment, the obstacles to therapeutic progress that might beset the client's change project.

Genuineness

Genuineness as a necessary therapist provided condition in CfD springs from Rogers' condition 'congruence'. Vigorous debate surrounds all of Rogers' therapeutic conditions, and none more so than congruence, since Rogers himself used the term in several different contexts to mean frankly different things. Rather than revisit these debates, we point readers to the work of Gill Wyatt (Wyatt, 2001) for the most comprehensive collection available debating congruence, and for a brief recent discussion, Cornelius-White (2013).

Readers will be familiar with some or all of the other terms used to describe genuineness, including: being real (rather than in a role), authentic, being 'all of a piece', natural, honest, unpretentious, transparent and so on.

The notion of genuineness sets CfD practice in contrast to some other therapeutic offerings in the 21st century. It ensures that CfD is seen primarily as a relational approach – that is, therapy in a relationship with a real person. It may seem nonsensical to readers unfamiliar with humanistic therapies to say 'with a real person', but it is worth noting that therapy is sometimes offered in settings where the professional role of the therapist, or the type of help offered, is likely to dictate that the helper will be experienced as a technical expert, adviser or educator, rather than a companion. Clients referred directly by medical practitioners might expect their therapist to be more like a doctor, and some will have already experienced the psychoeducation offered by self-help texts or computer software as sometimes impersonal and distancing.

Some therapists are, of professional necessity, two-faced. That is they are required to face in two directions at once: for example, they listen attentively to the client but do so feigning genuine interest in the person of the client in pursuit of information for a diagnosis. Even in the early 21st century, being genuine, authentic or 'real' might seem challenging and the idea that all psychological treatment practitioners should 'be themselves' without a professional façade is not a foregone conclusion.

Being genuine is another condition which demands a well-balanced touch from the counsellor. Gill Wyatt explains that genuineness has three facets (Wyatt, 2001: 84–5):

- *Being myself* means being real rather than putting on a professional facade, or acting out the role of counsellor. It also means that the counsellor can be relied upon to be truthful and give honest feedback if asked, rather than be polite in order to protect the client's feelings, for example. However, the counsellor must also judge the therapeutic benefit of such honesty on a moment-to-moment basis.
- *Psychological maturity* indicates the degree to which the counsellor is open to their own experience. In common-or-garden terms we might say that the counsellor is "sorted", "together", or the elements of their personality are integrated, in harmony – they do not behave defensively, are open to looking at, or reflecting on, their own behaviour and their own personal qualities. Most importantly, the more open the counsellor is to their experience, the less threatened they will be by the challenging ideas and behaviour of other people, making them more accepting of others.
- *The personal style of the therapist* refers to the notion that it's not necessarily *what* the counsellor does but *how* they do it – the counsellor's *manner* – are they comfortable, confident and safe? Clients are very good at detecting discomfort, inauthenticity or falseness and when they get a whiff of it the therapeutic relationship will suffer.

We would add a further quality to Wyatt's list: that of 'presence' – a quality closely allied with genuineness. This is yet another term with many meanings in person-centred and experiential psychology, but here we mean the quality of being wholly present in the moment. By 'wholly' we mean, in all of the possible domains of human relating: cognitively, emotionally, physically/viscerally. And by 'in the moment' we mean inhabiting and being fully aware in body and mind of, one's own experiences and offering this in the service of the client in the present moment. It is a state of alertness and intimate contact with the client's world that will be familiar to person-centred and experiential therapists. We associate presence with genuineness since it is virtually impossible to be inauthentic or lacking in genuineness when being present in the manner described. This is because the genuine and fully present therapist is also transparent, or open. In Counselling for Depression, there is a need to be congruent in the role of counsellor from within which we operate – integrated and committed to the responsibility of helping. There is simply no reason to *not* be transparent, open, fully present and genuinely involved. There is no danger in this, indeed it is a *requirement* in order to be effective and therapeutic.

Experienced person-centred and integrative person-centred therapists will be well-acquainted with the concepts of genuineness and presence and know that good practice is achieved through personal therapy, ongoing personal and professional development and supervision. It can sometimes be more difficult for therapists who have previously operated from a more rigid professional role to feel comfortable and competent when it comes to relating genuinely in the counselling room.

Collaboration

Collaboration is working with the awareness of what both the client and the counsellor can contribute towards the client achieving their therapeutic goals. In a more classical person-centred practice, active collaboration would ensue only at the request of the client. In Counselling for Depression, it is consciously acknowledged by the counsellor as one of the modus operandi of the relationship. The features of the collaborative relationship in CfD are:

- acknowledgement that the client knows what's best for them and has the ability to manage their own healing process
- acknowledgement that the counsellor has a set of understandings, skills and offerings that are intended to help clients locate and engage with their ability to self-heal and the counsellor is transparent about these
- the counsellor is an equal partner and companion in the therapeutic endeavour, not an expert with greater authority
- the client is encouraged to tell the counsellor when she is unhelpful or off the mark with her offerings
- the client is encouraged to be creative in their approach to their own hurts
- the counsellor's understanding that the client's experience is trustworthy and paramount
- the counsellor and client regularly review what is helpful and unhelpful in the sessions and both are prepared to act on this

Establishing a collaborative working relationship is particularly important in CfD since it is not simply 'person-centred therapy as usual', but an integrative approach which offers other techniques for specific issues that commonly affect people with depression. The counsellor must feel free to make offers of therapeutic techniques in the knowledge that the client is able to say 'yes' or 'no' to the offer from an emancipated position. Now, whilst there are no guarantees that this will be so, since the power relations in therapy are complex, establishing a collaborative alliance with the client is an important step towards this. The counsellor is working towards being trusted to make therapeutic offers in a non-authoritative, non-prescriptive way, leaving the client in control of the process. This is not window-dressing, or a technique to facilitate compliance. It is a theoretically consistent part of the process of building and maintaining a threat-free relationship.

The collaborative ethos is established as soon as possible so as to counter any expectations that the client might bring about the role of the therapist, e.g., that the counsellor is an expert on people's lives, or will be working from a medicalised frame-work, or will have all the answers, or prescribe exercises, etc. The CfD counsellor will establish this collaborative ethos partly by directly explaining what is likely to happen in CfD by way of introducing themselves, partly by their manner as a person and partly by their way of being as a counsellor. Although some therapeutic approaches do have a formal psychoeducational introduction, it would not be appropriate *formally* to set out the 'rules' of collaboration, or indeed any other aspect of the possible process of therapy, other than those aspects that would normally happen as part of the con-tracting process.

Formulation of therapeutic goals[2]

It is a simple enough aim to say that it is important that counsellors and clients establish a set of goals for the CfD sessions that they can both agree to. When we say 'both agree to' we mean that the therapist will have shared with the client the degree to which they think the goals are achievable. This should be a statement of gently realistic appraisal without brutally dashing clients' hopes on the one hand, whilst on the other holding the understanding that extraordinary change *is* possible. When we say 'a simple enough aim' we mean that it is too naïve to think that simply asking the client what their goals are and making a note, will in most cases, be effective. Many clients, on being asked 'What

---

[2] Throughout the book we use the terms therapeutic *goals* and therapeutic *aims*. Some definitions have goals as smaller steps towards larger aims. Others that a goal is a target, and the aim is the direction you take to 'hit' the target. Here, however, we are using both terms loosely to mean the same things, i.e., there is no difference in our usage between aims and goals. This loose usage is also more in keeping with the notion that clients will define their goals loosely and life itself is loose and forgiving in definitions.

would you like to achieve by the end of these sessions?' will offer a variation of the entirely reasonable answer 'I want to stop being depressed', or equally global, 'I want to put my life back together', or 'I want to feel happy again', and so on. While these are heartfelt expressions of how the client feels, it is the global, undifferentiated nature of these goals that is problematic. They are certainly understandable, but are not helpful in finding the road to resolution without further clarification and differentiation.

The skill of formulating goals is helping the client elaborate their experience and discriminate the elements within it that make the next step possible. Sometimes this might be metaphorically a small step forward, sometimes a step to the side and some-times a large step back. When the options are laid out, the client, in collaboration with the counsellor, will decide which step to take. This process will be reviewed frequently and U-turns or reformulation of the goals are also acceptable, if not inevitable steps along the way. Although we keep repeating the term 'goal', we do not want to imply that this activity is overly instrumental. We could rephrase it in terms of locating a focus for therapeutic process and movement.

When a client makes a general statement of their global goal, the counsellor helps them explore and unpack its undifferentiated, blanket nature by being empathic – in any or all of the forms discussed above. Goal-setting might appear to be a cognitive, logical activity, but counsellors must not limit themselves to verbal, cognitively oriented ways of being in this process. CfD good practice suggests that locating a focus for therapy is a creative process, wherein clients might be helped to evoke experiences on the edge of awareness or set themselves goals involving bodily sensations such as 'getting rid of the lump of lead in my gut'. It is the counsellor's responsibility to hold the goal-setting task during the early, and indeed subsequent stages of, the therapeutic relationship.

Assessment

Assessment is an integral part of CfD in a way that it has not been in traditional person-centred and experiential practice. There are a number of reasons for this. NHS psychological services are multi-professional and CfD is just one form of therapy offered within these services. This inevitably raises the question of how can clients be directed to the therapy that will provide them with most benefit. A collaborative assessment process founded on the use of the core conditions provides the best answer to this. Since assessment is linked to both diagnosis and CfD in stepped care, and working briefly, it is introduced and explained alongside stepped care in Chapter 4, pp. 61–3; and working briefly in Chapter 5, pp. 124–6.

Reviewing progress

Reviewing client progress and eliciting feedback from clients is an integral part of CfD and has become formalised with the use of sessional outcome measures such as those which make up the IAPT minimum dataset (PHQ-9,[3] GAD-7,[4] WSAS[5]). In Counselling for Depression there is more than one type or level of progress review serving more than one purpose. It is best practice that the CfD practitioner introduces the idea and forms of reviewing progress during the initial structuring of the relationship. Reviewing can focus on:

- progress towards goals, both in-session and between sessions
- how clients are experiencing therapy – its quality and usefulness (see also feedback-informed treatment (FIT) for another contemporary perspective on this (Miller, 2010))
- symptomatic levels of distress and subjective wellbeing

The review process can be carried out in a number of formal and informal ways, ranging from discussion to structured questionnaires/psychometric instruments. Some of these data collection protocols are required by IAPT services (see Chapter 10) and others may be service-specific or practitioner-specific for research or auditing purposes. Emerging best practice in the field recommends sessional data collection and this tends to be well received by the majority of clients.

Here we are concerned with the first two types of progress review: reviewing the progress of individual clients and choosing to incorporate the principles of feedback-informed treatment into our practice. Collecting outcome data for IAPT (see Chapter 10), an individual service or agency (refer to your service/agency), or for the purpose of auditing one's own personal practice (see, e.g. Sanders and Wilkins, 2010), are all dealt with elsewhere as indicated.

It is useful to distinguish between good CfD therapeutic practice and the professional responsibilities which must be accepted as a practitioner working within an IAPT service. Reviewing individual client progress is seen as an essential element of the CfD basic therapeutic stance. We also encourage counsellors to explore and consider FIT. Both were introduced in Chapter 7 'Working Briefly' since working briefly is facilitated by regular reviews to avoid cul-de-sacs in therapy which may be tolerated or even desirable in unlimited therapy relationships.

Reviewing client progress, quality and usefulness of the therapy, and subjective wellbeing

In-session reviewing of the client's progress and subjective wellbeing is both an informal and formal process. The process begins during structuring in the opening minutes of the first session. It also has a natural place, informally, when making a clear set of goals

---

[3] Patient Health Questionnaire 9. Available online at e.g. http://iapt.nhs.uk/silo/files/phq9-and-gad7.doc (retrieved 07/06/2013).

[4] Generalised Anxiety Disorder 7. Available online at e.g. http://iapt.nhs.uk/silo/files/phq9-and-gad7.doc (retrieved 07/06/2013).

[5] Work and Social Adjustment Scale (Mundt et al., 2002: 461).

or foci for the counselling process. To be blunt it could be seen as pointless to go to the trouble of setting achievable goals without finding out whether they have been achieved to the satisfaction of the client.

Informal reviewing of client progress is also a reflective assessment of the relationship itself and 'how it is going' as much as it is an evaluation of the extent to which the client's goals are/are not being achieved. By this we mean that it is effectively a joint review of progress, i.e. of the counsellor in question and the client in question – a tacit acknowledgement of the relational nature of the therapeutic project. As such it might involve any or all of the following.

Progress towards goals – possible questions

- Are the goals set earlier still the correct goals?
- To what extent does the client think they have achieved the goal(s) in question?
- To what extent does the counsellor think the client has achieved the goal(s)?

  - If the goals have not been met, how can this be worked with – do any strategies emerge?
  - If the client is disappointed, how can this be addressed?
  - If the goals have been achieved, have any new ones spontaneously arisen, is it appropriate to set new goals or to prepare for an ending?

- At this stage in therapy does this review suggest that more sessions or fewer sessions might be needed?

  - If more sessions, is it appropriate to offer them in CfD or should a referral to another approach or service be considered?

Quality and usefulness of the treatment – possible questions

- Has anything worked particularly well in therapy so far?

  - If so what?

- Has anything obstructed therapy or not been useful?

  - If so what?

- To what extent has the counsellor met the client's needs and expectations?
- To what extent has the counsellor met their own expectations?

Symptoms and subjective wellbeing – possible questions

A simple general question such as 'How have you felt in yourself this last week?' (taken from the Psychological Outcome Profiles questionnaire (PSYCHLOPS)[6]) can help get a sense of a client's overall sense of wellbeing and how this may change over time. More specific enquiries regarding particular symptoms that may trouble clients

---

[6] www.psychlops.org (retrieved 11/11/2013).

could include the type that are included in commonly used measures such as the PHQ-9 and GAD-7, e.g.:

- At the moment are you bothered by:
    - feeling down, depressed or hopeless?
    - having trouble falling or staying asleep?
    - feeling tired or having little energy?
    - feeling nervous, anxious or on edge?
    - not being able to stop or control worrying?
    - becoming easily annoyed or irritable?

Clients' general sense of wellbeing and their evaluation of their more specific symptoms are good indicators as to whether or not they feel they are improving in therapy.

This list of issues that may be raised in a review (above) is long and this is just a guide – it is not intended to be comprehensive. If tackled literally and sequentially it would take up a big chunk of the session and could be excessively formal in a relational therapy – being potentially out of character for the therapist and out of place in the relationship. We expect that practitioners will understand that informal review of a client's progress and implementing FIT informal narrative to evaluate the usefulness of the therapy is best integrated into the session where appropriate and as seamlessly as possible.

Formal review is a requirement of IAPT and also increasingly a requirement of individual agencies or services. It is usually done in a short portion of the session specially set aside, at the beginning or end – whatever is most convenient or appropriate. Counsellors and their clients should collaborate on review procedures appropriate to their relationship and personal styles.

The frequency of formal review is also determined by both IAPT and local agency protocols. It is a requirement in IAPT to complete measures in each session. If an agency or service decides to use a particular measure there will be a protocol relating to when the measure should be used, e.g. PSYCHLOPS has to be used pre-, mid-, and post-therapy. This should be brought to the client's attention during structuring in the first session. This doesn't however mean that the client has to complete the measures; they can refuse consent and opt out of them if they wish. But if they opt in they agree to complete them according to protocol.

Having taken the trouble to ask the client how things are going, how you the counsellor are doing, and to review the relationship and its effectiveness, it is surely sensible to treat responses seriously and act on them. This means considering a variety of possible actions, from simply doing the common-sense thing (doing more of what helps and less of what doesn't) through to taking particular issues to supervision and importantly, asking the client what they would like to have happen as a result of the review. Their responses become grist to the mill of the therapeutic relationship – pointing to different ways of doing things, to new goals, to revisiting old ones, to referral to a different type of counselling or treatment, or to the end of the counselling. Reviews also often point to the frequently non-linear, asystematic nature of the change process and this can be a revelation to some clients. They may also reveal that a large portion, possibly the majority, of therapeutic change takes place outside the counselling sessions, in everyday life.

Reviews can be surprising, revealing completely unexpected issues and processes. Insofar as it is possible, prepare for the unexpected.

Finally, it can be the case that the counsellor's thoughts and feelings in and about the review might be very different from the client's. Of the many possible and quite obvious reasons for this – and remember the starting position in any client-centred therapy is to follow the client and their assessments – is the fact that clients sometimes get 'review-weary'. That is, they get effectively 'tired' of frequent reviews, both in that they begin to lack enthusiasm for the reviews, but also they get less and less able to discriminate the improvements. In contrast, with the benefit of a possibly different type of reflection and professional supervision, the counsellor is more likely to be able to maintain a fresh perspective. It is important that the counsellor is able to identify this process, or at least be aware of it. It can be a difficult set of issues to disentangle, and supervision is the best, possibly the only, place to do this.

CfD auxiliary techniques

At the start of this chapter we explained how the CfD competence framework is represented by the CfD therapeutic stance and the auxiliary techniques. Having described the therapeutic stance we now turn to the auxiliary techniques which are outlined in the competence framework as the specific CfD competences:

Ability to:

- help clients access and express emotions
- help clients articulate emotions
- help clients reflect on and develop emotional meanings
- help clients make sense of experiences that are confusing and distressing[7]

These competences are predicated on the principle that healthy psychological functioning involves being able to bring our feelings into awareness, being able to express and communicate these where appropriate and finally being able to appreciate their significance in terms of our lives and how we function. Interruptions to this process are usually experienced as distressing or problematic. It follows that in working with clients to identify points of difficulty and helping to facilitate more optimal functioning, counsellors assist clients in their self-development.

The auxiliary CfD techniques aim to help the client at particular points in the client's process which may be identified by either the counsellor or the client. Hence if the counsellor notices the client is out of touch with how they feel it is at this level that they

---

[7] See p. 6, *Counselling for Depression Competency Framework*, Improving Access to Psychological Therapies, www.iapt.nhs.uk/silo/files/counselling-for-depression-competency-framework.pdf (retrieved 20/05/13).

will focus their interventions. Similarly if the client has expressed how they feel but is puzzling over what it all means, it is the task of making sense of the feelings that the counsellor will collaboratively engage in. Close empathic attunement allows the counsellor to respond to the client at the point in their process where they are currently striving to make progress. We continue to emphasise the collaborative method which reveals the signposts to the potential usefulness of these techniques. The most directive moment in the process is the tentative offer of a technique by the counsellor. This is not a clunky gear change in the session, but a natural part of the fluid moment-to-moment relationship which experienced therapists will navigate with ease.

Clearing a space

There are occasions when clients have difficulty in being in the right frame of mind, the right personal *space* for working. Then there are times when the client *is* ready to engage with their difficulties, but can't bring anything into the right kind of focus – the problem can be finding something to work on in that moment that has the right feel to it. Perhaps a client is caught like a rabbit in the headlights, unable to think or feel – overwhelmed by the enormity of the task and feelings associated with it. We can find no value in diagnosing these moments as being necessarily a symptom of *avoidance* – the more classical person-centred therapist would respectfully wait until the client was ready. When working briefly it might be necessary to utilise the time maximally and some clients can experience the difficulty of finding something to focus on as yet more evidence of the impossibility of their predicament, another symptom of their hopelessly defeating depression. Clearing a space is a constructive suggestion to the client to find the right space and energy to engage with their difficulty.

The activity 'clearing a space' was originated by Eugene Gendlin as the first step in 'focusing' (Gendlin, 1978/2003), and over the years, many have found that as a way of pausing and finding a safe place, it brings benefits when used to pay attention to any awareness-development task, or even just by itself as a momentary meditation. It is easy enough to do – in its most basic form the counsellor might suggest that the client simply 'finds a safe space' inside themselves, and this can be sufficient for some people. Safety and sufficiency are the characteristics of useful safe space, but each client will approach the suggestion differently and the counsellor might make a different suggestion for different tasks.

Elliott et al. (2004: 170–1) advise that the client:

- moves problems away from themselves by, e.g. pushing them into a corner of a room, or putting them at a safe distance
- imagines containing metaphors/images such a box, jar or cupboard that can be closed, locked or opened when necessary
- imagines a favourite safe space or activity in which the problems can be located
- imagines moving themselves physically away from the problems, putting a barrier, layer or 'clear blue water' between them and their problems

There is no formula for using a particular method for a particular difficulty, e.g., perhaps the client cannot choose which problem to work on, is feeling blank, or can't define a problem sharply enough – the counsellor and client will use trial and error to find something that works. Once achieved, the safe space so cleared can be remarkably robust and instantly effective. An example of using the technique is outlined in Chapter 9, p. 170.

Systematic evocative unfolding

This is a way of encouraging deep exploration of an experience. Originally advanced as a method by Laura Rice (Rice, 1974/2001; Rice and Saperia, 1984; see also p. 136, this volume) it involves evoking a re-experiencing of an event, situation or emotion. Whilst it has a general usefulness and is sometimes spontaneously undertaken by clients, it is particularly helpful in unpacking and clarifying confusing, problematic reactions.

Again, experienced practitioners may recognise systematic evocative unfolding as a hitherto natural, unnamed component of their practice. It consists of inviting the client to re-enter the confusing or problematic scene or situation and evoking an experiential response. This response is empathically tracked by the counsellor whilst they encourage further evocation of feelings, thoughts or sensations. As the experience is elaborated, it is hoped that the client becomes able to develop meaning, clarity or resolution to the puzzle. Its main distinguishing characteristic is the direct re-evocation of the experience – the client is invited to revisit, to relive the experience.

The counsellor simply and directly encourages the client to re-enter the situation by saying something like: 'I see, you walked into Sam's office and she said "sit down" … how were you feeling at that point?', or 'Going back to that morning, can you put yourself back there; the letter drops through the letter box … and you thought …?' The counsellor then helps the client move through the situation, step by step, letting the situation unfold in the client's experience, actively empathising, highlighting possible points of clarification and new understanding.

This is an *experiential* technique aiming to help the client access, relive an experience, allowing them to re-examine it and consider different options for response and action. This can evoke an intense response which might require a degree of emotion regulation, and so we can see how these techniques weave into a dynamic process – they should not be seen as a linear sequence of activities. Chapter 9, pp. 170–2 gives some examples of the use of systematic evocative unfolding.

Emotion regulation

Counselling for Depression theory places a high importance on the role of emotion in our lives. Emotions have the following functions:

- they facilitate goal-directed behaviour (Rogers, 1951: 492–3; Elliott et al., 2004: 24; Elliott, 2012: 109)
- they signal the importance/survival value of the behaviour they accompany (Rogers, 1951: 493; Elliott et al., 2004: 24; Elliott, 2012: 109)
- they signal needs (Elliott et al; 2004: 24; Elliott, 2012: 109)

From Rogers (e.g., Rogers, 1961), we note that in the psychologically healthy individual emotions are easily accessed, experienced without fear, expressed freely and appropriately with a satisfying result, and are available for processing and reformulation where necessary. Symptoms of depression are, as we have seen, often caused or exacerbated by problems processing emotions in adaptive ways. In this regard, one salient dimension of emotions and the processing of them is the relationship between the level of emotional arousal, or intensity, of emotion, and the person, situation and occasion. There is an optimal level of emotional arousal for different everyday tasks – similarly to general arousal – we can be over- or under-aroused for a specific task. Psychology research has tended to concentrate on the effect of general arousal on, e.g., learning, memory and other cognitive abilities, but emotional arousal similarly can impair a wide range of day-to-day functions. Managing the level of emotional arousal is an important tool in the repertoire of successful individuals. Emotion regulation is the self-explanatory term used in CfD to explain this capacity.

Often clients are only too aware of their difficulties regarding emotions. They know that they get overwhelmed with fear or sadness, or they are desperately in touch with their inability to feel joy. Furthermore, many will have tried to manage their emotional responses either globally or in given situations, and their inability to do this under their own steam will only add to their feeling of hopelessness. Other clients will have little or no awareness of the role that unregulated emotions play in their difficulties.

Problems regulating emotions can lead to repeatedly revisiting the same emotional material without, as Rogers (1961: 145) put it, the feeling flowing 'to its full result'. This cathartic expression of feeling is often portrayed as a caricature of therapy, but for many people a feeling, however intensely expressed, does need to be *processed*, rather than just expressed. It helps if the emotion is worked with in a way that allows it to become more adaptive, more 'fit for purpose' rather than inaccessible, unhelpful, obstructive or distressing. In order for helpful processing to take place the emotion must be at a manageable level, a level that is workable with, hence 'emotion regulation': the task of managing the level of emotional arousal. Strategies for accessing difficult emotions and managing under-arousal include:[8]

- exploring bodily sensations related to emotions or events (e.g. 'clearing a space', above)
- exploring, unpacking memories of events and previous emotional responses
- employing other vivid emotional cues, such as words or images
- exploring actions associated with emotions

---

[8] Adapted from *Learning Emotion-Focused Therapy* supplemental materials website: www.process-experiential.org/learning/supplemental/chap2.2.1.html (retrieved 18/03/2013).

Where we say 'exploring' this can mean verbally, but includes any medium of communication and expression – posture, movement, making non-verbal noises – indeed anything that helps access the emotion and heighten the level of arousal. As this work proceeds it is important that the counsellor is vigilant and helps the client keep the level of arousal within safe limits.

Strategies for managing over-arousal include:

- doing what in EFT might be termed 'self-soothing' – relaxing, meditating, self-comforting, self-supporting, self-caring
- getting support from others
- using language or imagery that helps contain or distance the emotion and its intensity
- temporarily distracting oneself with other activities
- naming and understanding emotions
- regulating the expression of emotion (letting out a little at a time)

Experienced practitioners will recognise some of these strategies as simply a part of their normal practice or things that clients have tried or currently use. Improving emotion regulation might be a matter of enhancing some of the strategies already in use, and note that we have included the apparently obvious 'getting support from others' since this is sometimes overlooked because it *is* so obvious. Less frequently used strategies include suggestions for self-soothing in the face of overwhelming emotions or using images and other non-verbal domains to contain or distance overwhelming emotions. Examples of these strategies can be found in Chapter 9, pp. 165–6 and 171.

Working with problematic dialogue between configurations of self

In Chapter 5 we explored the PCE theory regarding pluralism in personality structure. We noted that a range of psychological tension could result from problematic dialogue between configurations of self. Here we look at ways of working with such intrapersonal dialogue difficulties.

This area of therapeutic work is founded on two principles: first, that for a client to deepen their awareness of different aspects of themselves is therapeutic per se; second that to encourage dialogue between conflicting aspects of the self is transformational, in that new dialogue tends to change the nature of the conflicting configurations. From a practice point of view the starting point for this, as with all CfD practice, is empathic affirmation, attunement and following. When the client discloses or the counsellor discerns the emergence of multiple aspects of self, a number of options are opened up. Firstly, the nature of the configurations and the type or tone of dialogue can be important. Configurations can be supportive, protective, antagonistic, manipulative, critical and so on. Sensitively entering the internal frame of reference will help both the counsellor and client understand the nature of any conflicts between self-configurations, which can be associated with symptoms of depression. Thus in CfD we think of all 'splits' as potentially 'depressive splits', depending upon the unique experiences of each client, although the literature suggests that highly critical self-configurations can be particularly associated with depression (Greenberg and Watson, 2006).

Whilst empathic following can help map out the relationships between configurations and, with time, help reduce, resolve or creatively mediate in conflict, when working briefly, clients might appreciate the offer of more active interventions. EFT uses the gestalt therapy-derived 'chair work' to work with problematic self-configurations. Counselling for Depression practice does not employ chair work. Instead we simply use the imagination of the client – something which clients frequently spontaneously do, and which counsellors spontaneously encourage – which could be thought of as amounting to chair work in the mind.

There is no 'correct' way of working with configurations, except the general aim of deepening awareness of configurations, encouraging dialogue between them and thereby finding amelioration of distressing tension – CfD takes its lead from the work of Dave Mearns (Mearns and Thorne, 2000) and Robert Elliott and colleagues (Elliott et al., 2004). When, in the previous paragraph, we say 'active interventions', whilst this can simply be a matter of emphasis, we mean making the following types of suggestions within the collaborative style of CfD:

- help the client to identify the configurations that are polarised (e.g., the inner-critic and the vulnerable self that is on the receiving end of the criticism)
- encourage the client to name, visualise and describe the configurations as if they were real people
- ask the client if they are representative of real people or if they remind the client of a real person – this helps elaborate the experience and potentially distinguish internal dialogue from unfinished business with a real person
- encourage the client to inhabit or 'dwell' in the configurations, slowly and deliberately, one at a time, and become aware of any emerging experiences
- help the client to vocalise how the particular part of themselves thinks and feels and the kind of things they may say
- focus on how each configuration might feel on hearing the vocalisations of the opposing configuration
- suggest that the client dialogues with and between configurations, asking them what they want, if they have any intent, or have any messages
- notice any shifts in the content or tone of each configuration's communication and discuss with the client the significance of these
- help the client discover if tension can be resolved by encouraging dialogue between configurations, e.g. can bargains or alliances be made, or forgiveness offered and accepted, etc.

In EFT this is achieved by helping the client inhabit the configurations by imagining a self-configuration to be sitting in a chair in the therapy room and then inhabiting the configuration by literally sitting in 'its' place in the chair. The counsellor 'directs' the ensuing dialogue.

In CfD, the purpose is as much about encouraging dialogue between aspects of the self (as would be the case in EFT chair work) as it is about dwelling in the different aspects of the self and experiencing in a more differentiated way the thoughts, feelings and verbalisations associated with each particular aspect of the self. This deepening of experiencing is helpful in itself, regardless of whether constructive dialogue can be evoked.

This process is enacted entirely in the client's imagination and although the counsellor might make empathically led suggestions, the client remains in control of the process, with the counsellor facilitating. Examples of working with configurations are given in Chapter 9, pp. 160–3 and 178–81.

Creating meaning

Experienced practitioners will have been aware of a developing theme in this chapter. Again we begin by saying that many person-centred and integrative practitioners will recognise this way of working from their own practice. The only difference being they will not have named it 'creating meaning', rather seeing it as an activity that can occasionally spontaneously arise from the natural flow of work with a client. In Counselling for Depression we identify it as a discrete but connected task – connected to all other aspects of self in the matrix of meanings and emotions in the self-structure – which can be specifically addressed with a specific intervention. Meaning creation is a technique aimed at repairing the emotional damage done when a cherished life belief is destroyed. In EFT, these events are called 'meaning protests' or meaning crises and result in intense feelings of injustice, unfairness, anger, helplessness and betrayal and in terms of depression, can leave the client feeling, for example, that there is no purpose in life.

The meaning-creation process can be broken down into a series of steps:

- identify the cherished belief that has been shattered or destroyed
- explore the exact nature of the life belief that has been shattered or destroyed
- examine and evaluate the continued plausibility and utility of the life belief in question – many will have been formed in childhood and/or be introjects
- revise the life belief – this is the 'meaning creation' aspect, since it is replacing a maladaptive or untenable life belief with a more useful, flexible one

Person-centred practitioners will recognise the difference between the beginning and end point as a movement described by Rogers in his seven stages of process (Rogers, 1961: 125–59). Meaning creation does happen spontaneously, but in the time-limited context of CfD we consciously break it down into steps to achieve a theoretically grounded outcome, in collaboration with the client. Stating the process as a series of steps is intended as a helpful guide for practitioners, not an instruction to proceed mechanically through a series of pre-ordained steps. The natural character of the therapist and the flow of the relationship in question should be paramount.

Unfinished business

Finally, we turn our attention to helping the client complete what, increasingly in every-day discourse, is referred to as 'unfinished business'. It refers to unresolved interpersonal issues which the counsellor will become aware of through their empathic engagement with the client. Lingering unresolved feelings such as hurt and resentment relating to a person who was significant but may no longer be present in the client's life are usually indicative of unfinished business. Then the key intervention is to bring the missing third party into the room in the client's imagination.

What follows is similar to the process of working with a self-configuration, except that this time it is the absent third party who is engaged in dialogue in the client's imagination. Often, it can simply be a matter of saying what was left unsaid, or giving the other person a piece of your mind, and on other occasions, the client might engage in more complex dialogue with the missing person. It goes without saying that address-ing unfinished business head-on can be extremely difficult work for the client, and the counsellor must be ready to help the client regulate their emotions as the work proceeds.

Working with unfinished business can be a way of helping clients express long-held resentments relating to neglect and/or abuse, and resolve grief reactions, and again we remind readers that dialogue with a missing person need not be limited to verbal exchanges, and it is not even necessary for them to be completed in the therapy session. Some clients, especially those used to keeping diaries, might find it useful to write a letter to the missing person. It is not necessary to specify a series of stages for resolving or 'finishing' the unfinished business, other than to acknowledge that along the way clients might identify and work with unmet needs, revise their perception of the other, say goodbye or let go of the other (or find an adaptive way of holding them close), and so on. Resolution of unfinished business will almost certainly be signalled by a shift clearly felt by the client when the other person is called to mind. This is illustrated in Chapter 9, pp. 174–5.

9

Counselling for Depression in Practice

In this chapter we use three vignettes to illustrate CfD practice. The cases are fictional, informed by our experience as practitioners, but written primarily to communicate points of practice which make CfD unique: a distinctive integration of person-centred practice and emotion-focused therapy practice. The chapter is written with two assumptions in mind:

1. Although many readers may have had person-centred training, some will not, and the variety of UK person-centred courses will result in wide interpretations of person-centred-practice.
2. Many readers might not be familiar with emotion-focused therapy interventions and how these might integrate into a practice based on person-centred principles.

This gives us a chance to delineate, however loosely, the territory which we believe CfD comfortably inhabits.

Readers will notice each page is divided into three columns and shaded boxes occur occasionally throughout the text. The columns are arranged from the inside of the page – the spine of the book – outwards.

1. **The narrow left column** identifies the relevant Counselling for Depression competence – these are listed with the alphanumeric identifiers assigned by us in this book in Appendix 1, pp. 201–5. The humanistic and Counselling for Depression competency frameworks can be found in Figures 3.1 and 3.2 on pp. 26 and 30, or downloaded for printing from the IAPT website.[1] The competencies identified in this column are there to stimulate discussion, not offer a definitive analysis. What competences do you think are evidenced in this practice?
2. **The middle column** is the fictionalised transcript.
3. **The right column** is an intermittent commentary on the transcript.

---

[1] www.iapt.nhs.uk/silo/files/counselling-for-depression-competency-framework.pdf, retrieved 09/05/2013.

\mentary can be an insight into the therapist's thoughts and decisions, a note on \ects of theory are represented in the dialogue, or a comment on possibilities ... were not enacted.

Each vignette begins with a scene-setting box, and is punctuated with further boxes which summarise the action so far and/or fill in the intervening events. A final box brings the vignette to a close and says something about the outcome.

CfD is a high-intensity intervention, recommended in episodes of up to 20 sessions. Within the 20-session limit, endings should be agreed collaboratively with the client. All counsellors will know that counselling episodes end in a variety of circumstances, and we are not using these vignettes to illustrate different endings. All the vignettes are written to present CfD as a positive, active therapeutic enterprise, with examples of how it can work, rather than examples of how it may not work. As experienced practitioners, CfD counsellors will have an understanding of some of the many ways in which the therapeutic process can encounter difficulties, and specialist CfD supervision, described in Chapter 10, is the best place to resolve difficult therapy relationships. This is a 'how to' chapter rather than a 'troubleshooting' chapter.

There are several points we are trying to get across in this chapter:

- Firstly, CfD is predicated on the notion that successful therapy is dependent upon a collaborative relationship between the therapist and the client. This is the area of special expertise of those best placed to provide high-quality CfD, namely, person-centred therapists. CfD is founded on the essential ability to establish a therapeutic relationship based on the six therapeutic conditions described by Carl Rogers (Rogers, 1959) – this is the basis of the CfD therapeutic stance and taken as a given in the vignettes.
- Secondly, the therapeutic conditions proposed by Rogers can be sufficient in themselves, practised in the time-limited environment within which CfD is offered.
- Thirdly, the active offering of techniques within CfD is more of an art than a manual-driven set of therapist interventions. It is an art informed by person-centred and emotion-focused therapy theories, the relationship in question with the client in question, and the therapist's experience and clinical judgement.
- Fourthly, even though CfD has been described in terms of therapeutic tasks, therapeutic conditions and techniques in this book, in practice it is experienced by both therapists and clients as a fluid, seamless, unfolding relationship.
- Finally, although CfD has been presented in a logical, linear fashion in order to explain its rationale, in practice it is neither. It is unpredictable and sometimes impenetrable to the uneducated observer, with a local logic dictated by the world of the client which the counsellor must tune in to and follow. This apparently chaotic process has been simplified and caricatured in order to render it suitable as a teaching resource in these vignettes.

In the real world of CfD practice in NHS services, sessions and relationships rarely, if ever, develop in the ways we have presented in the vignettes. They have been idealised to illustrate particular aspects of CfD therapy and specific interventions that might be new to readers. Experience tells us that many clients with a diagnosis of depression in NHS services often have a combination of characteristics, including:

- a background of childhood abuse or neglect
- ongoing conflictual or disrupted interpersonal relationships
- living in challenging social and economic conditions

- experiencing a recent stressful event, or events that have triggered the current episode
- having experienced several episodes of depression throughout their lives, making self-care and the maintenance of wellbeing important issues
- having long-term medical conditions

Experienced practitioners in a range of services including primary care know this only too well, and should understand the challenges presented by this work. Working in multi-disciplinary teams to address these complex needs is a necessary skill which we assume CfD practitioners develop in situ or in ongoing training. Complexity and chronicity are the norms in this kind of work, especially with clients referred to counselling. Although they are the reality for many practitioners, such complex cases do not make good illustrative vignettes demonstrating individual interventions.

CASE EXAMPLE 1: Alan – Counsellor Jill

Alan is a white British 55-year-old engineering equipment salesman, married with two grown-up children. He arrives at his GP in something of a personal crisis. He has been sleeping poorly, has difficulty concentrating, is constantly tired, has lost interest in sex and has a persistent low mood. He has also lost interest in his work, which has previously been a source of interest and pride. He went to the doctor on the insistence of his wife who on two occasions found him asleep at his computer whilst working at home during the day. The final straw for her was when she found him weeping in the kitchen without being able to explain why.

Alan's GP, Dr Clayton, has been the family doctor for 15 years and a quick look through Alan's records showed that he was an infrequent visitor to the surgery, with a good level of general health. It was clear that Alan is intelligent, active and takes an interest in his health, so Dr Clayton immediately referred him to Prit in the Psychological Services Division for assessment.

Alan was not thought to pose any risks to himself or others and met the diagnostic criteria for counselling for depression. Prit referred him to Jill, the CfD counsellor.

Session 1

G4, G6

J: Hello Alan. My name's Jill. I see you've got the leaflet there explaining Counselling for Depression. Have you had a chance ro read it?

A: Yes, yes.

J: OK, There's a couple of things I need to go through with you before we get to talk properly about why you're here.

A: [*Nervous smile.*] OK.

Jill likes to make sure that clients are given the Department of Health booklet[2] as part of the assessment process or by the service receptionist.

Although not all the treatments are offered by her service, she finds that most clients do read through it. It can lead to productive discussion about what will happen in the sessions: for example, it gives her an opportunity to get some basic information about the client's expectations and later, for example, to introduce the time limited nature of CfD. Jill is also checking that CfD is a suitable approach for Alan.

---

[2] *Which Talking Therapy for Deprssion* www.iapt.nhs.uk/silo/files/which-talking-therapy-for-depression.pdf (retrieved 11/11/2013).

G10	J:	Did you choose CfD yourself, or did someone tell you it would be right for you? Maybe you looked at what was available and thought it would be the best for you?
	A:	Well, I don't know what would be best. The guy I saw before asked me and I didn't know then either. He told me about one other treatment but the waiting list was shortest for this and it looked OK. I think I want to talk about things, not read books about ... well ... you know ...
G4, G7, B6, B7	J:	No, of course, it is difficult to choose, it sounds as though the short waiting list was important and you wanted someone to actually talk to rather than get advice from a book, is that right?
	A:	Well, I went to the doctors because my wife was worried and I agreed with her that I needed to sort myself out. She was worried, so I thought I'd better get going as soon as possible. Is that OK?
B7	J:	Right, you wanted to do something about how you were feeling as quickly as possible because your wife was worried. And you agreed with her, that there was something to be concerned about, by the sound of things.
	A:	[*Nods.*] Yeah.
B5	J:	That's what brings you here today. So you've seen the leaflet, yes? [*Alan nods*] and you might have read that we've got up to twenty sessions to work together.
	A:	Mm, hmm.
B5	J:	Do you have any questions about what this counselling involves? Anything at all?
	A:	I've not been to counselling before so I don't know what to do. I suppose you'll give me suggestions about what to do, erm ... to feel, you know ... better.
B7, G8	J:	OK, it sounds as though you're a bit nervous, and you're guessing that I'll be giving you suggestions about how to deal with depression.
	A:	I suppose so.
B2 B6	J:	OK, well, it'll not be quite like that. Earlier, I said we'd be 'working together'.

Jill is spending the first part of the first session 'structuring' – see pp. 119–20 – setting the ground rules in both what she says and how she says it.

She responds empathically to get a clearer sense of what has brought Alan to the service in his own words.

Jill uses the fact that Alan has seen the leaflet to introduce the idea of his aims for the sessions and to find out, even at this early stage, that his expectations about CfD are in line with what she thinks is possible.

B5, G7	By that I mean ... that ... let's see, in Counselling for Depression there's a	This is quite direct structuring – Jill is explaining what is likely to happen in CfD, and again is taking the opportunity made by what Alan has said. Many such opportunities might arise in the first session.
G4, B1	couple of important things to know. One is that though you might not think it right	
B3, B5	now, I think that you will have some good ideas about what might work for you. Another is that I will give you plenty of time to talk about what's going on for you that you might think is important. That's where we'll start, me listening and you talking. In fact that is what we will do for most of the time. There might be a few times when I think of something that	
B5, S1	might be useful to do here in the session, and I'll say so. It'll be up to you if you think it's a good idea or not ... Also, talking like this can often bring up a lot of feelings, sometimes strong ones ... and that's completely normal.	It is important that Alan knows from the outset that CfD will probably bring up strong emotions – the counsellor needs to allow time to work with this. In CfD there are strategies to help clients regulate their emotional arousal if required.

A: Can I be honest?

B8, B9, G10	J: Of course, please do. That's important. I really want to hear what's going on for you ... whatever it is ...	Jill is emphasising and demonstrating that it's both safe and important for Alan to be honest and that she will treat his honesty, along with everything else he says, respectfully.
	A: I don't see how that will work. I erm ... I don't know. I don't know what would work.	
B8, B9, G2, B7, M4.2	J: You don't think just talking will work, is that it? And you sounded really, er, hopeless then ... not knowing what would work.	Jill is aware that feeling hopeless is also a common experience in depression.
	A: Did I? Yes, maybe. I need this to work.	
B6, B7	J: It's very important that these sessions actually help. You need this to work. And right now it just doesn't look as though it's going to.	Jill is achieving a number of things in these simple responses: she is making sure Alan is clear about what to expect from CfD, checking whether the therapy is really suited to him. She is making no attempt to 'shoe-horn' him into the therapy. She is leaving the decision-making up to him, and when he has made his decision she affirms this.
	A: Well, I ... I think ... I, er ... I'll give it a go. Like my Dad used to say, don't do it if you can't do it properly. I'll give it a go.	
B7, B8	J: OK Alan, what's coming through to me is that this is so important for you, it *must* work and you will give it your best shot.	
	A: What next?	
	J: OK, it sounds as though you want to get on. That's OK with me. And we can take a minute or two, well actually a few minutes	
B7, B8, B9, M1	at the end of each session to see how *we* think things are going – what, if	

G10
G12

anything, has been helpul and what has not. I'll also ask you to do a very short questionnaire – this is the official way of keeping track of whether the counselling is working or not. Does that sound OK?

A: Erm, OK, right, that's fine, but what if it's not working straightaway?

G7, M1, G12

J: Well, it's a good idea to give it a bit of a chance, a few sessions. So if you're concered that we'd just stop after the first session or two because these forms tell us it's not working, there's no need to worry. We'll give it plenty of time. It's also to collect information to research the best ways of helping people. [*Pause.*] I've been given the assessment report from your meeting with Prit, and it's got some detail of the

M1

symptoms you discussed.

A: [*Nods.*]

G6, G7, B3, G10

J: Right ... it's important we start off on the right foot, and what I would prefer to do is for you to tell me why you're here in your own words. It means I get to hear it from you, in your own words, since you know best why you're here, and second it might be that things have changed since you saw Prit, what, three weeks ago? You might feel better or worse, or different. Would that be OK?

A: Fine by me ... Now?

G6, B3, B8

J: Yes, in your own time, there's no need to rush.

A: [*Pause of about 30 seconds.*] Erm, it's difficult to know where to start. I don't really know where ... right now I feel OK, but that's because I'm here, talking to you. When I get home I'll just feel crap ...

Again, Jill takes her lead from issues raised by Alan. This time to introduce the fact that it is important to continuously evaluate the sessions, including what Alan does *not* find helpful. She also introduces the fact that there will be some formal measures to evaluate progress.

This is more structuring, here Jill is explaining and demonstrating that for her, Alan's story is paramount, his experience is the fuel for the therapeutic process, and that things can change. It also continues to show him that he is in control of the process.

Jill thinks that she and Alan have made good psychological contact and quickly formed the impression that he was able to actively engage with the therapeutic process – he was keen to 'sort himself out' as he put it on introducing himself.

After a stuttering start Alan talks about his symptoms. Nothing much has changed for him since the assessment interview. Jill is empathic, genuine and accepting. She notices that Alan sticks to his task. He is comfortable following instructions and doesn't stray far from simply doing as she asks. After about 10 minutes of Alan describing his symptoms in fairly distanced terms, she says ...

G7, B3,
B6, B7,
B8,
M4.1

J: I hope I've followed you there [*Alan nods.*] and I've got a question ... What do you want to achieve here, I mean, in these sessions? You might think there's an obvious answer to this, but I'd like to know in your own words, just like I want to hear all your experiences in your words.

A: [*After a short pause.*] I want to just get better, back to the way I was. But I can't see a way of doing that. I used to be organised, you know, get things done, enjoy going out ... the whole thing. Now I can't think straight and can't want to do anything. So ... just get back my old self.

Statements like 'get back to the way I was' and 'get my old self back' can be signposts to self-discrepancies – between ideal (old) self and experienced self. Jill makes a mental note but thinks it's too early to dive in to some work so early. Sometimes simply helping to unpack a person's goals helps them get a better handle on the problem, helps them get more detail. Jill won't use any goals Alan comes up with to tie up the therapeutic process or make it completely goal-oriented. It is a way into Alan's world and might provide useful signposts for them both as things unfold as an added benefit.

B6,
S2.3, B7

J: You put it very simply 'to get better', and 'get your old self back' – that's what you want, and at the same time, it seems almost impossible. You can't see how you can do it, and more than that

M2

you can't find either the right direction to go in, nor the motivation, the 'get-up-and-go'.

A: No, that's right, I don't know what to do and even if did, I'm not sure I'd actually do it when I get up in the morning. Don't know what to do ... it's like being in a fog, stumbling around.

S2.5

J: In a fog. You have to go slowly in a fog and sometimes you get lost. Is that how it feels?

Jill is helping Alan work with his own metaphor to help him articulate his feelings.

A: Well not slow, but, yes ... just lost and ... then hopeless. Like there's no way out.

Jill is patient and empathic, helping Alan elaborate and clarify his experience until a more specific goal emerges. Sometimes this doesn't happen and a client is left with an indistinct or global goal. Alan has goals 'to feel better' and get his old self back, but grinds to a halt.

B7

J: There's no way out. [*Flat reflection, not a question.*]

A: Like ... in a maze that's it, in a fog and in a maze. Just no way out, no point in looking, so just go to sleep. Well, I wish I could ... but ...

Alan talks until just over 10 minutes before the end of the session, Jill carries on offering the therapeutic conditions. Continuing to explore tentative goals and aims, Alan talks about work, especially how much pressure the whole sales team is under. Now the job is completely different from when he started. He started off talking about how everyone was suffering and moved on to talk about his own difficulties, just not having the time to get the job done the way he wants to – too much paperwork and not enough time talking to customers. He talked about being snowed under, putting jobs to one side and not fulfilling his quotas. He said the job was impossible.

He didn't talk at all about his family, except to say that he loved his wife and grown-up children. He then brought up the topic of his 'old self' again.

B4, B7

J: You mentioned 'your old self' earlier, but I didn't give you a chance to say much more about it. There seems to be an 'old you' you've lost touch with that used to be organised and get things done.

Jill thinks there's sufficient time left to at least start to work with this, so she returns to Alan's need to get back to his old self. It turns out to be a clear signpost to a discrepancy between the way he experiences himself now and the way he wants to be (his old self).

A: Yeah, I used to be 'Mr Organised', planned everything, and to be honest, I got it all done as well. I was good at that sort of thing. Everything sorted, you know.

J: Mr Organised ... sounds trustworthy ...

A: Yes, but not now ...

B7

J: Not now. Now ... you say you can't think straight and don't want to do anything ... this new you seems quite different from Mr Organised.

Empathic responding allows Alan to describe and clarify different configurations – bringing them into thoughtful awareness possibly for the first time. This in itself can be therapeutic.

A: Yeah. Just no comparison ... like two different people. Can't imagine what it was like ...

B7, S2.1

J: So on the one hand there's the organised trustworthy, old you, and now, today you feel all over the place, no get-up-and-go, can't think straight.

A: Yeah ...

Jill summarises the discrepancy between the old Alan and how he feels now to get a clearer sense of what 'getting my old self back' means to him (having more energy, being more organised, going out more and having fun). Alan and Jill tentatively set these as more specific goals for their time together. Then with barely 10 minutes to go ...

B3, B9,
M2, M7.2

J: I promised that we'd have a chance to see whether you think it's been useful today, whether anything in particular has helped or anything has not helped. Have you got any thoughts?

A: Erm, er ... yes, er ... well I've got something out of just talking. I just realised that I hadn't actually talked to anyone. I didn't want to worry my wife, didn't want to admit to feeling, you know, at work.

J: OK, so talking ...

A: I can't say it's ... made me feel, let's see ... better. No, but I do feel a bit, lighter. I thought at the beginning that it would be a waste of time, but I'll come back. Yes, it's been OK. Better than I thought.

Experienced practitioners know that sometimes, having the time and space to talk can help. The feeling of relief or 'lightness' might be short lived, or enduring – it's impossible to predict.

J: OK, so better than you thought it was going to be and you feel lighter. Anything that wasn't helpful?

A: No, not really.

G12 J: Right, finally there's just a minute or two left to fill these forms in. Would you like me to explain them?

A: Let's have a look ... [*Looks at the instructions.*] ... this looks OK. I do this here?

J: Yes, and I fill this bit in, but have a go and if you've any questions ...

It's a matter of choice when in the interview the formal evaluation instruments are completed. Some clients can take a long time filling them in and if done at the end of a session it can over-run.
Practitioners will have their own preferred way of managing this.

End of Session 1

Session 2

Alan arrived on time for his second session and started by telling Jill that he felt as though he had gone 'back to square one' the day after the first session. He was flat and disappointed and it only made him feel more hopeless and beyond help. It led in to him being able to talk about his symptoms, and he talked about them as though they were 'out there', things that had happened to him in the past, albeit only yesterday, and he described his experiences in a rather precise language almost as though he was describing something out of a textbook.

Jill listened empathically. She reflected the fact that he sounded flat and disconnected from the things he was talking about, but Alan did not take this up. She realised that there were several opportunities to use a technique to help Alan be more in touch with his experience, such as going inside and making a space, but she thought it was

(Continued)

161

(Continued)

more important to build a strong relationship and just as important to take any opportunities to tentatively enter Alan's world when invited.

About 35 minutes into the session, Alan returned to talking about work. Again he compared the past and the present, how much things had changed and how the company piled on the work. He was caught in a vicious cycle: the better he was at his job, the more they gave him to do, and although he was on commission, he didn't enjoy his work anymore. Then he paused, obviously deep in thought and distracted.

A: Work ... [*Deep sigh.*] ... I ... I feel beaten by it. I'm ... useless. [*Looks at Jill, then out of the window, looks uncomfortable and a little fearful.*]

B7, B8, S2.1

J: [*After a pause.*] Beaten by work and useless ... That's some combination ...

A: And I don't know what to do about it. Bloody useless!

S2.1, B7, M6.1

J: You've talked quite a lot about work in these sessions, and you sound a mixture of, almost angry, and then as you've just said, beaten and useless. In your voice you then sound angry with yourself for being useless. Would that be right?

A: Well, I, erm, yes, work is ... work is important isn't it? What else, well, the kids, of course, but you have to earn money don't you?

S2.3

J: It's important to earn money for your family. But you feel useless.

A: Yes. And I don't know what to do. That's why I'm useless.

S2.4, B7

J: So it's important for you to earn money for your family, but you feel useless because ... it sounds like you're at the end of your tether when you say you don't know what to do.

A: No, it's hopeless. I mean yes, I don't know what to do. It doesn't make sense. I get stuck thinking about it. Can't sort it out, make sense, do anything. What's the point? If it wasn't for the kids ...

J: That's a real dead end by the sound of it – nowhere to go – and if it wasn't for the kids ... ?

Jill is tentatively empathically responding to Alan's implicit feelings – carefully checking she is accurate in her reflections. These thoughts and feelings that Alan is expressing don't make a logical whole picture, but Jill isn't concerned. She's not looking for logic or reason, nor lack of, either. She's just trying to follow Alan, making sense where possible, or letting things hang where they are left. Counsellors can feel pushed to 'do something' when there are a specified number of sessions available, but Jill thinks that patience, empathy and building her relationship with Alan is the right thing to do. She has seen some small changes already in what he is talking about and the way he talks about it. For now, she is standing beside Alan in his 'not knowing what to do'. She doesn't judge this or suggest any solutions.

Jill continues to be aware that Alan's sense of hopelessness is a prominent experience for him, and is ready to pick this up if and when necessary.

B7, B8,
G10, G11

A: No, that's when I pull myself up short,
there's a part of me that thinks I have a
responsibility for them still, but then I hit
the deck again and still can't get anywhere.

J: There's a part of you that thinks you have
a responsibility for your children, even
though they're grown up, and that part of
you stops you from really, seriously
thinking about ... killing yourself? Is that
what you were not saying?

A: Well, yes, but it sounds worse when you say
it like that. I've thought about it. I think
about it a lot, but it's just thoughts. Really I'm
a coward. Then I say to myself – don't be so
f-ing stupid. What about the kids! I can hear
my Dad's voice saying 'it's the coward's way
out – be a man Al. Bloody pull yourself
together' ... he would think I was useless.

B7, S2.1,
S2.2

J: It sounds like there's a part of you that gets
really defeated, hopeless and helpless, then
another part of you that thinks of the kids
and pulls back from the brink. Is there
another part of you that almost speaks
with your Dad's voice, saying 'Be a man,
Al. Bloody pull yourself together!'?

B7, S2.2

A: Yes, and you know what? I just get lost in
the middle. Lost ...

J: And in the middle of it all you get lost –
not knowing which one to listen to,
maybe, or what to do.

A: [Nods.]

J: OK, Alan it's never a good time to draw
things to a close, and it might feel like it's
all hanging in mid-air, but if you would
like me to, I can remind you where we
finished off and see if any of this is around
for you at the beginning of the next
session. What do you think?

At this point, it would be routine for NHS
counsellors to risk assess and if appropriate
give advice about sources of support for
episodes of suicidal ideation. In this case,
Alan's risk factors are not critical. Although he
is a man, his age is not a risk factor, he is in a
stable relationship and employed (and so is
not socially isolated) has no history of self
harm or drug/alcohol abuse. He is talking in
measured terms about self – configuration
dialogue, rather than clear suicidal ideation.
Jill notes this though, and will keep a watchful
eye on any developments.

Jill can hear the parts of Alan's self – his
configurations of self – in dialogue here and
thinks it might help to make this a little clearer
in her reflections.

Jill draws the session to a close. Things are hanging in mid-air. She finishes off by asking
whether anything has been particularly helpful or unhelpful and whether Alan thinks it
is meeting his goals. He says he still doesn't know yet but will be back next time. Jill asks
if there's anything Alan would like to say or do to help him finish off before he goes back
outside into the 'real world'. He smiles and says he'll be fine.

End of Session 2

Session 3

G6, G7,
B7, B8, B9,
S2.2

J: Hi Alan, good to see you. I'm ready to listen to whatever you want to talk about, and I promised at the end of the last session to remind you of where we left off. Do you still want me to do that?

A: Yes, I remember. You don't need to remind me, I was thinking about it all the way home and for the next couple of days. What I was thinking about was my Dad. I think about him a lot.

J: Uh, huh. I see, would you like to talk more about that?

A: Yes ... I suppose I haven't actually talked about him since he died. But, then I, er, I don't really know why I should have.

J: You just saw no need to talk about your Dad.

G13

A: No, right but anyway, the thing is, I, I, [*Eyes moisten and catches breath in almost a sob.*] I, [*Strangles a sob tries to compose himself, but tears stream down his face.*]

B7, B8,
S1.1

J: Feelings about your dad are still very present, Alan, and very strong by the look of things ... and you seem to be taken by surprise ...

A: Yes, I, no, not really, just that I don't want to get into this [*Sobs more.*] ...

> Alan's feelings about his Dad looked as though they caught him by surprise, and they caught Jill by surprise too (she noted this and almost as soon as she spoke she realised that her reflection about being taken by surprise might have been her own surprise leaking out a little and decides to take it to supervision. Jill also realises that Alan's feelings are not clear at this moment. Strong, yes, but even though it looks like it, she doesn't want to jump to a conclusion that he might be sad or grieving. She waits for his feelings to become clear.

> Alan struggles for some time with his feelings. Every time he tries to talk about his Dad, he breaks down. Jill sits with him for several minutes while Alan continues to struggle and return to his Dad. Jill reflects that he is determined to talk about his Dad, even though it is very difficult. After about 10 minutes, Alan says that this is exactly why he never talks about his Dad – he just can't. He crumbles and becomes afraid that he might never stop crying, so he puts it all away and gets on with life. He has a respite from crying ...

S1.1, S1.5

J: It seems just too overwhelming to even try to talk about your Dad, and yet at the same time, you want to. The feelings are just too big, too much, too ... something, right?

A: Yes, I want to but it's like a big wave ...

S2.5

J: And you can't stand up to it.

A: Right.

> Here Jill has helped Alan clarify a therapeutic task (but there is no need for her to name it as such). He wants to talk about his Dad without being stopped in his tracks by the wave of emotion that accompanies every effort to talk. One possibility would be to wait until Alan is ready in his own time. This might take more time than is comfortably available in time-limited work like CfD.

J: So would you like to try something to get them to a manageable level, so you can feel the feelings, but be able to talk about your dad as well?

A: Yes, but I can't see how I can do that.

S1.1
S1.5

J: Well, if you want to give this a try, we can see how you do ... first, can you think of a safe place, may be from your childhood, it could be anywhere, any place ... there's not a correct answer, just a space or place that for you signifies safety ...

A: [*Pauses to think.*] ... er ... yes, I don't know if it's right, erm ... shall I say? [*Jill nods 'uh-huh'.*] Well, it's not from when I was little, but when I was about 14 or 15, we had a shed in the yard that had just junk in it, and I made a kind of workshop, with my engines in it: I used to have a few steam engines. It was my own place ... heaven.

What follows is 'emotion regulation' explained on pp. 147–9, and is specifically aimed at helping Alan manage the overwhelming emotions so that he can work on his issues about his Dad. Jill makes a tentative offer.

S1.2,
S2.1,
S2.4,
S2.5,
S4.2

J: OK, can you get a sense of it, what it was like, remember what it looked like, felt like?

A: Oh yes, easily. No problem! [*Enthusiatically.*] I can smell it!

J: OK, so in your imagination, now you can get a clear feeling of being there? [*Alan nods 'Mmmm'.*] And those strong feelings that come when you try to talk about your Dad, perhaps you can sense them, get a hint of them and how big and unmanageable they are? [*Alan nods 'Mmmm'.*] Try putting them somewhere safe, in that shed, it's up to you, erm, maybe in a cupboard if there are any, or ... what seems good to you?

Visualising or bringing to life a past experience can sometimes cause emotional over-arousal. Here, Jill is creatively helping Alan visualise an experience to help him regulate the feelings. In contrast, solid, straightforward empathic following keeps the emotional arousal at the level controlled by the client. This may be the preferred option in some situations.

A: [*After a pause of about 15 seconds.*] Yes, a tin box, in a tin. I used to put my bits in tins, old biscuit tins, and I think they can go in there. Shit! Oh bloody hell, that's actually worked. I can feel a relief.

J: So the feelings are safe in the tin, do you want to check to see that they're still there? [Alan: I know they are, I can see them through the side.] Now can you put the tin

S2.5

somewhere handy, but far enough away so as to be not in the way.

A: Yeah, on the shelf, easy. I can still ... no really, this is great ... God, what a relief, yeah.

S4.1

J: OK, a real relief, that sounds good, yes? And, so how about, now that they're there, safe, thinking about talking about your Dad a little ...

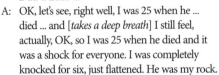

It's not necessary for Jill to give the emotion regulation idea a name (since there isn't any element of explicit psychoeducation in CfD), or extend it beyond the task of helping Alan work on the material relating to his Dad. He seems to adopt the idea very easily and so Jill can return to empathic following and counselling as usual.

A: OK, let's see, right well, I was 25 when he ... died ... and [*takes a deep breath*] I still feel, actually, OK, so I was 25 when he died and it was a shock for everyone. I was completely knocked for six, just flattened. He was my rock.

Alan spends the remaining time in the session talking about his Dad. He occasionally exclaims his surprise at being able to do so and Jill checks how he is doing with the feelings. A couple of times during the session he begins to cry a little and Jill stays with that, neither encouraging him to contain his feelings and put them away, nor get immersed in them. Alan seems able to regulate his feelings without any assistance or instruction, though Jill is ready to help with either should Alan get overwhelmed again.

Alan begins to talk about his conflicting feelings about his Dad, love and grief, and frustration bordering on anger. His love and affection for his Dad is tempered by Alan's growing sense of burden about his Dad insisting on Alan 'being a man'. It is a start. Jill's contribution is genuine, non-judgemental empathic following – nothing more, nothing less.

At the end of this session, Alan says that this time he does feel helped. He is very positive about the session. He is still incredulous that he can manage the feelings that he has been afraid of for so long.

End of Session 3

Session 4

J: Hi Alan, I'm ready to listen to whatever you want to talk about today.

A: Well, I actually felt better at the end of last week and it has stayed with me, sort of, so I'm feeling better. Know what I mean?

B6, B7, B8, S3.4

J: You felt better at the end of the session, and that feeling didn't die down like in previous weeks, and now you feel, erm, better about, and on top of, feeling better. Is that it?

A: Exactly. Yes. And I talked to Mary [Alan's wife] about it too.

Alan goes on to talk about his Dad, specifically, wanting his Dad's approval and trying to 'be a man' in his Dad's terms, but resenting this. He realises how much he carries his Dad's values and voice inside him and how he admonishes himself if he fails to live up to his Dad's expectations. At the same time, he finally grieves for his Dad.

Jill is empathic, genuine and non-judgemental, accompanying Alan as (in theory terms) his self-structure rearranges after realising how much he is influenced by his Dad's aims for him. This sounds easy, but took time and Alan hit a few very rough patches. Jill didn't intervene actively with techniques or suggestions. Alan was doing the work himself, after quickly realising that his powerful emotions didn't have to overwhelm him.

Freed from his Dad's expectations, he decides to ask his employer if he can take his retirement package early. They agree and Alan and Mary decide to 'downsize' and see if any part-time jobs come up to keep them active.

Towards the end of the ninth session, Alan volunteers the idea that he thinks he has met his aim. He doesn't feel completely back to his old self, but thinks it's best to see how he gets on without Jill.

Even though there are sessions left in Alan's allocation, it is good practice to let him decide when he feels the utility of CfD has come to an end. If Jill had any concerns about this, she would have raised them with Alan.

The end of Session 9

B6, B10   J: So let me check ... you feel you've achieved the goal you set at the beginning of the sessions, nine weeks ago. [*Alan nods.*] Now let me check a couple more things, since then, while we've looked at whether coming here has been helpful, we haven't talked about any other goals or aims you might have, or whether the one you set originally has changed. Has anything new come to mind that you'd like to look at or work on?

A: I haven't really thought. I just wanted to get this finished.

J: Right, just finishing these sessions was also a goal – almost like 'the quicker the better, then I can get away from here?'

A: Well, not quite [*Laughs.*] it sounds like I can't wait to get away, and I've actually, well, not enjoyed it exactly ...

J: So that wa ... [*Alan interrupts.*]

A: No I have enjoyed it. At least looked forward to the last couple of sessions. But I'm not sure if I want any more.

G9, B6,   J: I know you've got to looking forward to the sessions, so something positive, yes? And I simply wanted to check whether your goals for these sessions had changed, because you have changed some, otherwise you wouldn't want to stop, right?
S3.4, B10

If this were late in the 19th session, for example, it would not be a good idea to introduce the idea of new or unmet goals. Given that Alan has sessions to spare, so to speak, Jill offers him another opportunity to look back at his work and decide if there is anything else he would like to work on.

A: Yeah. True, that. I see. OK.

G9, B10   J: What do you think about going home to
think about any new things you want to
achieve and coming back next time to
discuss it with a view to making next time
the last time if you want?

> After a little further discussion Alan decides to return for one final session in which he
> says he doesn't have anything else he wants to 'sort out'. He feels better, but not 'great'.
> He reports sustained moderate improvement in all of his symptoms and he is enjoying
> going out socially with Mary. Most importantly for Alan, he feels motivated. He talks
> more about his plans for retirement and how Mary is also pleased with his 'new lease of
> life'. This tenth session is his last.

Note: the ending is agreed collaboratively between client and counsellor well within the
20-session limit for CfD in IAPT.

> **CASE EXAMPLE 2: Habiba – Counsellor Steph**
>
> Habiba is a 45-year-old woman whose parents came to the UK in 1954. Her father
> worked in heavy industry in the West Midlands and her mother was a full-time house-
> worker and mother to Habiba and her two brothers. Her parents were considered lib-
> eral Muslims who, given the somewhat precocious white British teenage culture at the
> time, did not subject Habiba to an arranged marriage after much debate and negotia-
> tion – she wanted to marry for love. She went to nursing college and met and married
> a doctor in her first year as a nurse. Her husband Rafiq, also Muslim, had come the
> England to train as a doctor and work in the NHS. They had two children, a girl and a
> boy, in quick succession, and a very happy family life.
>
> Five years ago, her husband left her and moved to a different part of the country to a
> new job. Habiba went into shock and was intensively supported by her mother, who
> moved in with Habiba and her teenage children. Since then, Habiba has not recovered.
> She lives like a robot, no joy, no pain, just going through the motions. She is unable to
> concentrate, sleeps poorly and her children complain about her mood swings. Her hus-
> band is still separated from her, not divorced, and this sham (her word) preserves a veil of
> honour and dignity for the extended family. She works in an old people's home in an
> unchallenging job where all that is required is that she goes through the motions.
>
> Referred for CfD, Steph learns that Habiba wants to feel more energy and get some
> zest for life back, and together they set that as her first therapeutic goal. She spends the
> first two sessions painstakingly going though her complaints about her husband but
> finds it impossible to talk about anything in any depth.

Session 3

S: Hi Habi, what would you like to talk about today?

H: Hi Steph, I've spent all week trying get him [*She always refers to her husband as 'him' or 'the children's father'.*] to sort the children's savings accounts out. We started them when they were born and now Aisha's 17 we have to think about university fees. I hate having to ask him for anything, but it's a complicated investment in his name and I hate having to talk to him [*Her face is mask-like, expressionless.*] and I ... I ... [*Trails off.*]

S: It sounds difficult, a real hassle to get Aisha's fees sorted. With all of the things you have complained about the children's father, I've never heard you look frustrated or angry or get angry, no angry tone in your voice at all. Of course you may not

B7, B8, B9, feel frustrated or angry, I realise that. It
M6.1, would help me understand if you could
M7.1 say some more about it ...

H: [*Pause of 20 seconds, looking blank.*] Not really. Just numb. No I used to, I think, at the beginning, I'm not sure, no, just nothing. Dead, really.

S1.1 S: Numb, dead, nothing – sounds detached and distant from all feelings.

H: [*Sits quietly, looking blank, unfocused and detached from what is being said.*] Yes, I suppose so.

M4.2, [*Silence for 55 seconds.*]
M6.1 H: So anyway, I finally got him to talk to Aisha about it but I don't like her having to ask. He should just have it there ready without all this, she shouldn't have to worry about the fees. She has her exams to worry about.

G8, S1.1 S: You talk about the children's father being, erm, obstructive, and not wanting Aisha to be worried. And somehow, you still seem to have no feelings yourself.

H: No. Not really. Just get through the ... what happens each day. Feelings get in the way. And anyway, what's the point? He's gone.

Habiba is not sufficiently emotionally aroused in order to do any productive work. Steph has respectfully, empathically stayed with Habiba for over two sessions. Steph gives her some feedback about how she looks whilst talking about her husband. Habiba might access some feelings if she can experience the discrepancy that Steph sees.

Steph keeps looking at Habiba, and occasionally meets her gaze without demanding anything. She waits attentively, conveying interest and concern.

S1.1   S: There's no point in feelings, you just get
        through each day. Feelings will only get in
G8   the way of getting things done, is that right?

        H: Yes, I suppose so.

        S: In the first session, we talked about getting   Steph takes it a step further reminding Habiba
S1.4   some energy back, some zest for life. When I   of the therapeutic goal they negotiated in
            listen to you, you seem so detached,   session 1.
B6, S2.3   disengaged. I wonder if there's anything you
            can think of that we could do to get
M8.2   something going. Am I helping or hindering,
            for example?

        H: Yes, I remember. I don't know what to do, I
            don't. It's not your fault. I should just give up.

S1.2, S1.3, S: I hear you saying how very, very difficult it   Whilst continuing to wait patiently and
S1.4,   is, and that you're at a loss as to what to   respectfully is an option, Steph decides that
M4.1,   do ... at the end of your tether. Would it be   since they have a reasonably strong
M4.2   OK for me to make a suggestion? You   relationship she will risk a more direct
            must tell me if it's not OK.   intervention.

        H: Alright.

        S: This numbness you feel when you think   Steph decides to offer a mixture of clearing a
            about the children's father, can you feel it   space and systematic evocative unfolding to
            now?   help Habiba access any feelings she might
                                                                have.
        H: I don't know.

S1.5,   S: Try closing your eyes and in your
S2.4   imagination find a place that's safe for
            you. You don't have to tell me where it is
            or what it's like. Just nod when you can
            feel safe inside. [*Habiba nods.*] OK, now
            take a moment to think about the
            childrens' father, maybe some of the
            conversations you've had with him this
            week.

        H: Oh. OK.

        S: Do any feelings come into your awareness?

        H: Just numb. Well, no, right next to the
            numbness is irritation.

S1.2, S1.3, S: Numbness and irritation right next to it.   Steph is ready to work with numbness as the
S1.4, S2.2, H: Yes, that's it exactly, and when I remember   main feeling, and is preparing to ask Habiba
M4.1,   what ... [*Habiba opens her eyes with a start*   to inhabit that numb feeling to see if it has
M4.2   *and bursts into tears, sobbing*   any meaning when something else happens ...
            uncontrollably.]

For the next 10 minutes Habiba is clearly overwhelmed with a mixture of feelings.
Habiba is unable to talk about them, since she seems to have gone from under-arousal
to over-arousal at the flick of a metaphorical switch. Steph tries to help Habiba get the

strong emotions down to a safe size with some emotion regulation in which Habiba is able to see the raging feelings in a glass bottle safely put about 100 yards away in an orchard. She is able to identify the emotions and very tentatively begin to work with them by looking into the bottle without risk of anything escaping. She identifies terrible humiliation, hurt, betrayal and raging anger.

H: I just don't know where to begin with these feelings. I feel too confused by it all, them all, everything. I want to just blank them all off again. It's best. Honestly.

Steph notes that Habiba's visualisation of the feelings in a glass bottle at a distance in an orchard indicates the strength of the feelings. It is a visualisation of a very *safe place.*

B7, S1.1, S1.5

S: It really does seem best to put it all away out of reach. You're not quite saying 'life would be simpler' if you could shut it all away again. Get back to being numb?

H: Yes. [*Looks down, shaking her head.*] No, no, that's not ... no. I need, I want to ... I don't know what to do with these feelings, but I must do something. This is just ruining everything.

S1.1, S1.5, B7, B8

S: These are really difficult feelings to understand, to experience without being afraid and overwhelmed. And let me check, first you want to somehow get to grips with them, whatever that means [*Habiba nods.*] and second they all, or most of them, started when the children's father left?

Steph is again gently checking that Habiba still wants to work actively with the goal she set in session 1.

H: Said he wanted to leave ... well, no let's see ...

S2.4

S: OK, would you like to try going back to that day, and, with me here with you, walking through it again, like a re-enactment of a crime.

Steph thinks that it might help to try some more systematic evocative unfolding, to relive the events whilst keeping the associated emotions to the fore. This way, in the safety of the relationship, Habiba might be put back in touch with the feelings and able to stretch her ability to experience these difficult feelings.

H: It was a crime! The swine! Why? What had I done? Nothing, that's what. He even said 'It's not your fault'.

S4.1, S4.2

S: OK, Habi, so it sounds as though you are right back there now. Where were you when this happened? And as you describe the scene, tell me the feelings that come up.

Beyond prompting Habiba to keep reliving the moment, Steph is doing no more than respectful, genuine, empathic following.

H: Well, right, it was, I remember it as though it was yesterday. [*She starts getting upset and takes a deep breath.*] He waited until the children had gone to my mother's for the weekend. It was Friday night and I'm sitting down on the sofa, just finished the washing up ...

> The systematic evocative unfolding goes well. In a short while, Habiba keeps hitting the notion that 'it's just not *fair* for him to leave'. She couldn't get past the idea that he wasn't fair, him leaving wasn't fair, life wasn't fair. He must have lied when he said he loved her when they first met. She could see no point in anything in the midst of all this injustice and broken dreams. Except her duty to the childern.

H: He *said* he loved me, but what changed? That doesn't change, does it? [*Looks imploringly at Steph.*] You can't fall out of love with someone can you? He *lied*! He never loved me, but I loved him.

To Steph, this sounds like a meaning protest. It sounds like Habiba has had a cherished belief about love, and how people in love conduct themselves, shattered by Rafiq's behaviour and the things he has said.

S1.1, S3.1, G5, M3.2

S: So love is forever? Is that a good way to put it? It never changes? You said a session or two ago that you married for love. Your parents weren't convinced at first but *you* believed in love. Have I got that right?

H: Yes, well, of course it's natural to think that isn't it. I was in love, I made a promise. I stuck by him, but he ... he ...

S3.1, B7

S: It's really important to you that *you*, *Habi* believe in love everlasting, loyalty, keeping promises. It sounds as though it's right at the centre of you at this moment.

The therapeutic task associated with meaning protest, is meaning creation (see p. 151) which looks similar to a cognitive therapy on paper. However, in the person-centred relational context, there is no judgement of rationality or refutation of cherished beliefs. Indeed, meaning creation begins with accepting and valuing the cherished beliefs that have been violated.

H: It is ... it just doesn't seem right ... how could he? He ruined everything.

B7

S: In that one moment, all that you held dear, and still hold dear, was ruined.

In CfD meaning creation can be simply being genuinely, respectfully empathic to the extent that the client can loosen their constrained introjects about, e.g. love, under their own steam. Sometimes, it might involve a slightly more active, persistent examination if the client will allow it.

H: That's it.

S: And there's no going back.

H: No. Of course not, Not now. But it still hurts. Like a broken heart. It sounds like a Disney movie, but it's true. It hurt my heart. It was ... is ... broken.

S3.1   S: Your heart was broken that day
            and it remains broken. You believe that
            love lasts forever, but he spoiled that
            forever.

        H: Yes, he did. [*Habiba's eyes moisten and she
            catches her breath.*]

M3.2   S: You fought hard for that belief, with your   Many therapeutic moments of movement are
            parents. You fought hard for love, rather   fleeting and as Steph follows Habiba she takes
            than tradition and an arranged marriage.   the opportunity to quickly move on to
            So the stakes were high.   respectfully examine the details of Habiba's
                                                             beliefs about love and the possibility of
        H: Yes, I did. Everyone must think   healing.
            how stupid ... humiliating, totally
            humiliated and ... how could he do it? I
            loved him.

        S: You were shamed, all that effort and   Steph still follows Habiba. She doesn't
            arguing, was open to ridicule.   challenge the rationality of Habiba's beliefs,
                                                             since she understands that Habiba's beliefs
        H: Yes, that's right. But what hurts most still   will have been forged at a time when they
            is the fact ... how could he do it? It was   were important and helpful. Questioning their
            supposed to be forever.   rationality would be non-therapeutic in that it
                                                             would threaten Habiba's self-structure. That
        S: It still hurts and it sounds as though   doesn't preclude gentle, respectful
            you are saying it can never be   examination of their continued viability,
            mended.   though this is a difficult line to tread.

        H: Broken is broken. Like a nice vase, or,
            erm, well, I suppose you *can* mend a vase
            but it never looks the same – always looks,
            you know, like it's been broken.

B7, B8, S: So are you saying that your heart might
S2.5   mend but will always have a mark or scar,
             or is that just about vases?

S1.6   H: [*Smiles.*] Ha ha. I see what you're saying. I
            don't know. Maybe. I don't know.

S3.2   S: When you think about that possibility, of   Steph continues to tread this line and take
            mending or changing your ideas about   opportunities to examine possible beliefs
            love, what happens inside, to your   about healing and how Habiba feels about
            feelings?   these ideas.

The remainder of the session, and the next two sessions, are taken up with similar
meaning creation work in which Habiba gradually does develop a different idea
about her ability to heal. She does not have to remain broken, but might carry a
scar. Although this work in CfD borrows the term *meaning creation* from emotion-
focused therapy, in many cases it simply describes what is already happening in

(Continued)

(Continued)

mainstream person-centred therapy. What CfD adds is the possibility of being slightly more active, while remaining gentle and respectful, and in a collaborative process with the client. As we explained, on paper, this can look quite cognitive, but in CfD is founded on understanding, acceptance and respect, not deliberate, mindful realigning of beliefs.

In the current session we have seen Steph be more active than a classical person-centred therapist in at least three ways: first, she helped Habiba identify and experience her emotions more strongly, then she helped her associate the feelings with specific events when Habiba felt lost. Finally, Steph responded to a meaning protest with non-intrusive meaning creation.

Therapeutic tasks are identified and responded to with 'techniques' in a fluid process and indeed, the commentary on this extract might be doing nothing more than naming components of person-centted work that naturally occur in the routine practice of many experienced counsellors.

Sessions five to eight see Habiba gaining in confidence slowly and tentatively. The meaning creation work also indicates that she has developed a slightly different way of understanding love which leaves her feeling less than *completely* violated and betrayed by her expectations. Having said that, there are no dramatic breakthroughs. She feels stronger in herself, less beaten up and betrayed and *thinks* about 'stepping outside the front door' – a metaphor she uses to describe getting more involved in a world beyond her children and reconnecting with her friends and community.

She identifies one remaining obstacle to her feeling able to try to 'step out' – her sense of shame, humiliation and worthlessness brought about by her husband's actions.

20 minutes into Session 9

H: It's his fault, I still think that, deep down. I can't find a way round it. He can't undo what he's done. He doesn't want to and I don't want him to. I hate him for it ... I'm sorry I keep saying that over and over, but it's true. I didn't do anything. He did and he's ... I'm too ashamed to ... I have very bad feelings for him.

S: You blame him, and you feel this very strongly that he *is* to blame. When you talk like this, it's almost as if he is in the room here. Would you like to try something to see if you can move past these feelings? Would that be a good idea?

Steph realises that not only are the feelings very present for Habiba, but that there might be an opporunity to complete some possibly unfinished business with her husband.

S1.4

H: It depends, but you're sort of right about him being here. I can see him clearly, even though it's been years.

S: OK, so it's not a big leap of your imagination to think what you would like to say to him if he really were here now. What would you say?

H: What, you mean here, now, like standing over there?

> Two chairs are not necessary to facilitate this kind of dialogue, especially when a client finds visualisation as easy as Habiba.

S: Yes, if that's what you can imagine.

H: Well, you … you bastard! I hate you! You lied to me, you have ruined my life and … I … want you to know that. To know *how much … how bad* you have been! You should be ashamed of yourself!

> Unfinished business can be finished in a number of ways, limited only by the creativity of the cilent and flexibility of the counsellor. Artwork and writing are commonly used by counsellors with expressive therapy experience.

S1.5   S: Wow, that was one barrel of your shot-gun, so to speak. But since you can see him, how about trying something a little more difficult, how about making it really personal and using his name.

> It is a risk to see if Habiba can tolerate using Rafiq's name. Steph uses her clinical judgement and moment-to-moment sense of where Habiba is up to.

[*Habiba looks at Steph intently for a second, gives a half-smile, takes a deep breath …*]

H: Rafiq, you bastard, it's you who should be ashamed, not me! *Not me*!!

Habiba rants at Rafiq for several minutes, with Steph following closely. During this time she begins to feel stronger in relation to the Rafiq in her imagination, and is able to shift her feeling of shame and humiliation. Subsequently, when the session returns to empathic following she feels stronger in herself. With this increase in confidence she plucks up the courage to 'step outside the front door'. To begin with this is still in the service of her children – she joins the parent–teacher group at their school and helps plan a fundraising event. She completes another two sessions with Steph, pleased with her progress.

CASE EXAMPLE 3: Aileen – Counsellor Mira

Aileen is a 25-year-old white Irish woman. Until she became pregnant 18 months ago, she worked for a national chain of fast food restaurants as a kitchen manager, and she intends to return to work soon. She was a keen hockey player at school, having played for her school team, she also played in the local town's team in the second eleven. She is married to Tim, also 25. She gave birth to Aisling, a healthy full-term baby 9 months ago.

Everything was fine for the first couple of months, even though Aisling was demanding and didn't sleep particularly well. Aileen started out very confident – Aisling was a planned baby and things couldn't have been better – but, in her own words, she slowly lost interest in being a mother. It wasn't dramatic, but the more distant and uninterested she became, the lower she began to feel. Over the next two months she felt guilty and useless, irritable and increasingly overwhelmed with responsibility.

The Health Visitor was the first to notice things weren't quite right and suggested that Aileen saw her GP who referred her for counselling for depression. Aileen's counsellor is Mira, an ex-Health Visitor herself. Aileen was clear in the first session that her aim was to start feeling happy again so that she could be a good mum.

The first two sessions comprised Aileen telling her story in a hopeless, detached way. She has felt isolated at home because she's been unable to talk to Tim about it – not because he is unsympathetic, but because she felt guilty and did not want him to know that she was struggling. So far it has been a relief to share it with Mira.

G6

M: What would you like to talk about today Aileen?

A: Well, I don't feel any better really. I nearly talked to Tim on Thursday, but I thought there'd be no point. It'd only worry him.

B7, B8, B9

M: So there's not been any change in your moods or feelings, and though you thought about talking to Tim, you then thought that it probably wasn't worth it because you didn't want him to worry.

A: [*In a flat, lifeless tone.*] Yeah. I mean there is no point, is there? I do feel a, well, a *tiny* bit better, I mean I feel better *here* and just after talking to you, but …

M: So, not much change, apart from brightening up a bit when you've been here and for a while afterwards. Then …

As this session gets under way, Mira is ready to follow Aileen empathically, and at the same time, feels it might be time for some more slightly active gently structuring of the session. She has no idea where Aileen will go, but is ready to gently probe and make suggestions if Aileen continues to be lifeless and detached. Even in this more active way of being, Mira will take her lead from Aileen.

Aileen's level of emotional arousal is too low for 'work' in CfD, though a more classical PC therapist would wait patiently, following Aileen empathically. Mira knows that helping Aileen access emotions and then help her increase her emotional arousal *might* be useful and holds the thought in readiness as the session unfolds.

back down to earth – bump ... but ... no,
B4, B7,
B8
not 'bump!' [*Accentuated in tone.*] You
sound *flat*, low, really flat.

A: Yeah, That's how I feel. Nothing to ...
[*Tails off.*]

M: Right now it looks pretty bleak. Nothing to
... ? I'm not sure if you wanted to finish that.

A: No not really. I just feel like a tyre that's
been punctured. Useless. Not fit for ...
what do they say?

M: Erm, not fit for anything?

A: Yeah. Fit for nothing, useless. A
disappointment.

B7, B8 M: A disappointment. [*Said in a level tone,
not as a question implying 'A
disappointment to whom?'*]

Talking about negative feelings is movement.
Aileen's flat tone has gone. She *feels*
disappointed and shows it. And the
metaphors and images she is using are
engaging and expressive.

A: Yeah. Inside I just feel I've let everyone
down.

S2.5 M: You've been a disappointment to
everyone. And that has punctured your
tyre. You can't get very far on a punctured
tyre.

A: No. Useless and oh, I don't know.

M: You *sound* punctured. A disappointment.
[*Pause of 30 seconds.*]

Mira wonders if Aileen can extend this slight
emotional arousal to sense what might be
happening inside her, to come closer to any
felt sense of this experience of
disappointment.

M: To *everyone.*

A: Yeah. That's what I feel inside.

S1.1 M: Inside, right now?

A: Yeah.

S1.2, S1.3, M: Is that a physical sensation? What does it
S1.4 feel like, the sense or physical feeling, to
be a disappointment?

S1.5, S2.1, A: Well, I suppose it's like a colour that stains
S2.2 everything. I look at myself and there's a
stain and mark, a black spot. Like a black
mark aganist me.

Helping give the experience more dimensions,
or make it more embodied, can help bring
things on the edge of awareness into the
foreground. Mira hopes that this expressive
imagery that Aileen is developing will help in
this process.

M: Like at school? A bad report.

S2.5 A: Yeah, like a criminal record.

M: That's strong stuff, a criminal record. More
than just blotting your copybook. A criminal
record. What did you do to get that?

B7, B8 A: I couldn't love my baby.

M: And that's a crime. [*Said as a statement.*]

A: Yes. Sort of. Yes. It's what I've always
wanted. It's what it means to be ... a
Brennan. A Brennan woman. Brennan's
my maiden name.

This is the first time Aileen has touched upon
anything that is a discrepancy between the
expectations embedded in her identity and
her lived experience. This is 'straightforward'
incongruence in terms of the person-centred
theory shared by CfD. The question Mira has
to deal with is 'How to work with it?'

S2.2   M: I see. That's a powerful tradition. Something to live up to, and it is such a disappointment to not be able to live up to it.

A: Yeah. Of course my mother was a saint.

B7, B8, B9   M: I'm not sure whether you are being ironic when you say that, 'a saint'?

A: No, really, she was just a great mum. I love her, but blooming heck, what an act to follow! And she still is now. She's been so supportive.

B7   M: So, your mum has been a great mum all the way through – all your life. And you really appreciate that.

A: I do. I don't know what I'd do without her. But I can't tell her. Oh no. No! I couldn't stand her *understanding*. She is so blooming *perfect*. It ... it's not her fault. It's me. I'm disappointed in myself.

M: So, let me see if I can get this ... the weight of tradition, of family expectations and your mother's ability to apparently embody those traditions and be everything you think a mother should be on the one side and then you, the realities of your life and your real experiences of motherhood on the other.

A: Yeah, that's about it. Shit, oh sorry! Such a disappointment.

B4, S.1.1   M: Oh, and the disappointment. Like a drip, drip.

A: Nagging at me. [*Sounds irritated, even a little angry.*]

S1.2, S1.3   M: So, it's not a drip, drip, it's nagging. And you sound angry when you say that. Is it nagging now?

A: Yes, right now. And yes, I am bloody cross, fed up with it. Just go away!

S1.4, S1.5   M: You're fed up and want it to go away right now. Can you hear it saying anything?

A: Yes, like, the Brennan women do this, do that. Are *quiet* and *good* wives. And *loving mothers*. And never want anything for themselves.

In theory terms this is a particular form of discrepancy between self-structure and experience. A self-critical part of Aileen's self structure takes shape. It coalesces around quite a catalogue of introjected expectations. Mira could wait to see if Aileen unpacks the bits herself or works with the whole in some other way. But, since these implicity self-critical statements of family expectations are so well-formed, she decides to see if Aileen can give them voice now and dialogue with them.

S1.2,
S1.4

M: Right. Does the nagging voice have anything else to say?

A: It just repeats itself.

M: Does it have a tone?

A: Well it's a kindly scolding. Sort of soft but insistent. It's a proud voice.

M: When you hear it now, inside, do you feel anything?

A: Actually it's me. It's my voice. Like a young me.

B7

M: The disappointed voice is you. A young Aileen. [*Statement, not question.*]

A: Yes.

M: Anything else?

A: Yes, she's so *certain,* so sure of herself. So sure she's got it right. But she hasn't.

S1.2,
S1.4,
S2.1

M: She hasn't got it right. You want her to know that. And your voice as you speak is now gentle, not angry any more. This is a conversation with that part of you, by the sound of it. Is that right, or have I got that wrong?

A: No, that's right. I'm not cross with her ... me.

S1.4,
S1.6

M: So you know what that part of you has to say [Aileen interjects: For now! She's got plenty more to say.] ... and ... she has to more to say, what do you want to do now? I was wondering if there was anything you wanted to say back? To tell her.

A: Erm, yes, well, OK ... I want her to know that it's not that simple. Life is miles more blooming complicated than that. You can't just say 'You're a Brennan woman and Brennan women get married, have kids, live like it's the 1950s' or something. It's not like that now'.

S3.1,
S3.4

M: The world is not like that any more. *I'm not like that* any more.

A: That's right I'm *not* like that. I just thought, actually, I remembered, well, I didn't forget, ... well ... maybe ... anyhow I, I [*Catches her breath and eyes fill up with tears.*]

S1.5

M: Take a minute ... these are strong feelings ... when you are ready ...

Mira is pursuing this work with the self-critic quite actively. She tries to bring the dialogue into the room – making it a spoken dialogue between parts of Aileen's personality and her lived experience.

Even though this is at the active end of CfD practice, Mira is respectful and doesn't push anything past the point at which Aileen is comfortable. She checks her understanding and ...

... is tentative in making suggestions to continue to move things along. She wonders whether encouraging dialogue in the session between Aileen and her 'younger self' configuration would be helpful. She is ready to let this pass or follow Aileen somewhere else if this is not acceptable or useful for Aileen.

A: [*Composes herself slightly.*] I, I feel frightened saying this [*Lowers her voice as if telling a secret.*] … I was not ready, really. Not ready to have children. Actually, I'm not sure I really wanted children. When I think of all the things I used to do and then BAM! I hit a brick bloomin' wall. Hit the bloody buffers good and proper.

M: You …

A: I've never said that before. I'm too ashamed, too guilty. Didn't … want …

B7, B8

M: Something you've kept inside …

A: Yes, I don't think I even really told myself. [*Laughs a weak laugh.*] Until now, the younger me, all certain there, well, bugger off! Life's just not like that! And before you ask, I don't feel anything, really. Just 'So go on, what do you think of that, little miss perfect!'

Now Aileen moves out of the process of dialogue and returns to disclosing a discovery from her immediate experience. These therapeutic tasks, processes and the techniques which facilitate them move fluidly, unannounced and without comment.

And now Mira returns to respectful empathic following, and continues to the end of the session, making no more suggestions.

5 minutes into Session 3

The remainder of the session, and further sessions, carry on in a similar vein, with Alieen slowly exploring her present thoughts and feelings about the experience of mother-hood. This is an alignment of the discrepancy between her self-structure and experi-ence. In this case, some of her experience in the world and content of her self-structure were intially just out of awareness. A combination of the safety of the therapeutic rela-tionship and the 'soft' techniques of identifying self-critical parts of her personality and encouraging dialogue between the discrepant elements of her self-structure and expe-rience allow alignment and reconciliation.

Aileen was also able to talk about the things she missed and resolved to get back into some sort of sport. This was her incentive to tell Tim that she wasn't coping as well as she had led him to believe. This relieved more pressure on her.

Aileen returned in session 7 to talk more about her 'young self' and discovered that the intention of the younger 'configuration of self' was to protect her and arm her for a successful and contented life. A brief, calm, even respectful dialogue ensued for a few minutes before the younger Aileen just disappeared. Aileen believed that this was because she had done her job, so to speak.

After eleven sessions, Aileen and Mira decided to finish the counselling. Aileen was feeling much more in touch with her feelings and was able to talk to Tim who helped more with the childcare in small, but important ways. Not spectacular, but effective.

Epilogue

We hope these vignettes have drawn together the theory and practice of CfD and breathed some life into it. Our intention was to reassure experienced person-centred practitioners that their established attitudes and skills are entirely in harmony with the CfD therapeutic stance, whilst introducing the more active interventions and demonstrating how they might be integrated into sessions. Most importantly, we needed to illustrate how, although a competence-based therapy, CfD in practice follows the client's experience in a flexible, flowing relationship. The relationship is paramount – not just the substrate for therapy, but the substance, the essential essence of it as well. Our principal message is that CfD competences are not to be used instrumentally in a clunky counselling-by-numbers manner. Readers may now better understand how the competences in the narrow margins are illustrative and disputable, not prescriptive and rigid. Our intent is that the vignettes start expansive discussions about good and better practice, not constraining discussions about what is right and wrong.

10

Training, Supervision and Research: Developing Counselling for Depression

In evidence-based practice there is perhaps too much emphasis placed on the question of which type of therapy is the most effective, at the expense of considering other aspects of therapy delivery. The process of making psychological therapies available can be viewed as a system containing a number of important elements additional to the therapeutic approach taken:

- opportunities for the client to access the therapy
- what the client brings in terms of motivation and personal resources
- the skills and personal qualities of the therapist
- opportunities for the therapist to access high-quality training
- the quality of supervision provided to the therapist
- research into the practice and outcomes of therapy

All of these have a bearing on the impact and outcomes of psychological services and, while all are important, the latter three form the focus of this chapter.

Training

As depression is the most common single psychological problem in the UK and CfD is recommended by NICE for the treatment of this area of distress, it follows that counsellors working and training within the person-centred and experiential tradition should have widespread opportunities to train in CfD. Training in CfD should be available both to those undergoing initial counsellor training as well as to qualified and experienced practitioners. In both of these cases considerable underpinning skill and knowledge is required for the CfD competences to be mastered and implemented effectively. Hence, where a CfD module forms part of an initial training programme, it is important for it to be scheduled towards the end of the programme of study to allow for the prior acquisition of the necessary skill and understanding. Similarly, where CfD training is offered as continuing professional development (CPD) to qualified and experienced counsellors, it is essential to ensure that those entering the programme have the appropriate foundational knowledge and skill to be successful and benefit from the training.

The elements of fundamental knowledge and skill fall into a number of general areas. Training in CfD builds on core professional competence, requiring proficiency in a number of areas (described in more detail in Chapter 3): knowledge of common mental health problems; ability to work ethically within professional guidelines; ability to work effectively with individuals from a diverse range of backgrounds; ability to undertake a generic assessment; ability to assess and manage risk of suicide and self-harm; ability to use measures to guide therapy and to monitor outcomes; ability to make use of supervision. Theoretical knowledge of the person-centred and experiential approach is likewise very important, as a solid grounding in this theoretical perspective supports the learning of the more novel aspects of CfD. Along with theoretical knowledge, the ability to implement the person-centred relational stance using the therapeutic conditions (Rogers, 1957) is central to learning the CfD approach. Since training in CfD rests upon these areas of skill and knowledge, experienced practitioners trained in the person-centred approach and trainees on dedicated person-centred training or integrative training based around person-centred therapy are best placed to deliver CfD.

A training curriculum[1] for CfD has been developed and is likely to be of interest to trainers, trainee counsellors and counsellors considering taking up the training. It is illustrative rather than prescriptive and the structure of this book maps closely onto the subject areas covered in the curriculum. Assessment of trainee competence on the training programme focuses on practice with clients. As the CfD competence framework provides the link to evidence of effective practice, as set out in the research literature, it follows that the assessment of trainees should be based on how far they implement the competences with real clients in therapy sessions. This is achieved by trainees submitting audio recordings of sessions and implementation of the competence framework measured by use of a standardised tool, the PCEPS developed at Strathclyde University (Freire et al., 2013). As competence necessitates not only knowledge but the application of this to complex real-life situations, counsellor competence can only be truly assessed using real sessions with clients as opposed to role-plays, written case studies or essays. Hence the importance of the PCEPS and the opportunity it provides to assess either live or recorded therapy sessions.

The use of scales such as the PCEPS to assess the effectiveness of therapeutic practice is not a new idea in person-centred therapy. Out of concerns that therapeutic practice was not always effective and that the training of therapists was often too academic and theoretical, Truax and Carkhuff (1967) sought to identify from the research and theoretical literature the effective components common to all forms of psychotherapy, develop operational descriptions of these and produce scales which could then be

---

[1] Curriculum available at: www.iapt.nhs.uk/silo/files/curriculum-for-counselling-for-depression.pdf (retrieved 18/11/2013).

applied to both live and audio-recorded therapy sessions, to determine the effectiveness of the therapist. This, they argued, would improve training programmes and the overall standard of therapeutic practice. Empathy, non-possessive warmth and genuineness were identified as being the effective common factors (thereafter often referred to as the 'core conditions') and a rating scale was developed for each, based on grade descriptions denoting levels of each condition. Over the last 40 years these scales, and similar adapted versions of them, have been widely used in person-centred training and many counsellors will have used them to hone their ability to implement the core conditions.

There are parallels between Truax and Carkhuff's work and the development of CfD and the PCEPS scale. The CfD project has sought to use the research literature to iden-tify effective interventions and translate these into practice through training. Like the core condition rating scales, the PCEPS aims to promote effective practice by providing an objective method to assess how successfully trainees are implementing the main principles of the approach. The development of the PCEPS began in March 2010, led by Beth Freire, Robert Elliott and Graham Westwell at Strathclyde University and sup-ported by seed-corn research funding from the BACP. The driving force behind the project was the challenge to person-centred counselling presented by the evidence-based paradigm (see Chapter 2) and the need for a measure which could be used to assess the competence of therapists in RCTs of person-centred and experiential counsel-ling. RCT methodology requires a demonstration that the psychological treatment tested in trials is delivered in a way that is faithful to the treatment manual; often referred to as *treatment fidelity*. The first part of the process of developing the measure involved constructing a set of high-order competences that capture the essence of the therapeutic approach, using archived audio recordings of therapy to assess the validity of the competences. Once the items on the scale were agreed, teams of raters used the scale with a standard set of recorded therapy sessions to determine whether different raters came up with similar scores, thus testing the reliability of the measure. An initial version of the scale consisted of 15 items with two subscales: (a) person-centred process and (b) experiential process. These two subscales represented the division between non-directive person-centred therapy and more experiential approaches derived from emo-tion-focused therapy. Long-held theoretical understanding depicted these areas of practice as distinct and so it was originally planned that the measure would need to differentiate between the two. Items on the person-centred subscale included 'Client Frame of Reference/Track', 'Core Meaning', 'Client Flow', 'Warmth', 'Accepting Presence' and 'Genuineness', and items on the experiential subscale included 'Collaboration', 'Experiential Specificity', 'Emotion Focus', 'Client Self-Development' and 'Emotion Regulation Sensitivity'.

Testing the reliability and validity of the measure was carried out using 120 audio-recorded segments of therapy sessions, systematically selected from 20 clients seen by 10 therapists, three of whom were EFT practitioners and the other seven person-cen-tred. The audio recordings were rated independently by six raters, divided into two teams of three raters each. All raters were person-centred counsellors, three being qualified and experienced and the other three trainees. Each rater scored 60 audio-recorded segments and results were compared across the group. Results indicated that the PCEPS had good internal consistency and reliability. Interestingly, an exploratory factor analysis did not support the distinction between person-centred and experiential practices which had been hypothesised by the authors of the measure (Freire et al., 2013). This meant that items in both the person-centred and experiential subscales were equally applicable across both person-centred and EFT practitioners. It was also felt that the scale was too long and could usefully be abridged.

As a result of these findings the scale was reduced to 10 items and the subscales taken out (see Figure 10.1 on pp. 186–91). A number of conclusions can be drawn from the fact that the subscales were not found to be valid. It suggests that person-centred practitioners implement experiential interventions as a natural part of their practice, in the same way that EFT practitioners naturally use person-centred methods in their way of working. The two areas are much more convergent in practice than they appear when conceptualised theoretically and person-centred and experiential competences can be grouped together to form a coherent model of practice, which is a principle central to the development of CfD.

Further research needs to be carried out on the PCEPS to see whether current findings are replicated. The measure has the potential to be extremely useful in training and research and field trials of the measure suggest that distinctions between person-centred and experiential approaches are more theoretically and ideologically driven than rooted in therapeutic practice.

To date, several cohorts of counsellors have undergone training in CfD and have had their competence assessed using the PCEPS. In the interest of improving the training programme and developing a better understanding of trainees' perspectives, a formal evaluation of the initial roll-out of the training was conducted (Pearce et al., 2012). The training was initially delivered by a network of accredited providers across England.[2] The CPD training, aimed at experienced counsellors who already hold an initial qualification in person-centred or humanistic counselling/psychotherapy, consisted of a five-day taught programme followed by 80 hours of supervised and assessed counselling practice.[3] Trainees who had completed both the five-day programme and the 80 hours of practice were invited to participate in the evaluation which aimed to assess their responses both to the training programme and the competence framework. The evaluation consisted of a survey by questionnaire and follow-up telephone interviews with six participants who had taken part in the survey. The questionnaire asked about sense of self as practitioner pre-training, expectations of the CfD training, experience of the five-day taught CfD training programme, attitudes to the CfD competence framework, experience of supervised practice, experience of the assessment of counselling practice and the impact of the CfD training on their practice. Of the 60 counsellors contacted to take part in the evaluation, 30 completed the questionnaire online. The majority worked as high-intensity therapists in IAPT services, often in part-time roles.

---

[2] The Metanoia Training Institute, London; University of Keele; University of York St John.
[3] Curriculum available at: www.iapt.nhs.uk/silo/files/curriculum-for-counselling-for-depression.pdf (retrieved 18/11/2013).

Figure 10.1

PERSON-CENTRED & EXPERIENTIAL PSYCHOTHERAPY SCALE-10 (v. 1.2, 12/12/12)

© 2011, 2012, Robert Elliott & Graham Westwell. (Permission is granted to reproduce this form for educational, training, or supervision purposes, on the condition that it is not changed or sold).

Client ID:	Session:
Rater:	Segment:

Rate the items according to how well each activity occurred during the therapy segment you've just listened to. It is important to attend to your overall sense of the therapist's immediate experiencing of the client. Try to avoid forming a 'global impression' of the therapist early on in the session.

1. CLIENT FRAME OF REFERENCE/TRACK:

How much do the therapist's responses convey an understanding of the client's experiences as the client themselves understands or perceives it? To what extent is the therapist following the client's track?

Do the therapist's responses convey an understanding of the client's inner experience or point of view immediately expressed by the client? Or conversely, do therapist's responses add meaning based on the therapist's own frame of reference?

Are the therapist's responses right on client's track? Conversely, are the therapist's responses a diversion from the client's own train of thoughts/feelings?

---

1. **No tracking:** Therapist's responses convey no understanding of the client's frame of reference; or therapist adds meaning based completely on their own frame of reference.
2. **Minimal tracking:** Therapist's responses convey a poor understanding of the client's frame of reference; or therapist adds meaning partially based on their own frame of reference rather than the client's.
3. **Slightly tracking:** Therapist's responses come close but don't quite reach an adequate understanding of the client's frame of reference; therapist's responses are slight 'off' of the client's frame or reference.
4. **Adequate tracking:** Therapist's responses convey an adequate understanding of the client's frame of reference.
5. **Good tracking:** Therapist's responses convey a good understanding of the client's frame of reference.
6. **Excellent tracking:** Therapist's responses convey an accurate understanding of the client's frame of reference and therapist adds no meaning from their own frame of reference.

---

2. PSYCHOLOGICAL HOLDING:

How well does the therapist metaphorically hold the client when they are experiencing painful, scary, or overwhelming experiences, or when they are connecting with their vulnerabilities?

High scores refer to therapist maintaining a solid, emotional and empathic connection even when the client is in pain or overwhelmed.

Low scores refer to situations in which the therapist avoids responding or acknowledging painful, frightening or overwhelming experiences of the client.

Figure 10.1 (Continued)

---

1. **No holding:** Therapist oblivious to client's need to be psychologically held: avoids responding, acknowledging or addressing client's experience/feelings.
2. **Minimal holding:** Therapist seems to be aware of the client's need to be psychologically held but is anxious or insecure when responding to client and diverts or distracts client from their vulnerability.
3. **Slight holding:** Therapist conveys a bit of psychological holding, but not enough and with some insecurity.
4. **Adequate holding:** Therapist manages to hold sufficiently the client's experience.
5. **Good holding:** Therapist calmly and solidly holds the client's experience.
6. **Excellent holding:** Therapist securely holds client's experience with trust, groundedness and acceptance, even when the client is experiencing, for example, pain, fear or overwhelmedness.

---

3. EXPERIENTIAL SPECIFICITY:

How much does the therapist appropriately and skilfully work to help the client focus on, elaborate or differentiate specific, idiosyncratic or personal experiences or memories, as opposed to abstractions or generalities?

E.g., by reflecting specific client experiences using crisp, precise, differentiated and appropriately empathic reflections; or asking for examples or to specify feelings, meanings, memories or other personal experiences.

---

1. **No specificity:** therapist consistently responds in a highly abstract, vague or intellectual manner.
2. **Minimal specificity:** therapist seems to have a concept of specificity but doesn't implement adequately, consistently or well; therapist is either somewhat vague or abstract or generally fails to encourage experiential specificity where appropriate.
3. **Slight specificity:** therapist is often or repeatedly vague or abstract; therapist only slightly or occasionally encourages experiential specificity; sometimes responds in a way that points to experiential specificity, at times they fail to do so, or do so in an awkward manner.
4. **Adequate specificity:** where appropriate, therapist generally encourages client experiential specificity, with only minor, temporary lapses or slight awkwardness.
5. **Good specificity:** therapist does enough of this and does it skilfully, where appropriate trying to help the client to elaborate and specify particular experiences.
6. **Excellent specificity:** therapist does this consistently, skilfully, and even creatively, where appropriate, offering the client crisp, precise reflections or questions.

---

4. ACCEPTING PRESENCE:

How well does the therapist's attitude convey an unconditional acceptance of whatever the client brings?

Do the therapist's responses convey a grounded, centred, and acceptant presence?

(Continued)

Figure 10.1 (Continued)

---

1. **Explicit nonacceptance:** Therapist explicitly communicates disapproval or criticism of client's experience/meaning/feelings.
2. **Implicit nonacceptance:** Therapist implicitly or indirectly communicates disapproval or criticism of client experience/meaning/feelings.
3. **Incongruent/inconsistent nonacceptance:** Therapist conveys anxiety, worry or defensiveness instead of acceptance; or therapist is not consistent in the communication of acceptance.
4. **Adequate acceptance:** Therapist demonstrates calm and groundedness, with at least some degree of acceptance of the client's experience.
5. **Good acceptance:** Therapist conveys clear, grounded acceptance of the client's experience; therapist does not demonstrate any kind of judgement towards client's experience/behaviour.
6. **Excellent acceptance**: Therapist skilfully conveys unconditional acceptance while being clearly grounded and centred in themselves, even in face of intense client vulnerability.

---

5. CONTENT DIRECTIVENESS:

How much do the therapist's responses intend to direct the client's content?

Do the therapist's responses introduce explicit new content? E.g., do the therapist's responses convey explanation, interpretation, guidance, teaching, advice, reassurance or confrontation?

---

1. **'Expert' directiveness:** Therapist overtly and consistently assumes the role of expert in directing the content of the session
2. **Overt directiveness:** Therapist's responses direct client overtly towards a new content.
3. **Slight directiveness:** Therapist's responses direct client clearly but tentatively towards a new content.
4. **Adequate nondirectiveness:** Therapist is generally nondirective of content, with only minor, temporary lapses or slight content direction.
5. **Good nondirectiveness:** Therapist consistently follows the client's lead when responding to content.
6. **Excellent nondirectiveness:** Therapist clearly and consistently follows the client's lead when responding to content in a natural, inviting and unforced manner, with a high level of skill.

---

6. EMOTION FOCUS:

How much does the therapist actively work to help the client focus on and actively articulate their emotional experiences and meanings, both explicit and implicit?

E.g., by helping clients focus their attention inwards; by focusing the client's attention on bodily sensations; by reflecting toward emotionally poignant content, by inquiring about client feelings, helping client intensify, heighten or deepen their emotions, by helping clients find ways of describing emotions; or by making empathic conjectures about feelings that have not yet been expressed. Lower scores reflect ignoring implicit or explicit emotions; staying with non-emotional content; focusing on or reflecting generalised emotional states ('feeling bad') or minimising emotional states (e.g., reflecting 'angry' as 'annoyed').

(Continued)

Figure 10.1 (Continued)

---

1. **No emotion focus:** therapist consistently ignores emotions or responds instead in a highly intellectual manner while focusing entirely on non-emotional content. When the client expresses emotions, the therapist consistently deflects the client away from them.
2. **Minimal emotion focus:** therapist seems to have a concept of emotion focus but doesn't implement adequately, consistently or well; therapist may generally stay with non-emotional content; sometimes deflects client away from their emotion; reflects only general emotional states ('bad') or minimises client emotion.
3. **Slight emotion focus:** therapist often or repeatedly ignores or deflects client away from emotion; therapist only slightly or occasionally helps client to focus on emotion; while they sometimes respond in a way that points to client emotions, at times they fail to do so, or do so in an awkward manner.
4. **Adequate emotion focus:** where appropriate, therapist generally encourages client focus on emotions (by either reflections or other responses), with only minor, temporary lapses or slight awkwardness.
5. **Good emotion focus:** therapist does enough of this and does it skilfully, where appropriate trying to help the client to evoke, deepen and express particular emotions.
6. **Excellent emotion focus:** therapist does this consistently, skilfully, and even creatively, where appropriate, offering the client powerful, evocative reflections or questions, while at the same time enabling the client to feel safe while doing so.

---

7. DOMINANT OR OVERPOWERING PRESENCE:

To what extent does the therapist project a sense of dominance or authority in the session with the client?

Low scores refer to situations in which the therapist is taking charge of the process of the session; acts in a self-indulgent manner or takes over attention or focus for themselves; interrupting, talking over, silence or controlling the process; or acting in a definite, lecturing, or expert manner.

High scores refer to situations in which the therapist offers the client choice or autonomy in the session, allows the client space to develop their own experience, waits for the client to finish their thoughts, is patient with the client, or encourages client empowerment in the session.

---

1. **Overpowering presence:** Therapist overpowers the client by strongly dominating the interaction, controlling what the client talks about or does in the session; clearly making themselves the centre of attention; or being patronising toward the client.
2. **Controlling presence:** Therapist clearly controls the client's process of the session, acting in an expert, or dominant manner.
3. **Subtle control:** Therapist subtly, implicitly or indirectly controls what and how the client is in the session.
4. **Noncontrolling presence:** Therapist generally respects client autonomy in the session; therapist does not try to control client's process.
5. **Respectful presence:** Therapist consistently respects client autonomy in the session.
6. **Empowering presence:** Therapist clearly and consistently promotes or validates the client's freedom or choice, allowing client space as they desire.

(Continued)

Figure 10.1 (Continued)

8. CLARITY OF LANGUAGE:

How well does the therapist use language that communicates simply and clearly to the client?
E.g., therapist's responses are not too wordy, rambling, unnecessarily long; therapist does not use language that is too academic or too abstract; therapist's responses do not get in the client's way.

1. **No clarity:** Therapist's responses are long-winded, tangled, and *confusing*.
2. **Minimal clarity:** Therapist's responses are wordy, rambling or *unfocused*.
3. **Slight clarity:** Therapist's responses are *somewhat clear*, but a bit too abstract or long.
4. **Adequate clarity:** Therapist's responses are *clear but a bit too long*.
5. **Good clarity:** Therapist's responses are *clear and concise*.
6. **Excellent clarity:** Therapist's responses are *very clear and concise*, even elegantly capturing subtle client experiences in a few choice words.

9. CORE MEANING:

How well do the therapist's responses reflect the core, or essence, of what the client is communicating or experiencing in the moment?
Responses are not just a reflection of surface content but show an understanding of the client's central/core experience or meaning that is being communicated either implicitly or explicitly in the moment; responses do not take away from the core meaning of client's communication.

1. **No core meaning:** Therapist's responses address only the cognitive content or stay exclusively in the superficial narrative.
2. **Minimal core meaning:** Therapist's responses address mainly the cognitive content or the superficial narrative but bring occasional glimpses into the underlying core feeling/experience/meaning.
3. **Slight core meaning:** Therapist's responses partially but incompletely address the core meaning/feeling/experience that underlies the client's expressed content.
4. **Adequate core meaning:** Therapist's responses were close to the core meaning/feeling/experience that underlies the client's expressed content, but do not quite reach it.
5. **Good core meaning:** Therapists' responses accurately address the core meaning/feeling/experience that underlies the client's expressed content.
6. **Excellent core meaning:** Therapists' responses address with a high degree of accuracy the core meaning/feeling/experience that underlies the client's expressed content.

10. EMOTION REGULATION SENSITIVITY:

How much does the therapist actively work to help the client adjust and maintain their level of emotional arousal for productive self-exploration?
Client agency is central; this is not imposed by the therapist. There are three possible situations:
(a) If the client is overwhelmed by feelings and wants help in moderating them, does the therapist try to help the client to manage these emotions? E.g., by offering a calming and

(Continued)

Figure 10.1   (Continued)

holding presence; by using containing imagery; or by helping the client self-soothe vs. allowing the client to continue to panic or feel overwhelmed or unsafe.
(b) If the client is out of touch with their feelings and wants help in accessing them, does the therapist try to help them appropriately increase emotional contact? E.g., by helping them review current concerns and focus on the most important or poignant; by helping them remember and explore memories of emotional experiences; by using vivid imagery or language to promote feelings vs. enhancing distance from emotions.
(c) If the client is at an optimal level of emotional arousal for exploration, does the therapist try to help them continue working at this level, rather than deepening or flattening their emotions?

---

1. **No facilitation:** therapist consistently ignores issues of client emotional regulation, or generally works against client emotional regulation, i.e., allowing client to continue to feel overwhelmed or distanced.
2. **Minimal facilitation:** therapist seems to have a concept of facilitating client emotional regulation but doesn't implement adequately, consistently or well; therapist either generally ignores the client's desire to contain overwhelmed emotion or to approach distanced emotion; sometimes they misdirect the client out of a productive, optimal level of emotional arousal, into either stuck or overwhelmed emotion or emotional distance or avoidance.
3. **Slight facilitation:** therapist often or repeatedly ignores or deflects client away from their desired level of emotional regulation productive for self-exploration; therapist only slightly facilitates productive self-exploration. While they sometimes respond in a way that facilitates client productive emotional regulation, at times they fail to do so, or do so in an awkward manner.
4. **Adequate facilitation:** where appropriate, therapist generally encourages client emotional regulation (e.g., by helping them approach difficult emotions or contain excessive emotional distress as desired by client), with only minor, temporary lapses or slight awkwardness.
5. **Good facilitation:** therapist does enough emotional regulation facilitation and does it skilfully and in accordance with client's desires, where appropriate trying to help the client to maintain a productive level of emotional arousal.
6. **Excellent facilitation:** therapist does this consistently, skilfully, and even creatively, where desired, offering the client evocative or focusing responses to help the client approach difficult emotions when they are too distant and to contain overwhelming emotions, all within a safe, holding environment.

The survey found that most respondents felt that they had a good understanding of person-centred theory and practice pre-training. Very few felt that they had equal status to therapists from other modalities, particularly CBT, in their service context. Accessing the CfD training was generally seen as a way to address this and gain enhanced status. The use of the competence framework, together with the PCEPS, as a basis for training and practice were viewed positively and there was broad agreement that the CfD competence framework accurately described both the person-centred and experiential approach and how to work effectively with depressed clients. The majority of participants valued the role that supervision played throughout the assessed practice period in helping them align their practice with the CfD competence framework. Opinion was, however, more divided about participants' experience of having their practice assessed, which some trainees found stressful. However, the majority of trainees agreed that feedback from tutors on assessed practice was clear and supported their development as CfD therapists.

In terms of the impact of the training programme, the majority of respondents reported being more confident in working with depressed people and approximately half of respondents felt that participating in CfD training had enhanced their status as a therapist. For the majority of participants, the training changed how they practised and had deepened their understanding of how to work with depressed clients. Data from the qualitative interviews tended to support the findings of the survey: 'This training has empowered me. And in the setting of our trust, I'm now respected more.' There was also an interest in learning the more experiential competences derived from EFT, which for many trainees represented a developing edge to their practice. There was, however, some frustration among trainees at not being able to implement what they had learned on the training programme when they returned to practise in their services: 'The minute the course was finished, it was back to normal, back to try and get clients, you know, patched up in four or five sessions ... I didn't really get a chance to ... really engage in what I'd learnt.' The problem here seemed to be that some services were restricting the number of counselling sessions to a maximum of six, despite the fact that on the CfD programme counsellors had trained in a high-intensity intervention recommended for up to 20 sessions.

On a more positive note, a number of trainees experienced the training as helping them to reconnect with the person-centred and experiential approach and, interestingly, as equipping them to work with clients in greater emotional and relational depth. 'It was going home to a way of working that I had somewhat, not strayed from, but somehow, because of working in a very pressurised environment, I'd actually lost some of ... the spirit of it.' For experienced practitioners, who had developed a number of different ways of working, the training seemed to help them realign their practice with the main principles of the person-centred and experiential approach.

Supervision

The role of supervision is to support ethical and effective practice and, more specifically, in the case of CfD, ensure that counsellors' practice is aligned with the competence framework, as this provides a link to evidence of effectiveness. This can be viewed as part of the normative function of supervision. Supervision of CfD practice requires specialist appreciation of the approach and so a dedicated CfD supervision training is recommended. As with CfD counsellor training, CfD supervisor training builds on core supervisory skills and knowledge. Knowledge of the person-centred and experiential approach is essential and so it is important for CfD supervisors to have undergone initial training in this modality. Likewise familiarity with the CfD competence model is important and so it is desirable for supervisors themselves to have trained as CfD counsellors. Significant experience of working as a therapist is essential, particularly within healthcare settings. It is also helpful for CfD supervisors to have an understanding of multidisciplinary working and the stepped care model used in IAPT services. This type of knowledge can support counsellors in assessing clients and making appropriate referrals. Supervisors' understanding of depression and the elevated risk of suicide among this population of clients can be essential in helping counsellors identify and manage risk of self-harm among their clients. In their competence framework for supervisors, Roth and Pilling (2009) describe a wide range of core skills and knowledge, too exhaustive to set out here. Some examples, however, include: ability to enable ethical practice; ability to foster competence in working with difference; ability to form and maintain a supervisory alliance; ability to structure supervision sessions; ability to help the supervisee present information about clinical work; ability to help the supervisee to reflect on his/her work and on the usefulness of supervision; ability to use a range of methods to give accurate and constructive feedback; ability to manage serious concerns about practice.

In addition to these areas of core knowledge and skill there are a number of supervision competences which have been adapted from Roth and Pilling's (2009) supervision framework that are of specific relevance to the supervision of person-centred and experiential counsellors and particularly to the supervision of CfD counsellors. They fall into three areas, outlined below.

Understanding and application of CfD

Supervisors need to draw upon a sound knowledge of the principles underpinning the person-centred and experiential approach and the CfD model. In the CfD competence framework the overarching competence which attempts to summarise the whole approach is *an ability to offer a therapeutic relationship that facilitates experiential exploration within a relational context*. This descriptor emphasises two key elements. The first is that 'experiencing' is at the centre of human psychological functioning. Experiencing is defined as thinking, perceiving, sensing, remembering and feeling, along with the inherent meanings and actions associated with these. It follows, therefore, that effective therapy should track and explore the client's experiencing.

The second element is that people are essentially relational beings and are best helped through authentic, person-to-person relationships. The implication of this is that the therapeutic relationship is the major vehicle for change. Additional, but no less important principles are that human beings are free to act in relation to their worlds, and consequently therapeutic change will be largely founded on self-direction.

Also people tend to be motivated towards self-maintenance, psychological growth and development, and hence the realisation of their potential, a process which operates throughout the life span. Knowledge of depression and the ability to conceptualise this condition from the person-centred and experiential perspective (see Chapter 6) are also important. Supervisors need to be able to draw upon these principles to help supervisees review and apply their own knowledge of CfD and link concepts and principles to therapeutic strategies and methods.

The CfD supervisory stance

The relational stance adopted by the supervisor needs to place the primary focus on the exploration of client issues and the therapist's experience of the client, rather than on developing immediate solutions to problems. Hence the ability empathically to understand the supervisee's perceptions, experience and responses to their work, including those which may be on the edge of awareness, is of paramount importance. Allied to this is the ability to be reflective and to self-monitor the emotional and interpersonal processes associated with supervisor-supervisee interactions.

Maintaining the CfD therapeutic focus

Part of the role played by supervision is also to help the supervisee maintain a primary focus on clients' affective experience and for the supervisee to reflect on their own experience of the therapeutic relationship (including their affective, cognitive and somatic reactions to the client). This is central to an experiential approach to therapy and is mirrored in the experiential approach to supervision. In maintaining an empathic and challenging supervisory relationship which supports supervisees' capacity to be honest and open about their experience of offering therapy, supervision can help supervisees become more flexible and spontaneous in their therapeutic role. The modelling of the core conditions (empathy, non-possessive warmth, genuineness) in the supervisory relationship is also an important aspect of maintaining an experiential focus.

Throughout this book, we have emphasised how the use of measures can support effective and reflective practice. This principle applies equally to CfD supervision. For example, not only is the PCEPS a valuable tool for research and training but it can also be useful in the supervisory context. Significant learning can emerge from reviewing recordings of therapy sessions in supervision and applying the PCEPS in a collaborative and reflective manner. This can help to identify areas of strength and weakness and provide a basis for further training and skills development. The shared use of a standardised tool also ensures that practice remains 'on model' and doesn't become randomly eclectic. Additionally, in IAPT and other psychological therapy services it has become the norm to use sessional measures to track and monitor the client's progress. This provides important data on how services are being used, who the clients are that are using the service and how effective the service is in reducing clients' levels of distress. While accepting the general benefits of this process, individual therapists have at times expressed concern that the collection of this data may disrupt the client–counsellor relationship. Asking clients to complete questionnaires when they are distressed, or have urgent concerns to discuss, can take valuable time away from the session. However, used judiciously, measures can provide an additional support to the therapeutic process. Brief sessional measures of depression, anxiety and functional ability such as those used in IAPT services (PHQ-9, GAD-7, WSAS) together consist of 21 items and can be completed by clients in just a few minutes. They can then serve as a basis for reviewing with the client how they have been feeling since the last session. Problem areas, such as 'feeling nervous, anxious or on edge' or 'feeling bad about yourself' (both items contained in the measures mentioned above) can be identified and focused on, if the client wishes this, and more nuanced and subjective discussions of the problem areas entered into. Repeating this process on a sessional basis encourages clients to review their progress and reflect on their levels of wellbeing over time. This tends to foster self-reflection and self-care, helping clients manage themselves and their problems with a greater degree of autonomy. Bringing data from these measures into supervision can similarly produce benefits, where the discussion can focus on key areas of difficulty for the client and creative ways of working with such difficulties.

The outcome data can also provide an indication of which clients seem to be doing well and which are either not improving or deteriorating. Studies have found (Harmon et al., 2007) that around 8% of clients in psychological services deteriorate and that routine outcome data is more reliable in identifying clients who deteriorate than counsellors' own professional judgement alone. As such these data represent a valuable additional source of information that can be used in supervision to benefit clients. Accurately identifying clients who are not doing well can prompt supervisors to focus on providing support to supervisees, helping them to adapt the way they are working with a deteriorating client or make an appropriate referral. The active use of this data in supervision can help to reverse the process of deterioration and lead to improvements in the overall effectiveness of services. Given the elevated risk of suicide among clients who deteriorate and the high costs of hospitalisation where a client can no longer be treated as an outpatient, this is an important role supervision can play.

Two experiences of CfD training, supervision, assessment and practice

Bill Miller

First impressions

Arriving on day one I felt pleased to step off the treadmill of full-time counselling work to spend time engaging with some core therapeutic values in a supportive learning environment. The course structure allowed time and space for reflection on theory and practice. During the week I began walking each day after lunch reflecting on each morning's work; a challenging and refreshing process.

The training week

The training involved taught sessions that explained the origins of IAPT, evidence-based practice and counselling's position within this new context. This set the scene for referring to the recently developed CfD competence framework which articulates the features of counselling that are evidently effective in 'treating' depression. This

(Continued)

(Continued)

framework has been designed to describe the skills that are brought into use by effective counsellors working with depression. These competences are explained in clear and accessible terms and are linked to evidence of effective practice.

Many course participants expressed a sense of being marginalised by the recent and growing dominance of the CBT approach. Even though counsellors are valued within many NHS services, without NICE recognition and ongoing approval as an evidence-based therapy counselling will not continue to be commissioned. CBT's success is based on the findings of many randomised control trials and it has developed its own competence framework; a manual laying out the skills involved in that approach.

The competence framework for Counselling for Depression, based on a person-centred/experiential model is the result of painstaking efforts to capture the essential attitudes and skills of this approach. This work, I would argue, has significantly improved the prospects for counsellors working within the NHS.

This framework was explored during the training week, through many experiential exercises and discussions. As a fundamentally person-centred practitioner I felt at ease in this process. However for others whose approach was more integrative, there seemed to be more anxiety about practising within the framework. The subtlety of the person-centred approach was similarly illustrated, discussed and practised in various exercises related to the competence framework.

The course provided ample time for discussion and practice and at the end of the week we worked in pairs as counsellors and clients, video recording sessions that were assessed for adherence to the competence framework.

Reflecting on my practice

On returning to my counselling work I began audio recording counselling sessions with those of my NHS clients who gave consent. With up to twenty clients a week I felt relaxed about producing four recordings that evidenced my adherence to the CfD competence framework to pass the course. I was able to review many of these recordings, becoming newly aware of how I actually work. I learned, for example, that my genuineness was consistently evident, along with warmth and acceptance. I also realised that when feeling pressured to get results I can, without sufficient self-awareness, be prone to losing touch with my client's perspectives in favour of my own. I found this to be a very helpful learning process.

Supervision and post-qualification experience

Trainees proceed to a period of supervised practice following assessment of their video recordings on the taught course. Feedback from tutors on audio-recorded sessions was usefully discussed in supervision. From initial supervision sessions, recordings were eligible for assessment and feedback received and acted on. I found feedback from tutors, my use of supervision and my ability to self-assess supported my use of the competence framework which boosted my confidence. In fact my CfD adherence

(Continued)

(Continued)

scores were mostly well above the pass mark so I could trust in my ability to practise, reducing my anxiety about having to fit in with an external framework. This eventually led to my being awarded the certificate of competence later in the year.

Since being awarded the certificate of competence I have attended CfD supervision training and visited a CfD training course, passing on some practical tips and encouragement to new CfD trainees. My sense is that CfD is at the forefront of developing counselling in terms that are consistent with NICE clinical guidelines.

Louise Harper

As soon as I arrived at the course, I realised how good it was to be with like-minded colleagues. It felt good to stop, meet new people from different localities with stories like mine. What was really comforting was being in an atmosphere that was respectful and in which I felt listened to without that now-familiar sense of being judged.

The five days of CfD training were varied and engaging, beginning with some context setting on the political background of IAPT and the development of CfD as a NICE-approved, evidence-based approach. I did not appreciate at the time how important this information was to be to me in the near future. A main focus was on the embodiment of the competences in practice, which was challenging and most importantly supportive. To my surprise, having arrived with considerable cynicism, there wasn't anything in the competences I disagreed with.

At the end of the week, practice sessions were video recorded as a first assessment. This process was very nerve-racking. It took me some time to realise that this was only what I do every day. None of my previous counselling training had used audio taping so I had no idea how this would impact me. Initially it took some time to 'forget' that the recorder was there, experiencing a kind of performance anxiety. I had never heard myself counselling before and had to get over hearing the sound of my own voice. My clients didn't seem to mind being recorded. In fact, many were curious about my results.

With CfD supervision, there was no reliance on memory or my report, or my own filtered narrative but in surround sound on my CfD supervisor's sound system with other CfD therapists listening and holding the competency sheets. The first time I took a taped session was difficult but, on the whole, validating feedback was given along with practice-focused feedback on specific areas, which was not too onerous. In fact the subtleties others picked up were very helpful. The competency framework encouraged a focus on what we were actually doing as therapists, rather than what we remembered. Knowing that others were to listen and measure, brought sharpness to supervision and through time my anxiety lessened.

Waiting for the result was different because the process felt a long time in coming and I found myself getting frustrated and impatient. When adherence assessment recording feedback came, it was always valuable and gave excellent points to review. Assessors sometimes picked up different things on the recordings than peers and the

(Continued)

(Continued)

supervisor, sometimes valuing pieces of tape we might have missed and sometimes raising points that we had not recognised. I put in my last recordings without waiting for review by peers and the supervisor because I felt that they were good enough, trusting my own assessment of adherence to the increasingly familiar competences.

I returned to my work in GPs' surgeries with increasing optimism, endeavouring to let doctors and managers know that actually NICE 'had approved'. Practice managers mentioned a fund that we could apply to for continuing counselling at the surgeries. That was when all the CfD background information, political overview and evidence became valuable. I was equipped to be articulate about the approach in discussion with my managers so that they could go back to their managers and argue the case to support counselling. I could also write the funding application form with confidence. The outcome of which was that I was given a contract for a further year to work in two surgeries. I did, and using the IAPT minimum data set outcome monitoring, my recovery rates were over 80%.

The change in my practice was an increase in my confidence and a reminder of how to be, not to do. Perhaps this sort of CPD is something that we therapists should schedule in a bit like an annual service on a motor vehicle.

Critical engagement

Having read the preceding chapters, CfD may seem like old wine in a new bottle. Its development is certainly a deliberate attempt to integrate some of the well-established principles of the person-centred and experiential approach with more contemporary research and practice and, in doing so, acknowledge some of the inevitable, but hopefully creative, tensions between the old and the new. Like all other models of counselling/psychotherapy, the PCE approach has its own distinct values and philosophy which often resonate very personally with members of this professional community. These inevitably clash with other philosophies and epistemologies, particularly the rationalist and positivist principles underpinning evidence-based practice and the taxonomies of psychological conditions and treatments that guide the delivery of NHS psychological therapy. One possible response to this is to oppose the philosophies we disagree with and withdraw into the comfort of our own values and way of being. The inevitable consequences of this position, faced with the dominance of some of these other paradigms, are the marginalisation of the person-centred and experiential approach, a consequential reduction in employment opportunities for PCE counsellors, and reduced access to this form of therapy for clients who may benefit from it. By way of a contrast, in developing CfD, a position of critical engagement has been adopted, where the gaps between the worlds of public healthcare, evidence-based practice and PCE counselling are acknowledged and attempts made to build meaningful bridges across these spaces. This process has involved the adaptation of aspects of the person-centred and experiential approach, but, we argue, without compromising the integrity of its fundamental principles. Adapting to a changing environment is part of the inevitable evolution of the approach, necessary for its survival and good health.

Values and philosophy will always be important but counsellors must consider holding these tentatively and be prepared to review and revise them in the light of experience. The notion of flexibility and adaptability is central to good psychological health in person-centred psychology and we mindfully extend this principle to the values underpinning the approach itself. There needs to be a similar relationship between the person-centred and experiential approach and the empirical findings that emerge from research, whether quantitative or qualitative. In this way the approach will remain open to new knowledge and notions of what works for clients. This requires practitioners being prepared to be surprised and challenged by research findings and to adapt accordingly, as opposed to holding on to ways of thinking that cast the principles of the approach as unchanging articles of faith. The CfD project has this adaptable stance at its core, where new research findings can lead to additions or amendments to the competence framework and these changes then be translated into training and practice. The ongoing evaluation of practice can then feed back into this process, leading to an integration of research, training and practice. This virtuous circle is centred on the needs of clients, seeking to improve the quality of therapy and, in turn, helping them towards greater levels of psychological wellbeing.

Research

In many ways the person-centred and experiential approaches have lagged behind other approaches, particularly CBT, in terms of the amount of research they have produced, which takes us back to the arguments set out at the beginning of this book as to why a critical engagement with evidence-based practice is necessary. We argue that person-centred and experiential therapies need further evidence from RCTs to support and promote them. The fact that in CfD we now have a clearly defined, competence-based therapy, together with a standardised training programme based on these competences and, in the form of the PCEPS, a measure to assess adherence to the therapy, provides distinct benefits for the design and conduct of RCTs. There is now a very clear and standardised integrative form of PCE counselling that can be tested in trials, along with a mechanism to ensure the therapy is implemented as intended. In designing future RCTs, it is worth bearing in mind that decades of counselling and psychotherapy research tell us that when psychological therapy is compared with no-treatment, therapy tends to be superior. And so to test CfD against no-treatment control groups will probably tell us very little we don't already know. As CBT is the recommended treatment for depression, and many other conditions, the key question is whether CfD is as effective as CBT. Additionally, the current NICE (2009a) recommendation tends to restrict counselling to 6–10 sessions for mild-moderate depression. So an important question for future RCTs to address is whether CfD is effective in a greater number of sessions (say 16) with more severely depressed clients. For CfD to continue to be viewed as an evidence-based intervention, it is essential for future research to address these questions.

As RCTs tend to require large amounts of funding and high levels of academic expertise, they are generally not the type of studies in which practitioners can readily engage. A more feasible form of engagement is to become a member of a practice-research network (PRN) (Barkham et al., 2010). A PRN is defined as a 'group of practising clinicians that co-operates to collect data and conduct research studies' (Zarin et al., 1997). An example of this is the PRN hosted by BAPCA.[4] Within such networks members agree to collect and pool data relating to clinical outcomes using a standardised set of measures. This facilitates the building of large, clinically relevant databases on which practice-based research can be carried out. Along with large-scale quantitative research on the outcomes of therapy, PRNs also provide opportunities for members to collaborate on small-scale, contextualised, qualitative and case study research. Such networks have the benefit of engaging practitioners in research activity that is clinically meaningful and relevant to local contexts. Similarly, the large outcome datasets they can produce usefully complement the findings of RCT research, providing evidence for the effectiveness of interventions in routine, naturalistic settings as opposed to the more controlled context of the RCT. For CfD practitioners to join such networks and pool routine data on their practice, a number of benefits would accrue, including improving the quality of therapy offered to clients, expanding our knowledge and understanding of CfD and how it works, and firmly establishing the approach as an evidence-based therapy, delivered by open-minded, curious and research-informed practitioners.

---

[4] www.bapca.org.uk/blog/538-bapca-practice-research-network.html (retrieved 11/11/2013).

Appendix 1

Lists of Competences

Generic

G1-Knowledge and understanding of mental health problems
G2-Knowledge of depression
G3-Knowledge of, and ability to operate within, professional and ethical guidelines
G4-Knowledge of a model of therapy, and the ability to understand and employ the model in practice
G5-Ability to work with difference (cultural competence)
G6-Ability to engage client
G7-Ability to foster and maintain a good therapeutic alliance, and to grasp the client's perspective and 'world view'
G8-Ability to work with the emotional content of sessions
G9-Ability to manage endings
G10-Ability to undertake a generic assessment
G11-Ability to assess and manage risk of self-harm
G12-Ability to use measures to guide therapy and to monitor outcomes
G13-Ability to make use of supervision

Basic

B1-Knowledge of the philosophy and principles that inform the therapeutic approach
B2-Knowledge of person-centred theories of human growth and development and the origins of psychological distress
B3-Knowledge of the person-centred conditions for, and goals of, therapeutic change
B4-Knowledge of the PCE conceptualisation of depression
B5-Ability to explain and demonstrate the rationale for counselling
B6-Ability to work with the client to establish a therapeutic aim

B7-Ability to experience and communicate empathy

B8-Ability to experience and to communicate a fundamentally accepting attitude to clients

B9-Ability to maintain authenticity in the therapeutic relationship

B10-Ability to conclude the therapeutic relationship

Specific

S1-Ability to help clients to access and express emotions

S1.1-An ability to identify the ways in which clients manage and process their emotions, including the ability to recognise when clients are finding it difficult to access these

S1.2-An ability to help clients experience feelings which may be out of current awareness, e.g.:

- by helping clients focus their attention inwards in order to become more aware of their feelings
- by helping clients find ways of describing emotions which seem difficult to access
- by listening empathically for feelings that are implicit and not yet fully in awareness
- by focusing the client's attention on bodily sensations
- by making empathic conjectures about feelings that have not yet been expressed

S1.3-An ability to judge when it is appropriate to help clients reduce the extent to which they avoid experiencing underlying feelings

S1.4-An ability to use methods that help clients increase contact with avoided emotion e.g.:

- by helping clients explore what might be making it difficult for them to acknowledge and/or experience feelings
- by identifying moments when clients seem to be having difficulty acknowledging and/or experiencing underlying feelings and drawing their attention to this
- by helping clients explore the ways in which they avoid acknowledging and/or experiencing underlying feelings, and possible factors that may influence this e.g.:

  o previous negative experiences of expressing emotions to others
  o cultural and family attitudes to the expression of emotion

S1.5-An ability to help clients achieve a level of emotional arousal that is optimal for exploring their feelings, e.g.:

- helping clients who are overwhelmed by feelings e.g. by offering a calming and containing presence, containing imagery, or help to self-soothe
- enabling clients who are out of touch with their feelings to increase emotional contact, for example by:

- ○ helping them review current concerns and focus on the most significant
- ○ helping them bring to mind and discuss previous episodes when they experienced heightened emotion
- ○ the counsellor using vivid imagery or language aimed at promoting feelings in the client
- ○ suggesting active methods that promote emotional expression (e.g. encouraging clients to repeat a phrase more forcefully)

S1.6-An ability to help the client differentiate between feelings that are appropriate to (and hence useful for) dealing with a current situation and those that are less helpful to them, for example:

- because they are emotional responses relating to previous experiences rather than the present context
- because they are reactions to other, more fundamental, emotions

S2-Ability to help clients articulate emotions

S2.1-An ability to help the client clarify and find appropriate words to describe their emotions
S2.2-An ability to help the client verbalise the key concerns, meanings and memories which emerge out of emotional arousal
S2.3-An ability to help the client identify and verbalise the wishes, needs, behaviours and goals associated with feelings and emotions (i.e. the 'action tendency' inherent in emotions)
S2.4-An ability to suggest imagery and metaphor to help the client become more aware of and to articulate the meaning of their experiences
S2.5-An ability to work with images or metaphors in a way that is helpful to clients: by communicating in a manner that helps clients focus on their experiencing:

- by checking the 'fit' of images or metaphors with the client's experience
- by working with the client to elaborate the image or metaphor

S3-Ability to help clients reflect on and develop emotional meanings

S3.1-An ability to help clients explore their implicit central assumptions about self, others and the world
S3.2-An ability to help clients adapt central assumptions in the light of experience
S3.3-An ability to help the client explore alternative ways of understanding their emotional difficulties and the ways in which they experience themselves and others
S3.4-An ability to help clients explore and evaluate new perspectives on their experiences in order for them to:

- develop alternative ways of understanding their experiences
- revise their views of themselves
- develop new narratives relating to themselves and their world

S3.5-An ability to help the client develop metaphors for themselves that fit with their newly-emerging experience
S3.6-An ability to help the client reflect on any new meanings that emerge:

- to check the accuracy of meanings against experience
- to assess the implications of the new meanings
- to re-examine behaviour and where appropriate consider alternative forms of action

S3.7-An ability to help clients evaluate new perspectives in terms of their social context, personal values and goals in life

S4-Ability to help clients make sense of experiences that are confusing and distressing

S4.1-An ability to recognise and to help clients reflect on reactions that they experience as problematic and/or incongruent (e.g. when they over- or underreact to a situation, or react in ways which they describe as being out of character)
S4.2-An ability to help the client describe both their emotional reactions and the external situation, in ways that encourage the client:

- to identify how they were feeling before they encountered the situation
- to re-imagine the situation
- to identify the moment when the reaction was triggered
- to explore their reaction to the situation
- to make links between their reactions and the way they construed the situation
- to develop new ways of understanding the situation and their responses to it

Metacompetences

M1-Capacity to implement CfD in a flexible but coherent manner
M2-Capacity to adapt interventions in response to client feedback
M3-Working with the whole person

M3.1-An ability, when working with clients, to maintain a holistic perspective (recognising the integral nature of intrapersonal, interpersonal, contextual, and spiritual aspects of the person)
M3.2-An ability to take fully into account the clients' cultural and social context in order to empathise with their frame of reference

M4-Maintaining a person-centred stance

M4.1-An ability to balance any tensions between the maintenance of the therapeutic relationship and the achievement of therapeutic tasks

M4.2-An ability to maintain a balance between directive and non-directive dimensions of the therapeutic process
M4.3-An ability for the counsellor to adopt an accepting and non-judgemental attitude towards the client while acknowledging their feelings for, and reactions to, the client.

M5-Maintaining safety in the therapeutic relationship

M5.1-An ability to balance the maintenance of a person-centred stance with the need to attend to issues of client safety and risk
M5.2-An ability to hold authority and contain the therapeutic process while sharing power appropriately with the client

M6-Maintaining psychological contact

M6.1-An ability to establish and maintain psychological contact with the client at both explicit and implicit levels

M7-Capacity to balance therapeutic tasks

M7.1-An ability to balance the need for warmth and acceptance with the need to be congruent and transparent with clients
M7.2-An ability to attend to both process and content in the therapeutic relationship
M7.3-An ability to balance emotional arousal with the need for understanding and meaning making in the therapeutic relationship
M7.4-An ability to balance levels of support and challenge in the therapeutic relationship
M7.5-An ability to hold in mind and to monitor the client's emotional needs and capacities when devising and undertaking therapeutic tasks

M8-Integrating the therapist's experience into the therapeutic relationship

M8.1-An ability for the counsellor to make use of 'metacommunication' (describing the impact of the client's behaviour and communications on them), and a capacity to:

- judge when metacommunication might be helpful to the client
- convey the intention behind the counsellor's communication
- explore the impact of the counsellor's communication on the client

M8.2-An ability for the counsellor to recognise their own contribution to the construction of meaning in the therapeutic relationship

Appendix 2

Data from Elliott et al.'s (2013) Meta-Analysis of PCE for Depression Research

Table A   Person-Centred-Experiential Psychotherapy for Depression: Pre-post Effect Sizes

Study	Treatment[a] (length)	Population (n of completers)	Type of Measure[b]	Mean Change E.S.[c]
1. Client-Centered:				
Cooper et al. (2003)	Nondirective (10)	Post-partum Depression (48)	SSy, Imp, Rel	Post: 0.94 FUearly: 1.79 FUlate: 1.26
Fleming & Thornton (1980)	Group CC (16)	Depression (9)	SSy, Adj, Scm	Post: 2.15 FUearly: 2.59
Greenberg & Watson (1998) 'York I'	CC (16)	Depression (17)	Ssy, Scm, Adj, TC	Post: 1.81 FUearly: 1.80 FUlate: 1.34
Goldman et al. (2006) 'York II'	CC (18)	Depression (19)	SSy, Adj, Scm	Post: 1.05 FUearly: 1.48 FUlate: 1.03
Holden et al. (1989)	Rogerian (9)	Post-partum depression (26)	CSy, SSy	Post: 0.75
McNamara & Horan (1986)	Rogerian (8)	Depressed (10)	Adj, Scm, PC	Post: 0.97 FUearly: 1.39
King et al. (2000); Ward et al. (2000)	CC (7)	Depression in Primary Care 1. 3-way RCT: 62 2. 2-way RCT: 50 3. Pref trial: 52	SSy, Adj, Cost	1. FU2mo: 0.84 FU10mo: 0.94 2. FUearly: 1.12 FUlate: 1.20 3. FUearly: 0.99 FUlate: 0.94

(Continued)

Table A (Continued)

Study	Treatment[a] (length)	Population (n of completers)	Type of Measure[b]	Mean Change E.S.[c]
Morrell et al. (2009)	Person-Centred (8)	Post-natal depression (131)	SSy	Post: 3.41
Teusch et al. (2003)	Inpatient CC program (60)	Treatment refractory depression (28)	CSy, Exp	Post: 1.03 FUlate: 1.13
Wickberg & Hwang (1996)	Nondirective (6)	Post-natal depression (20)	CSy	Post: 1.64
2. Supportive:				
Beutler et al. (1991)	Supportive/Self-directed (plus self-help books) (20)	Depressed (20)	CSy, SSy	Post: 0.97 FUearly: 1.21
Brent et al. (1997); Kolko et al. (2000)	Nondirective Supportive (16)	Depressed adolescents (35)	CSy, SSy, Adj, Scm, Rel	Post: 0.62 FUlate: 0.81
Lerner & Clum (1990)	Group Supportive (10)	College students with suicidal ideation (9)	CSy, PC	Post: 0.65 FUearly; 0.64
Maynard (1993)	Group Nondirective Supportive (12)	Depressed women (8)	CSy, Scm	Post: 0.09
Mohr et al. (2005)	Telephone-administered supportive emotion-focused (16)	Multiple sclerosis and depression (64)	CSy, SSy	Post: 0.92 FUearly: 1.36 FUlate: 1.22
Propst et al. (1992)	Pastoral Counseling (religious content) (18)	Depressed Religious (10)	Adj, CSy,SSy	Post: 1.29 FUearly: 1.50 FUlate: 1.72
Shaw (1977)	Group Nondirective (8)	Depression (8)	CSy, SSy	Post: 0.88
Stice et al. (2006, 2010)	Supportive-expressive group (4)	Experiencing sadness (19)	SSy	Post: 1.56 FUearly: 1.50
Wilson (1990)	Nondirective supportive (4)	Depressed prisoners (5)	SSy, PC	Post: 0.61 FUearly: 1.04
3. Process-Experiential/Emotion-Focused:				
Dessaulles (1991, 2003)	EFT Couples (16)	Couples with Depressed female (7)	SSy, Rel	Post: 0.74
Diamond et al. (2002)	Attachment-based Family therapy (8)	Depressed teenagers (16)	CSy, SSy, Rel	Post: 0.97

(Continued)

Table A   (Continued)

Study	Treatment[a] (length)	Population (n of completers)	Type of Measure[b]	Mean Change E.S.[c]
Gibson (1998)	Feminist PE (12)	Depression (6)	SSy, CSy, Adj	Post: 0.46
Greenberg & Watson (1998) 'York I'	PE (16)	Depression (17)	SSy, Scm, Adj, TC	Post: 2.43 FUearly: 1.84 FUlate: 1.68
Goldman et al. (2006) 'York II'	PE (18)	Depression (19)	SSy, Adj, Scm	Post: 1.80 FUearly: 1.79 FUlate: 2.12
Jackson & Elliott (1990)	PE (16)	Depression (15)	Adj, CSy, Exp, Scm, SSy, TC	Post: 1.32 FU6mo: 2.00 FU18mo: 1.75
Mestel & Votsmeier-Röhr (2000)	Integrative Experiential Inpatient Program (6 weeks)	Depression (412)	SSy, Adj, Exp	Post: 1.11 FU22mo: 0.98
Watson et al. (2003)	Process Experiential (16)	Depression (33)	SSy, Adj, Scm, PC	Post: 0.89
4. Gestalt Therapy:				
Beutler et al. (1991)	Gestalt group (20)	Depressed (22)	CSy, SSy	Post: 1.05 FU3early: 1.80
Tyson & Range (1987)	Group Gestalt empty chair dialogues (4)	Mild depression (11)	SSy, PC	Post: 0.53 FU7wk: 0.85
5. Other Experiential (emotive, psychodrama):				
Mohr et al. (2001)	Supportive-Expressive Group (16)	Depression + multiple sclerosis (22)	Adj, CSy, SSy	Post: 0.73 FUearly: 1.39
Rezaeian et al. (1997)	Intensive Psychodrama (60)	Depressed males (18)	Scm	Post: 1.51
Tyson & Range (1987)	Active expression group (4)	Mild depression (11)	SSy, PC	Post: 0.36 FUearly: 0.04

[a] Individual treatment unless otherwise noted; number of sessions given in parentheses; CC: Client-Centered Therapy; EFT: Emotionally-Focused Therapy; PE: Process-Experiential Therapy.

[b] Adj: social adjustment or interpersonal problems measures; CSy: clinician ratings of symptoms; Exp: measures of experiential functioning; Imp: estimates based on improvement ratings or per cent recovered; PC: measures of personality and coping style; Rel: measures of relationship quality (e.g., marital); Scm: schematic/self image measures; SSy: self ratings of symptoms; TC: Target complaint or individualised problem measures.

[c] ESs for multiple outcome measures were first averaged within instruments (e.g., 8 scales of Freiberg Personality Inventory), then across instruments for each treatment group and each assessment period. FUearly: Follow-up < 1 yr; FUlate: Follow-up 1+ yr; mo=month.

Table B Summary of Overall Pre-post Change, Controlled and Comparative Effect Sizes for Depressed Clients

	n	m	se
Pre–Post Change ES (mean d)			
By Assessment Point:			
Post	31	1.13	0.12
Early Follow-up (1–11months)	20	1.38	0.13
Late Follow-up (12+ months)	16	1.34	0.10
Overall (mES):			
Unweighted	34	1.20	0.11
Weighted by n	1287[a]	1.27	0.11
Controlled ES (vs. untreated clients)[b]			
Unweighted mean difference	8	0.34	0.17
PCE mean pre-post ES	8	0.80	0.17
Control mean pre-post ES	8	0.46	0.07
Weighted mean difference	107[a]	0.42	0.18
Comparative ES (vs. other treatments)[b]			
Unweighted mean difference	37	0.02	0.01
PCE mean pre-post ES	37	1.25	0.01
Comparative treatment mean pre-Post ES	37	1.23	0.01
Weighted mean difference	755[a]	−0.02	0.08
Comparative ES (more vs. less process-guiding PCE)			
Unweighted	4	0.45	0.07
Weighted by n	69[a]	0.44	0.02

Note. Hedge's d used. Where indicated, number of clients in humanistic treatment conditions used as weighting variable (corrects for small sample bias).
[a] Total number of clients in studies combined.
[b] Mean difference in change ESs for conditions compared, except where these are unavailable; positive values indicate pro-humanistic therapy results.

Table C Controlled Outcome Research on Person-Centred Experiential Psychotherapies

Study	PCE Treatment	Control Condition	Mean Difference in Effect Size
1. Client-Centered:			
Holden et al. (1989)	Rogerian	Treatment as Usual	0.55
Shaw (1977)	Nondirective	Waitlist	0.25

(Continued)

Table C (Continued)

Study	PCE Treatment	Control Condition	Mean Difference in Effect Size
2. Supportive:			
Maynard (1993)	Group Nondirective Supportive	No treatment	−0.14
Propst et al. (1992)	Pastoral Counseling	Waitlist	0.59
Stice et al. (2006, 2010)	Supportive-expressive group	Waitlist	1.10
3. Emotion-Focused:			
Diamond et al. (2002)	Attachment-based family therapy	Waitlist	0.67
4. Gestalt Therapy:			
Tyson & Range (1987)	Group Gestalt empty chair dialogues	No treatment	0.10
5. Other Experiential:			
Tyson & Range (1987)	Active expression group	No treatment	−0.39

Note. ES values given are differences in change ESs (averaged across measures and assessment periods).

Table D Comparative Outcome Research on Person-Centred-Experiential Psychotherapies

Study	Experiental Treatment	Comparison Treatment	Mean Difference in Effect Size
1. Client-Centered:			
Cooper et al. (2003)	Nondirective	CBT	−0.12
Cooper et al. (2003)	Nondirective	Psychodynamic	−0.05
Cooper et al. (2003)	Nondirective	Treatment as Usual	−0.03
Fleming & Thornton (1980)	Nondirective group	Coping skills training	0.47
Fleming & Thornton (1980)	Nondirective group	Cognitive therapy	0.48
King et al. (2000); Ward et al. (2000) (1. 3-way trial; 2. 2-way trial; 3. Preference trial)	CC	CBT	1: −0.18 2: −0.16 3: −0.06
King et al. (2000); Ward et al. (2000)	CC	Treatment as Usual (Primary care physician)	0.10

(Continued)

Table D (Continued)

Study	Experiental Treatment	Comparison Treatment	Mean Difference in Effect Size
McNamara & Horen (1986)	Rogerian	Behaviour therapy	−0.94
McNamara & Horen (1986)	Rogerian	Cognitive therapy	−0.72
McNamara & Horen (1986)	Rogerian	CBT	−0.77
Morrell et al. (2009)	Person-Centred	CBT	0.00
Morrell et al. (2009)	Person-Centred	Treatment as usual	0.37
Shaw (1977)	Nondirective	Cognitive therapy	−1.08
Shaw (1977)	Nondirective	Behavioural therapy	0.20
Wickberg & Hwang (1996)	Nondirective	Treatment as usual	1.33
2. Supportive:			
Beutler et al. (1991)	Supportive/Self-directed (bibliotherapy)	Cognitive Therapy Group	−0.18
Brent et al. (1997); Kolko et al. (2000)	Nondirective supportive	CBT	−0.13
Brent et al. (1997); Kolko et al. (2000)	Nondirective supportive + Information	Systemic behaviour family therapy	−0.07
Lerner & Clum (1990)	Group Supportive	CBT	−1.34
Maynard (1993)	Group Nondirective Supportive	CBT	−1.12
Mohr et al. (2005)	Telephone-administered supportive emotion-focused	Telephone CBT	−0.29
Propst et al. (1992)	Pastoral Counseling	Cognitive Therapy (non-religious or religious)	0.04
Stice et al. (2006, 2010)	Supportive-expressive group	Bibliotherapy	0.36
Stice et al. (2006, 2010)	Supportive-expressive group	CBT	0.44
Stice et al. (2006, 2010)	Supportive-expressive group	Expressive writing	0.62
Stice et al. (2006, 2010)	Supportive-expressive group	Journalling	0.73
Wilson (1990)	Nondirective supportive	CBT	0.38

(Continued)

Table D (Continued)

Study	Experiental Treatment	Comparison Treatment	Mean Difference in Effect Size
3. Process-Experiental/Emotion-Focused:			
Dessaulles (1991)	EFT Couples	Antidepressant medication	1.37
Watson et al. (2003)	PE	Cognitive behavioural	0.11
4. Gestalt Therapy:			
Beutler et al. (1991)	Focused Expressive group	Cognitive Therapy Group	0.16
Tyson & Range (1987)	Group Gestalt empty chair	Theatre workshop	0.51
5. Other Experiential:			
Mohr et al. (2001)	Supportive-Expressive Group	CBT	−0.72
Mohr et al. (2001)	Supportive-Expressive Group	Medication (Sertraline)	−0.58
Tyson & Range (1987)	Active expression group	Theatre workshop	−0.82

Note. Multiple treatments for a given study listed separately. Effect sizes are differences in change effect sizes (averaged across measures and assessment periods). Types of experiential treatment correspond to main headings in Table A. Abbreviations: CBT: Cognitive-Behavioural Therapy; CC: Client-Centered Therapy; EFT Emotionally-Focused Therapy; PE: Process-Experiential.

Table E Research Comparing Less vs. More Process-guiding Person-Centred-Experiential Psychotherapies

Study	More Process-Guiding	Less Process-Guiding	Mean Difference in Effect Size
Beutler et al. (1991)	Focused Expressive group	Supportive/Self-directed (bibliotherapy)	0.34
Greenberg & Watson (1998) 'York I'	EFT	Client-centred	0.33
Goldman et al. (2006) 'York II'	EFT	Client-centred	0.71
Tyson & Range (1987)	Gestalt	Active Expression	0.51

Note. Effect sizes are differences in change effect sizes (averaged across measures and assessment periods). Abbreviations: CC: Client-Centered Therapy; EFT Emotionally-Focused Therapy.

Appendix 3

Manuals and Texts used in the Development of Roth, Hill, and Pilling (2009) *The Competences Required to Deliver Effective Humanistic Psychological Therapies*

1 Essential texts

Elliott, R., Watson J.C., Goldman, R.N. and Greenberg L.S. (2004) *Learning Emotion-Focused Therapy: The Process-Experiential Approach to Change.* Washington, D.C.: American Psychological Association.

Greenberg, L.S. and Watson, J.C. (2006) *Emotion-Focused Therapy for Depression.* Washington, D.C.: American Psychological Association.

King, M. (unpublished) *Counselling Manual,* as employed in: King, M., Sibbald, B., Ward, E., Bower, P., Lloyd, M., Gabbay, M. and Byford, S. (2000) 'Randomised controlled trial of non-directive counselling, cognitive-behaviour therapy and usual general practitioner care in the management of depression as well as mixed anxiety and depression in primary care.' *Health Technology Assessment,* 4 (19).

Mearns, D. and Thorne, B. (2007) *Person-Centred Counselling in Action,* 3rd edn. London: Sage.

Rennie, D. (1998) *Person-Centred Counselling: An Experiential Approach.* London: Sage.

Rogers, C.R. (1951) *Client-Centered Therapy.* Boston: Houghton Mifflin.

Sanders, P. (2006) *The Person-Centred Counselling Primer.* Ross-on-Wye: PCCS Books.

Sanders, P. (2007) *The Contact Work Primer.* Ross-on-Wye: PCCS Books.

Tolan, J. (2012) *Skills in Person-Centred Counselling and Psychotherapy,* 2nd edn. London: Sage.

2 Background texts – drawn on as helpful sources of information regarding humanistic approaches

Barrett-Lennard, G.T. (1998) *Carl Rogers' Helping System. Journey and Substance.* London: Sage.

Cain, D. and Seeman, J. (2002) *Humanistic Psychotherapies: Handbook of Research and Practice.* Washington, D.C.: American Psychological Association.

Cooper, M. (2003) *Existential Therapies*. London: Sage.

Cooper, M., O'Hara, M., Schmid, F. and Wyatt, G. (eds) (2007) *The Handbook of Person-centred Psychotherapy and Counselling*. Basingstoke: Palgrave Macmillan.

Evans, K. and Gilbert, M. (2005) *An Introduction to Integrative Psychotherapy*. Basingstoke: Palgrave Macmillan.

Gendlin, E.T. (1996) *Focusing-oriented Psychotherapy. A Manual of the Experiential Method*. New York: Guilford Press.

Scott, T. (2004) *Integrative Psychotherapy in Healthcare: A Humanistic Approach*. Basingstoke: Palgrave Macmillan.

Stern, D.N. (2004) *The Present Moment in Psychotherapy and Everyday Life*. New York: W.W. Norton & Co.

References

American Psychiatric Association (2000) *Diagnostic and Statistical Manual of Mental Disorders. Fourth Edition – Text Revision*. Washington, D.C.: American Psychiatric Association.

American Psychiatric Association (2013) *Diagnostic and Statistical Manual of Mental Disorders. Fifth Edition*. Washington, D.C.: American Psychiatric Association.

Anderson, S. and Hasler, J. (1979) 'Counselling in general practice.' *Journal of the Royal College of General Practitioners*, 29: 352–6.

Andrade, L., Caraveo-Anduaga, J.J., Berglund, P., Bijl, R.V., De Graaf R., Vollebergh, W., Dragomirecka, E., Kohn, R., Keller, M., Kessler, R.C., Kawakami, N., Kilic, C., Offord, D., Ustun, T.B and Wittchen, H-U. (2003) 'The epidemiology of major depressive episodes: results from the International Consortium of Psychiatric Epidemiology (ICPE) surveys.' *International Journal of Methods in Psychiatric Research*, 12 (1): 3–21.

Appleby, L. (2004) *The National Health Service Framework for Mental Health: Five Years On*. London: Department of Health.

BACP (2010) *Counselling for Depression (CfD) General Information*. Available at: www.bacp.co.uk/learning/Counselling%20for%20Depression/ (accessed 20/02/14).

Barrett-Lennard, G.T. (1962) 'Dimensions of therapist response as causal factors in therapeutic change.' *Psychological Monographs*, 76 (43, Whole, No. 562).

Barrett-Lennard, G.T. (2003) *Steps on a Mindful Journey: Person-centred Expressions*. Ross-on-Wye: PCCS Books.

Barkham, M., Hardy, G.E. and Mellor-Clark, J. (eds) (2010) *Developing and Delivering Practice-Based Evidence: A Guide for the Psychological Therapies*. Chichester: Wiley-Blackwell.

Bayne, R., Horton, I., Merry, T., Noyes, E. and McMahon, G. (1999) *The Counsellor's Handbook*, 2nd edn. Cheltenham: Stanley Thornes.

Bedi, N., Chilvers, C., Churchill, R., Dewey, M., Duggan, C., Fielding, K., Gretton, V., Miller, P., Harrison, G., Lee, A. and Williams, I. (2000) 'Assessing effectiveness of treatment of depression in primary care.' *British Journal of Psychiatry*, 177: 312–18.

Bentall, R. (2009) 'People or plants? The myth that psychiatric diagnoses are meaningful.' In R. Bentall, *Doctoring the Mind: Why Psychiatric Treatments Fail*. London: Penguin, pp. 89–112.

Beutler, L.E., Engle, D., Mohr, D., Daldrup, R.J., Bergan, J., Meredith, K. and Merry, W. (1991) 'Predictors of differential response to cognitive, experiential, and self-directed psychotherapeutic procedures.' *Journal of Consulting and Clinical Psychology*, 59: 333–40.

Biermann-Ratjen, E-M. (1998) 'On the development of persons in relationships.' In B. Thorne and E. Lambers (eds) *Person-Centred Therapy: A European Perspective*. London: Sage.

Bohart, A. and Tallman, K. (1998) *How Clients Make Therapy Work: The Process of Active Self-healing*. Washington: American Psychological Association.

Bohart, A. and Tallman, K. (2010) 'Clients as active self-healers: implications for the person-centered approach.' In M. Cooper, J.C. Watson and D Hölldampf (eds) *Person-Centered and Experiential Psychotherapies Work: A Review of the Research on Counseling, Psychotherapy and Related Practices.* Ross-on-Wye: PCCS Books, pp. 91–131.

Bower, P. and King, M. (2000) 'Randomised controlled trials and the evaluation of psychological therapy.' In N. Rowland and S. Goss (eds) (2000) *Evidence-Based Counselling and Psychological Therapies.* London: Routledge.

Bower, P. and Rowland, N. (2006) 'Effectiveness and cost effectiveness of counselling in primary care.' *Cochrane Database of Systematic Reviews.* Issue 3. Art. No: CD001025. DOI: 10.1002/14651858.CD001025.pub2

Boyle, M. (2007) 'The problem with diagnosis.' *The Psychologist,* 20: 290–92. Available at: www.thepsychologist.org.uk/archive/archive_home.cfm/volumeID_20-editionID_147-ArticleID_1184-getfile_getPDF/thepsychologist%5C0507dia1.pdf

Bozarth, J.D. (1984/2001) 'Beyond reflection: emergent modes of empathy.' In R.F. Levant and J.M. Shlien (eds) *Client-Centered Therapy and the Person-Centered Approach: New Directions in Theory, Research and Practice.* Westport, CT: Praeger, pp. 59–75. Reprinted in S. Haugh and T. Merry (eds) *Rogers' Therapeutic Conditions, Volume 2: Empathy.* Ross-on-Wye: PCCS Books, pp. 131–54.

Bozarth, J. (1998) *Person-Centered Therapy: A Revolutionary Paradigm.* Ross-on-Wye: PCCS Books.

Brent, D.A., Holder, D., Kolko, D., Birmaher, B., Baugher, M., Roth, C. and Johnson, B. (1997) 'A clinical psychotherapy trial for adolescent depression comparing cognitive, family, and supportive treatment.' *Archives of General Psychitary,* 54: 877–85. Also reported in Kolko, D.J., Brent, D.A., Baugher, M., Bridge, J. and Birmaher, B. (2000) 'Cognitive and family therapies for adolescent depression: Treatment specificity, mediation, and moderation.' *Journal of Consulting and Clinical Psychology,* 68: 603–14.

Brettle, A., Hill, A. and Jenkins, P. (2008) 'Counselling in primary care: a systematic review of the evidence.' *Counselling and Psychotherapy Research,* 8 (4): 207–14.

Broadhead, W.E., Blazer, D.G., George, L.K. and Tse, C.K. (1990) 'Depression, disability days, and days lost from work in a prospective epidemiological survey.' *JAMA,* 264: 2524–8.

Brodley, B.T. (2002) 'Observations of empathic understanding in two client-centered therapists.' In K.A. Moon, M. Witty, B. Grant and B. Rice (2011) (eds) *Practicing Client-Centered Therapy: Selected Writings of Barbara Temaner Brodley.* Ross-on-Wye: PCCS Books, pp. 328–56.

Budman, S.H. and Gurman, A.S. (1988) *Theory and Practice of Brief Therapy.* New York: Guildford Press.

Cain, D.J. (2002) *Classics in the Person-Centered Approach.* Ross-on-Wye: PCCS Books.

Cameron, R. (2003) 'Psychological contact' (Chapters 7 and 8). In J. Tolan (ed.) *Skills in Person-Centred Counselling and Psychotherapy.* London: Sage, pp. 87–109.

Centre for Economic Performance Mental Health Policy Group (2006) *The Depression Report: A New Deal for Depression and Anxiety Disorders.* London: London School of Economics and Political Science.

Chambless, D.L. and Hollon, S.D. (1998) 'Defining empirically supported therapies.' *Journal of Consulting and Clinical Psychology,* 66: 7–18.

Cochrane, A.L. (1972) *Effectiveness and Efficiency: Random Reflections on Health Services.* London: Nuffield Provincial Hospitals Trust.

Cooper, M. (2001) 'Embodied empathy.' In S. Haugh and T. Merry (eds) (2001) *Rogers' Therapeutic Conditions, Volume 2: Empathy.* Ross-on-Wye: PCCS Books, pp. 218–29.

Cooper, M. (2008) *Essential Research Findings in Counselling and Psychotherapy.* London: Sage.

Cooper, P. J., Murray, L., Wilson, A., and Romaniuk, H. (2003) 'Controlled trial of the short- and long-term effect of psychological treatment of post-partum depression.' *British Journal of Psychiatry,* 182: 412–19.

Cornelius-White, J. (2013) 'Congruence.' In M. Cooper, M. O'Hara, P.F. Schmid and A. Bohart (eds) *The Handbook of Person-Centred Psychotherapy and Counselling*. Basingstoke: Palgrave Macmillan.

Cuijpers, P., De Graaf, R. and Van Dorsselaer, S. (2004) 'Minor depression: risk profiles, functional disability, health care use and risk of developing major depression.' *Journal of Affective Disorders*, 79: 71–9.

Cushman, P. (1995) *Constructing the Self, Constructing America*. Cambridge, MA: Da Capo Press.

Department of Health (1999) *National Service Framework for Mental Health*. London: Department of Health.

Dessaules, A. (1991) *The Treatment of Clinical Depression in the Context of Marital Distress*. Unpublished doctoral dissertation. University of Ottawa. Available at: http://scholar.lib.vt.edu/theses/available/etd-04262002-132402/unrestricted/Dissertation1.pdf

Dessaules, A., Johnson, S.M. and Denton, W. (2003) 'Emotion-focused therapy for couples in the treatment of depression: a pilot study.' *The American Journal of Family Therapy*, 31: 345–53.

Diamond, G.S., Reis, B.F., Diamond, G.M., Siqueland, L. and Isaacs, L. (2002) 'Attachment-based family therapy for depressed adolescents: a treatment development study.' *Journal of the American Academy of Child and Adolescent Psychiatry*, 41: 1190–6.

Elliott, R. (2012) 'Emotion Focused Therapy.' In P. Sanders (ed.) *The Tribes of the Person-Centred Nation: An Introduction to the Schools of Therapy Associated with the Person-centred Approach*. Ross-on-Wye: PCCS Books, pp. 103–30.

Elliott, R., Watson, J.C., Goldman, R.N. and Greenberg, L.S. (2004) *Learning Emotion-Focused Therapy: The Process-experiential Approach to Change*. Washington DC: American Psychological Association.

Elliott, R., Watson, J.C., Greenberg, L.S., Timulak, L. and Freire, E. (2013) 'Research on humanistic-experiential psychotherapies.' In M.J. Lambert (ed.) *Bergin & Garfield's Handbook of Psychotherapy and Behavior Change*, 6th edn. New York: Wiley, pp. 495–538.

Fava, M. and Kendler, K. (2000) 'Major depressive disorder.' *Neuron*, 28: 335–41.

Fleming, B.M. and Thornton, F. (1980) 'Coping skills training as a component in the short-term treatment of depression.' *Journal of Consulting and Clinical Psychology*, 48: 652–4.

Freire, E., Elliott, R. and Westwell, G. (2012) 'Measuring the immeasurable.' *Therapy Today*, 23 (4): 22–6.

Freire, E., Elliott, R. and Westwell, G. (2013) 'Person-Centred and Experiential Psychotherapy Scale: development and reliability of an adherence/competence measure for person-centred and experiential psychotherapies.' *Counselling and Psychotherapy Research: Linking research with practice*. DOI: 10.1080/14733145.2013.808682

Friedli, K., King, M.B., Lloyd, M. and Horder, J. (1997) 'Randomised controlled assessment of non-directive psychotherapy versus routine general-practitioner care.' *Lancet*, 350: 1662–5.

Gendlin, E.T. (1978/2003) *Focusing*. Revised and updated 25th anniversary edition (2003). London: Rider.

Gendlin, E.T. (1998) *Focusing-oriented Psychotherapy: A Manual of the Experiential Method*. New York: Guilford Press.

Gibbard, I. (2004) 'Time-limited person-centred therapy.' *Person-Centred Practice*, 12 (1): 42–7.

Gibbard, I. (2007) '"In the World, But Not of It": person-centred counselling in primary care.' In K. Tudor (ed.) *Brief Person-Centred Therapies*. London: Sage, pp. 113–23.

Gibson, C. (1998) *Women-centered Therapy for Depression*. Unpublished doctoral dissertation. Department of Psychology, University of Toledo.

Gilbody, S. and Sowden, A. (2000) 'Systematic reviews in mental health.' In N. Rowland and S. Goss (eds) (2000) *Evidence-Based Counselling and Psychological Therapies*. London: Routledge, pp. 147–70.

Glass, G.V., McGaw, B. and Smith, M.L. (1981) *Meta-analysis in Social Research*. Beverly Hills, CA: Sage.

Glover, G., Webb, M. and Evison, F. (2010) *Improving Access to Psychological Therapies: A Review of the Progress Made by Sites in the First Rollout Year.* Durham: North East Public Health Observatory. Available at www.iapt.nhs.uk/silo/files/iapt-a-review-of-the-progress-made-by-sites-in-the-first-roll8208-out-year.pdf (accessed 05/12/13).

Goldman, R.N., Greenberg, L.S. and Angus, L. (2006) 'The effects of adding emotion-focused interventions to the client-centred relationship conditions in the treatment of depression.' *Psychotherapy Research*, 16: 537–49.

Grant, B. (1990/2002) 'Principled and instrumental nondirectiveness in person-centered and client-centered therapy.' *Person-Centered Review*, 5 (1): 77–88. Reprinted in D. Cain (ed.) (2002) *Classics in the Person-Centered Approach.* Ross-on-Wye: PCCS Books, pp. 371–6.

Greenberg, L.S. and Watson, J.C. (1998) 'Experiential therapy of depression: differential effects of client-centred relationship conditions and process experiential interventions.' *Psychotherapy Research*, 8: 210–24.

Greenberg, L.S. and Watson, J.C. (2006) *Emotion-Focused Therapy for Depression.* Washington D.C.: American Psychological Association.

Greenberg, L.S., Elliott, R. and Lietaer, G. (1994) 'Research on humanistic and experiential psychotherapies.' In A.E. Bergin and S.L. Garfield (eds) *Handbook of Psychotherapy and Behaviour Change*, 4th edn. New York: Wiley, pp. 509–39.

Haddad, P.M. and Anderson, I.M. (2007) 'Recognising and managing antidepressant discontinuation symptoms.' *Advances in Psychiatric Treatment*, 13: 447–57.

Harmon, C., Lambert, M.J., Smart, D.M., Hawkins, E., Nielsen, S.L., Slade, K. and Lutz, W. (2007) 'Enhancing outcome for potential treatment failures: therapist-client feedback and clinical support tools.' *Psychotherapy Research*, 17(4): 379–92.

Harray, A. (1975) 'The role of the counsellor in a medical centre.' *New Zealand Medical Journal.* 82: 383–5.

Healy, D. (2005) *Psychiatric Drugs Explained*, 4th edn. Oxford: Churchill Livingstone/Elsevier.

Helfin, C.M. and Iceland, J. (2009) 'Poverty, material hardship and depression.' *Social Science Quarterly*, 90 (5): 1052–71.

Higgins, E.T. (1987) 'Self-discrepancy: a theory relating self and affect.' *Psychological Review*, 94: 319–40.

Hill, A. (2010) *The Competences Required to Deliver Effective Counselling for Depression (CfD).* London: Department of Health. Available at www.ucl.ac.uk/clinical-sychology/CORE/Counselling_for_depression_Framework.htm

Holden, J.M., Sagovsky, R. and Cox, J.L. (1989) 'Counselling in a general practice setting: controlled study of health visitor intervention in treatment of postnatal depression.' *British Medical Journal*, 298: 223–6.

Howard, K.I., Kopta, S.M., Krause, M.S. and Orlinsky, D.E. (1986) 'The dose-effect relationship in psychotherapy.' *American Psychologist*, 41: 159–64.

Jackson, L. and Elliott, R. (June, 1990) 'Is experiential therapy effective in treating depression? Initial outcome data.' Paper presented at Society for Psychotherapy Research, Wintergreen, VA.

James, W. (1890/1983) *Principles of Psychology*, with introduction by George A. Miller. Cambridge, MA: Harvard University Press.

Kendrick, T., Sibbald, B., Addington Hall, J., Brenneman, D. and Freeling, P. (1993) 'Distribution of mental health professionals working on site in English and Welsh general practices.' *British Medical Journal*, 307 (6903): 544–6.

Kessler, D., Bennewith, O., Lewis, G. and Sharp, D. (2002) 'Detection of depression and anxiety in primary care: follow up study.' *British Medical Journal*, 325: 1016–17.

Kessler, R.C., Berglund, P., Demler, O., Jin, R., Koretz, D., Merikangas, K.R., Rush, A.J., Walters, E.E. and Wang, P.S. (2003) 'The epidemiology of major depressive disorder: results from the National Comorbidity Survey Replication (NCS-R).' *Journal of the American Medical Association,* 289: 3095–105.

King, L. and Moutsou, C. (2010) *Rethinking Audit Cultures: A Critical Look at Evidence-based Practice in Psychotherapy and Beyond.* Ross-on-Wye: PCCS Books.

King, M., Sibbald, B., Ward, E., Bower, P., Lloyd, M., Gabbay, M. and Byford, S. (2000) 'Randomised controlled trial of non-directive counselling, cognitive-behaviour therapy and usual general practitioner care in the management of depression as well as mixed anxiety and depression in primary care.' *Health Technology Assessment,* 4 (19): 1–83.

Kirschenbaum, H. (2007) *The Life and Work of Carl Rogers.* Ross-on-Wye: PCCS Books.

Kirschenbaum, H. and Henderson, V.L. (1990) *The Carl Rogers Reader.* London: Constable.

Kohut, H. (1971) *The Analysis of the Self.* New York: International Universities Press.

Kovacs, M. (1996) 'Presentation and course of major depressive disorder during childhood and later years of the life span.' *Journal of the American Academy of Child and Adolescent Psychiatry,* 35: 705–15.

Kupfer, D. J. (1991) 'Long-term treatment of depression.' *Journal of Clinical Psychiatry,* 52 (Suppl. 5): 28–34.

Kupfer, D.J., Frank, E. and Wamhoff, J. (1996) 'Mood disorders: update on prevention of recurrence.' In C. Mundt and M.J. Goldstein (eds) *Interpersonal Factors in the Origin and Course of Affective Disorders.* London: Gaskell/Royal College of Psychiatrists, pp. 289–302.

Lerner, M.S. and Clum, G.A. (1990) 'Treatment of suicide ideators: a problem-solving approach.' *Behavior Therapy,* 21: 403–11.

Marriott, M. and Kellett, S. (2009) 'Evaluating a cognitive analytic therapy service; practice-based outcomes and comparisons with person-centred and cognitive-behavioural therapies.' *Psychology and Psychotherapy,* 82: 57–72.

Maynard, C.K. (1993) 'Comparison of effectiveness of group interventions for depression in women.' *Archives of Psychiatric Nursing,* 7: 277–83.

McCrone, P., Dhanasiri, S., Patel, A., Knapp, M. and Lawton-Smith, S. (2008) *Paying the Price: The Cost of Mental Health Care in England to 2026.* London: King's Fund.

McNamara, K. and Horan, J.J. (1986) 'Experimental construct validity in the evaluation of cognitive and behavioral treatments for depression.' *Journal of Counseling Psychology,* 33: 23–30.

Mearns, D. (1999) 'Person-centred therapy with configurations of the self.' *Counselling,* 10 (2): 125–30.

Mearns, D. (2003) *Developing Person-Centred Counselling,* 2nd edn. London: Sage.

Mearns, D. and Cooper, M. (2005) *Working at Relational Depth in Counselling and Psychotherapy.* London: Sage.

Mearns, D. and Thorne, B. (2000) *Person-Centred Therapy Today: New Frontiers in Theory and Practice.* London: Sage.

Mellor-Clark, J. (2000) *Counselling in Primary Care in the Context of the NHS Quality Agenda: The Facts.* Rugby: BACP.

Merry, T. (2002) *Learning and Being in Person-Centred Counselling,* 2nd edn. Ross-on-Wye: PCCS Books.

Mestel, R. and Votsmeier-Röhr, A. (June, 2000) 'Long term follow-up study of depressive patients receiving experiential psychotherapy in an inpatient setting.' Paper presented at meeting of Society for Psychotherapy Research, Chicago, IL.

Miller, S.D. (2010) 'Psychometrics of the ORS and SRS. Results from RCTs and meta-analyses of routine outcome monitoring and feedback: The available evidence.' Available at www.scottd-miller.com/?q=blog/1&page=2

Mohr, D.C., Boudewyn, A.C., Goodkin, D.E., Bostrom, A. and Epstein, L. (2001) 'Comparative outcomes for individual cognitive-behavior therapy, supportive-expressive group psychotherapy, and sertraline for the treatment of depression in multiple sclerosis.' *Journal of Consulting and Clinical Psychology*, 69: 942–9.

Mohr, D.C., Hart, S.L., Julian, L., Catledge, C., Honos-Webb, L., Vella, L. and Tasch, E. T. (2005) 'Telephone-administered psychotherapy for depression.' *Archives of General Psychiatry*, 62: 1007–14.

Moore, M., Yuen, H.M., Dunn, N., Mullee, M.A., Maskell, J. and Kendrick, T. (2009) 'Explaining the rise in antidepressant prescribing: a descriptive study using the general practice research database.' *British Medical Journal*, 339, doi: http://dx.doi.org/10.1136/bmj.b3999

Morrell, C.J., Slade, P., Warner, R., Paley, G., Dixon, S., Walters, S.J., Brugha, T., Barkham, M., Parry, G. and Nicholl, J. (2009) 'Clinical effectiveness of health visitor training in psychologically informed approaches for depression in postnatal women: pragmatic cluster randomised trial in primary care.' *British Medical Journal*, 338, a3045.

Mundt, J.C., Marks, I.M., Shear, M.K. and Greist, J.H. (2002) 'The Work and Social Adjustment Scale: a simple measure of impairment in functioning.' *British Journal of Psychiatry*, 180: 461.

National Collaborating Centre for Mental Health (2010) *The NICE Guideline for the Treatment and Management of Depression in Adults, Updated Edition.* Leicester & London: The British Psychological Society and The Royal College of Psychiatrists. Available at www.nice.org.uk/nicemedia/live/12329/45896/45896.pdf

National Institute for Health and Clinical Excellence (2009a) *Depression: Treatment and Management of Depression in Adults, Including Adults with a Chronic Physical Health Problem. Quick Reference Guide.* Available at www.nice.org.uk/nicemedia/live/12329/45890/45890.pdf

National Institute for Health and Clinical Excellence (2009b) *Clinical Guideline 90: Depression in Adults: The Treatment and Management of Depression in Adults.* Available at http://publications.nice.org.uk/depression-in-adults-cg90 (retrieved 19/10/12).

Office for National Statistics (2001) *Psychiatric Morbidity Among Adults Living in Private Households, 2000.* London: HMSO.

Office for National Statistics (2009) *Psychiatric Morbidity Among Adults Living in Private Households, 2007.* London: HMSO.

Ostler, K., Thompson, C., Kinmonth, A.L.K., Peveler, R.C., Stevens, L. and Stevens, C. (2001) 'Influence of socioeconomic deprivation on the prevalence and outcome of depression in primary care: the Hampshire Depression Project.' *British Journal of Psychiatry*, 178: 12–17.

Pearce, P., Sewell, R., Hill, A., Coles, H., Pybis, J., Hunt, J., Robson, M., Lacock, L. and Hobman, P. (2012) 'Evaluating Counselling for Depression.' *Therapy Today*, 23 (10), Dec.

Petticrew, M. and Roberts, H. (2006) *Systematic Reviews in the Social Sciences: A Practical Guide.* Oxford: Blackwell.

Porta, M. and Last, J.M. (2008) *A Dictionary of Epidemiology*, 4th edn. Oxford: Oxford University Press.

Poston, J.M. and Hanson, W.E. (2010) 'Meta-analysis of psychological assessment as a therapeutic intervention.' *Psychol Assess*, 22 (2): 203–12, doi: 10.1037/a0018679

Probst, J.C., Laditka, S., Moore, C.G., Harun, N. and Powell, M.P. (2005) *Depression in Rural Populations: Prevalence, Effects on Life Quality, and Treatment-Seeking Behavior.* Columbia, SC: South Carolina Rural Health Research Center.

Propst, L.R., Ostrom, R., Watkins, P., Dean, T. and Mashburn, D. (1992) 'Comparitive efficacy of religious and nonreligious cognitive-behavioral therapy for the treatment of clinical depression in religious individuals.' *Journal of Consulting and Clinical Psychology*, 60: 94–103.

Purton, C. (2004) *Person-Centred Therapy: The Focusing-oriented Approach.* Basingstoke: Palgrave.

Rezaeian, M.P, Mazumdar, D.P.S. and Sen, A.K. (1997) 'The effectiveness of psychodrama in changing the attitudes among depressed patients.' *Journal of Personality & Clinical Studies,* 13: 19–23.

Rice, L.N. (1974/2001) 'The evocative function of the therapist.' In D.A. Wexler and L.N. Rice (eds) *Innovations in Client-Centered Therapy.* New York: Wiley, pp. 289–311. Reprinted in S. Haugh and T. Merry (eds) (2001) *Rogers' Therapeutic Conditions, Volume 2: Empathy.* Ross-on-Wye: PCCS Books, pp. 112–30.

Rice, L.N. and Saperia, E.P. (1984) 'Task analysis and the resolution of problematic reactions.' In L.N. Rice and L.S. Greenberg (eds) *Patterns of Change.* New York: Guilford Press, pp. 29–66.

Rogers, C.R. (1951) *Client-Centered Therapy.* Boston: Houghton Mifflin.

Rogers, C.R. (1957/1990) 'The necessary and sufficient conditions of therapeutic personality change.' In H. Kirschenbaum and V.L. Henderson (eds) (1990) *The Carl Rogers Reader,* London: Constable, pp. 219–35.

Rogers, C.R. (1959) 'A theory of therapy, personality and interpersonal relationships, as developed in the client-centred framework.' In S. Koch (ed.) *Psychology: A Study of a Science, Vol. 3: Formulation of the Person and the Social Context.* New York: McGraw-Hill, pp. 184–256.

Rogers, C.R. (1961) *On Becoming a Person: A Therapist's View of Psychotherapy.* London: Constable.

Rogers, C.R. (1976) Interview with Anthony Clare. *All in the Mind.* BBC Radio. Available at www.bbc.co.uk/radio4/science/allinthemind_20070710.shtml (downloaded 12/05/08).

Rogers, C.R. (1980) *A Way of Being.* London: Constable.

Rogers, C.R. (1986/2002) 'Reflection of feelings.' *Person-Centered Review,* 1 (4): 375–7. Reprinted in D. Cain (ed.) (2002) *Classics in the Person-Centered Approach.* Ross-on-Wye: PCCS Books, pp. 13–14.

Rogers, C.R., Gendlin, E.T., Kiesler, D.J. and Truax, C.B. (1967) *The Therapeutic Relationship and Its Impact: A study of psychotherapy with schizophrenics.* Madison, WI: University of Wisconsin Press.

Romme, M., Escher, S., Dillon, J., Corstens. D. and Morris, M. (2009) *Living with Voices: 50 Stories of Recovery.* Ross-on-Wye: PCCS Books.

Roth, A.D., Hill, A. and Pilling, S. (2009) *The Competences Required to Deliver Effective Humanistic Psychological Therapies.* London: Department of Health.

Roth, A.D. and Pilling, S. (2008) 'Using an evidence-based methodology to identify the competences required to deliver effective cognitive and behavioural therapy for depression and anxiety disorders.' *Behavioural and Cognitive Psychotherapy,* 36: 129–47.

Roth, A.D. and Pilling, S. (2009) *A Competence Framework for the Supervision of Psychological Therapies.* London: University College, London. Available at www.ucl.ac.uk/clinicalpsychology/CORE/supervision_framework.htm

Sackett, D.L., Rosenberg, W.M.C., Gray, J.A.M., Haynes, R.B. and Richardson, W.S. (1996) 'Evidence-based medicine: what it is and what it isn't.' *British Medical Journal,* 312: 71–2.

Samaritans (2004) *Samaritans Information Resource Pack.* Ewell, Kent: Samaritans.

Samaritans (2012) *Samaritans Information Resource Pack.* Ewell, Kent: Samaritans. Available at www.samaritans.org/sites/default/files/kcfinder/files/2012%20information%20resource%20pack.pdf

Samaritans (2013) *Samaritans Suicide Statistics Report.* Ewell, Kent: Samaritans. Available at www.samaritans.org/sites/default/files/kcfinder/files/research/Samaritans%20Suicide%20Statistics%20Report%202013.pdf

Sanders, P. (2006) *The Person-Centred Counselling Primer.* Ross-on-Wye: PCCS Books.

Sanders, P. (2012) 'Mapping person-centred approaches to counselling and psychotherapy.' In P. Sanders (ed.) *The Tribes of the Person-Centred Nation: An Introduction to the Schools of Therapy Related to the Person-centred Approach.* Ross-on-Wye: PCCS Books, pp. 233–46.

Sanders, P. and Wilkins, P. (2010) *First Steps in Practitioner Research: A Guide to Understanding and Doing Research in Counselling and Health and Social Care.* Ross-on-Wye: PCCS Books.

Seeman, J. (1983) *Personality Integration: Studies and Reflections.* New York: Human Sciences Press.

Shafran, R., Cooper, Z. and Fairburn, C.G. (2002) 'Clinical perfectionism: a cognitive-behavioural analysis.' *Behaviour Research and Therapy*, 40: 773–91.

Shaw, B.F. (1977) 'Comparison of cognitive therapy and behavior therapy in the treatment of depression.' *Journal of Consulting and Clinical Psychology*, 45: 543–51.

Shlien, J.M. (1997/2001/2003) 'Empathy in psychotherapy: vital mechanism? Yes. Therapist's conceit? All too often. By itself enough? No.' In A.C. Bohart and L.S. Greenberg (eds) *Empathy Reconsidered.* Washington, D.C.: American Psychological Association, pp. 63–80. Reprinted in S. Haugh and T. Merry (eds) (2001) *Rogers' Therapeutic Conditions, Volume 2: Empathy.* Ross-on-Wye: PCCS Books, pp. 38–52. Reprinted in J.M. Shlien (2003) *To Lead an Honorable Life.* Ross-on-Wye: PCCS Books, pp. 173–90.

Sibbald, B., Addington Hall, J., Brenneman, D. and Freeling, P. (1993) 'Counsellors in English and Welsh general practices: Their nature and distribution.' *BMJ*, 306 (6869): 29–33.

Simon, G. E., Goldberg, D. P., von Korff, M. and Ustün, T.B. (2002) 'Understanding cross national differences in depression prevalence.' *Psychological Medicine*, 32: 585–94.

Simpson, S., Corney, R., Fitzgerald, P. and Beecham, J. (2003) 'A randomised controlled trial to evaluate the effectiveness and cost-effectiveness of psychodynamic counselling for general practice patients with chronic depression.' *Psychological Medicine*, 33: 229–39.

Singleton, N., Bumpstead, R., O'Brien, M., et al. (2001) *Psychiatric Morbidity Among Adults Living in Private Households, 2000.* London: The Stationery Office.

Stice, E., Burton, E., Bearman, S.K. and Rohde, P. (2006) 'Randomized trial of brief depression prevention program: An elusive search for a psychosocial placebo control condition.' *Behaviour Research and Therapy*, 45: 863–76.

Stice, E., Rohde, P., Gau, J.M. and Wade, E. (2010) 'Efficacy trial of a brief cognitive-behavioral depression prevention program for high-risk adolescents: Effects at 1- and 2-year follow-up.' *Journal of Consulting and Clinical Psychology*, 78: 856–67.

Stiles, W.B., Barkham, M., Twigg, E., Mellor-Clark, J., Cooper, M. (2006) 'Effectiveness of cognitive-behavioural, person-centred and psychodynamic therapies as practised in UK National Health Service settings.' *Psychological Medicine*, 36 (4): 555–66.

Taft, J. (1937) *The Dynamics of Therapy in a Controlled Relationship.* New York: MacMillan.

Teusch, L., Böhme, H., Finke, J., Gastpar, M. and Skerra, B. (2003) 'Antidepressant medication and the assimilation of problematic experiences in psychotherapy.' *Psychotherapy Research*, 13: 307–22.

Thomas, C.M. and Morris, S. (2003) 'Cost of depression among adults in England in 2000.' *British Journal of Psychiatry*, 183: 514–19.

Timonen, M. and Liukkonen, T. (2008) 'Management of depression in adults.' *British Medical Journal*, 336 (7641): 435–9.

Torgerson, D.J. and Torgerson, C.J. (2008) *Designing Randomised Trials in Health, Education and the Social Sciences.* Houndmills: Palgrave Macmillan.

Truax, C.B. and Carkhuff, R. (1967) *Toward effective counselling and psychotherapy: training and practice.* Chicago: Aldine

Tudor, K. (2008) (ed.) *Brief Person-Centred Therapies.* London: Sage Publications.

Tudor, K. and Merry, T. (2002/2006) *Dictionary of Person-Centred Psychology.* London: Whurr. Re-published in 2006 by PCCS Books, Ross-on-Wye.

Tudor, K. and Worrall, M. (2006) *Person-Centred Therapy: A clinical philosophy.* Hove: Routledge.

Tyson, G.M. and Range, L.M. (1987) 'Gestalt dialogues as a treatment for mild depression: Time works just as well.' *Journal of Clinical Psychology,* 43: 227–31.

Wampold, B.E. (2001) *The Great Psychotherapy Debate.* Mahwah: Lawrence Erlbaum Associates.

Waraich, P., Goldner, E.M., Somers, J.M. and Hsu, L. (2004) 'Prevalence and incidence studies of mood disorders: a systematic review of the literature.' *Canadian Journal of Psychiatry,* 49: 124–38.

Ward, E., King, M., Lloyd, M., Bower, P., Sibbald, B., Farrelly, S., Gabbay, M., Tarrier, N. and Addington-Hall, J. (2000) 'Randomised controlled trial of non-directive counselling, cognitive-behaviour therapy, and usual general practitioner care for patients with depression.' *British Medical Journal,* 321: 1383–8.

Warner, M.S. (1997) 'Does empathy cure? A theoretical consideration of empathy, processing and personal narrative.' In A.C. Bohart and L.S. Greenberg (eds) *Empathy Reconsidered.* Washington, D.C.: American Psychological Association, pp. 124–40.

Warner, M. (2005) 'A person-centered view of human nature, wellness and psychopathology.' In S. Joseph and R. Worsley (eds) *Person-centred Psychopathology: A Positive Psychology of Mental Health.* Ross-on-Wye: PCCS Books, pp. 91–109.

Watson, J.C., Gordon, L.B., Stermac, L., Kalogerakos, F. and Steckley, P. (2003) 'Comparing the effectiveness of process-experiential with cognitive-behavioral psychotherapy in the treatment of depression.' *Journal of Consulting and Clinical Psychology,* 71: 773–81.

Watson, N., Bryan, B.C. and Thrash, T.M. (2010) 'Self-discrepancy: comparisons of the psycho-metric properties of three instruments.' *Psychological Assessment, 22* (4), 878–92. Available at http://watsonresearch.wm.edu/Self-Discrepancy_Comparisons_Watson_Bryan_Thrash.pdf (note that this study is freely available online).

Westen, D. and Bradley, R. (2005) 'Empirically supported complexity: rethinking evidence-based practice in psychotherapy.' *Current Directions in Psychological Science,* 14: 266–71.

Whelton, W. and Greenberg, L.S. (2002) 'Psychological contact as dialectical construction.' In G. Wyatt and P. Sanders (eds) *Rogers' Therapeutic Conditions: Evolution, Theory and Practice. Volume 4: Contact and Perception.* Ross-on-Wye: PCCS Books, pp. 96–114.

Wickberg, B. and Hwang, C.P. (1996) 'Counselling of postnatal depression: a controlled study on a population based Swedish sample.' *Journal of Affective Disorders,* 39: 209–16.

Wilson, G.L. (1990) 'Psychotherapy with depressed incarcerated felons: a comparative evaluation of treatments.' *Psychological Reports,* 67: 1027–41.

World Health Organization (1992) *The ICD-10 Classification of Mental and Behavioural Disorders.* Geneva: World Health Organization.

World Health Organization (2001) *World Health Report 2001. Mental Health: New Understanding, New Hope.* Geneva: World Health Organization. Available at www.who.int/whr.

World Health Organization (2012) www.who.int/mediacentre/events/annual/world_health_day/en/index.html (retrieved 10/10/12).

Wyatt, G. (ed.) (2001) *Rogers' Therapeutic Conditions: Evolution, Theory and Practice. Volume 1: Congruence.* Ross-on-Wye: PCCS Books.

Zarin, D.A., Pincus, H.A., West, J.C. and McIntyre, J.S. (1997) 'Practice-based research in psychiatry.' *American Journal of Psychiatry,* 154: 1199–208.

Zimring, F. (2000/2001) 'Empathic understanding grows the person ...' *Person-Centered Journal,* 7 (2): 101–13. Reprinted in S. Haugh and T. Merry (eds) (2001) *Rogers' Therapeutic Conditions, Volume 2: Empathy.* Ross-on-Wye: PCCS Books, pp. 86–98.

Index